SCHOOL BOARD LEADERSHIP

THE RIGHT WAY

A Comprehensive Professional Resource for School Board Members

LAURA ZORC

DR. KAREN HILTZ

Published by Best In Ed
20 F Street NW, Suite 700
Washington DC 20001
www.BestInEd.org

ISBN 979-8-218-59227-1

Library of Congress Control Number 2025900469

First Edition

Table of Contents

Introduction

In an era of constant flux in education, school board roles have never been more demanding. ***School Board Leadership: The Right Way* is designed as a beacon for current and aspiring school board members**, expertly guiding them over hurdles of governance, accountability, and community engagement.

The pages are filled with comprehensive professional learning resources, skillfully prepared by Laura Zorc and Dr. Karen Hiltz—both former school board members—who offer invaluable insights and practical strategies to assist you in your important role. Unlike many existing resources on the market today that often come from the perspectives of consultants, former administrators, superintendents, or professors, this book is a foundational resource grounded in the lived experiences of school board members and uniquely written *by* school board members *for* school board members. It gives insights backed by over 40 years of collective wisdom from school board members across the country. Integrating the experiences of both new and veteran members asserts a comprehensive perspective that gives a clearer understanding of areas to look out for and questions to ask in making informed decisions and driving positive change in our communities.

Sir Isaac Newton once famously stated, *"If I have seen further than others, it is by standing upon the shoulders of giants."* This acknowledgment highlights that progress is rarely achieved in isolation. The "giants" are the researchers, visionaries, and mentors who have cleared the way before us. By recognizing and learning from those we trust and by becoming the giants others can rely upon, you can build a strong foundation for your success as a school board member.

Whether you feel satisfied with the current state of management and leadership within your local public education system or are frustrated by the endless cycle of ineffective practices that yield slight improvement, you are in the right place. This book will inspire you to ask vital questions such as: "Why are we doing what we do?" and "Is there a logical reason for our practices, or are we adhering to them simply because they have always been done this way?"

As stewards of local education, you must deal with complex challenges while championing the interests of students, families, and the community. This book lays the groundwork for effective leadership by providing essential knowledge about state statutes, governance structures, and the myriad responsibilities accompanying your role. From understanding the subtleties of board dynamics to cultivating a culture of transparency and trust, each chapter will enhance your capacity to lead with confidence and integrity.

About the Authors and Contributors

Authors

Laura Zorc – Biography

Laura Zorc is a prominent leader in education reform and a recognized grassroots strategist, currently serving as the President and Founder of Best In Ed, a nonprofit organization based in Washington, D.C. In this role, she bridges the gap between national educational policy and local community decision-making, focusing on enhancing school board leadership and community advocacy.

Zorc has been instrumental in developing the first professional development program specifically tailored for school board members by their peers, emphasizing principles such as limited government, accountability, fiscal responsibility, and transparency. This initiative has significantly strengthened the effectiveness of school boards nationwide.

Her leadership experience includes serving as a school board member and chairman for the Indian River County School Board in Florida, where she governed a $320 million budget and championed transformative accountability measures. Through her commitment to improving education, Zorc faced significant political pushback while advancing fiscal responsibility and accountability. Despite the challenges, her resilience is a testament to what is possible through steady leadership, leading to enhancements in student services, expansion of vocational and technical education programs, and the development of alternative education pathways. Her tough governance approach has laid the groundwork that transformed her school district into one of the highest-performing and best-managed school districts in the nation.

Since leaving the school board in 2020, Laura Zorc has remained committed to education, sharing invaluable lessons by mentoring over 1,000 members about their essential roles in local school boards, culminating in this book. Through Best In Ed, she has expanded her influence nationwide in post-COVID education reform, spearheading initiatives to enhance educational outcomes and promote local control. This commitment includes a movement involving parents and community education leaders, where the Best team coaches aspiring candidates on effective campaign strategies through the School Board Candidates Academy and advocates for transformative education policies at both state and federal levels. Their testimony shapes policies that encourage local decision-making, improve student outcomes, and contribute to state committees driving meaningful legislation.

With a blend of business acumen, operations management expertise, and a background in forensic accounting, Zorc is dedicated to advancing educational outcomes through fiscally responsible policy and proactive governance across the country. Frequently featured in national media, she provides insightful commentary informed by her extensive experience and strong connections within grassroots education communities.

Dr. Karen Hiltz – Biography

Dr. Karen Hiltz is a dedicated public servant and expert in educational governance. She is known for her commitment to enhancing the quality of education through leadership and strategic planning. From 2016 to 2020, she served a four-year term on the Franklin County School Board in Virginia, where she focused on vital areas such as policy development, strategic planning, and contract and agreement management.

Dr. Hiltz's tenure exemplified her dedication to creating a transparent and accountable educational environment. A veteran of the U.S. Navy, Dr. Hiltz brings a wealth of experience from her military service and a successful career in federal procurement. This background has equipped her with a unique perspective on governance and the importance of effective resource management in public institutions.

Dr. Hiltz's expertise extends beyond her service on the school board. She is actively involved in mentoring school board members nationwide, sharing her knowledge and experience to promote effective leadership. She plays an important role in creating school board leadership curricula that emphasize principles such as limited government, accountability, transparency, and responsibility—key tenets for modern educational governance. Her commitment to service is further demonstrated through her roles as a Planning and Zoning Commissioner and Community College Advisory Board member. Dr. Hiltz has also contributed to private education as a school board member and has advised various non-profit organizations, leveraging her expertise to benefit her community.

An accomplished author, Dr. Hiltz has written numerous articles and two influential books: *The Case for Choice: One Size Fits All – An Outdated Education Model for the 21st Century* and *The Apple Report: Diary of a Public School Board Member*. She holds a Bachelor of Science and a Master of Business Administration in Management, as well as a Doctorate in Leadership Studies. Currently residing in Florida, Dr. Hiltz continues to advocate for educational reform and effective governance, firmly believing in the power of informed leadership to transform educational systems.

Contributors

Anniece Barker – Anniece Barker was elected to the Central Valley School District outside Spokane, Washington, in 2023. Barker received a Bachelor of Science in Psychology from Brigham Young University in Idaho. She has focused on her own children's schooling while also striving for the exceptional academic education of all students. As an active parent volunteer, Barker is the founding chair of A Voice for Washington Children, formed in 2020 to help protect parent's rights in their children's education. As a mom of four boys, Barker advocates for community values, fiscal stewardship, parent involvement, and high academic standards.

Evelyn Brooks – Evelyn Brooks is the Texas State Board of Education representative for District 14, having served since 2022. Brooks has extensive experience educating and helping youth to develop a Biblical worldview, challenging them to strive for excellence, to think independently, and to develop self-discipline and self-control. Evelyn's mission is to ensure that all children have access to a quality education that is grounded on the preservation of the liberties and rights of citizens and is free from indoctrination. She promises to protect children's innocence and be the voice of the unheard.

Amy Carney – Amy Carney is an experienced leader serving a four-year term on the Scottsdale, Arizona, school board. Previously, she was the Deputy Director of Building Education for Students Together (BEST), a national program dedicated to improving the quality of education K-12 and parental rights in education, reflecting her passion for improving education in America. As a mother of six, Carney actively engages with parents on intentional parenting and is the author of *Parent on Purpose*. Her work with the American City County Exchange (ACCE) Executive Committee further enriches her expertise in local governance.

Thomas (Tom) Hach – Tom Hach is currently in his fourth term as a veteran Ohio school board member and serves as the State Director of the Ohio Freedom Action Network, having previously held the position of Executive Director for Free Ohio Now. Through these roles, he has collaborated with dedicated individuals to unite like-minded leaders across Ohio. After retiring as an IT program manager and completing a 21-year career in the Navy Reserve, which included service in Iraq from 2006 to 2007, Tom has also earned a BS in Chemistry from Miami (Ohio) University and an MBA from Case Western Reserve University.

Jacqueline "Jackie" Rosario – Jackie Rosario is a school board member, serving a second term in Florida, since 2018. She brings over three decades of educational experience to her roles, which began as an English as a Second Language teacher and included positions such as Assistant Principal, Professional Learning Facilitator, and Instructional Leader. She holds two permanent certifications from New York: one as a Teacher of English as a Second Language and the other as a School District Administrator. Passionate about education, as a homeschooling mother, Jackie advocates for school choice and parental rights while mentoring other school board members in policy writing.

Sherri Story – Sherri Story has dedicated her life to education, serving as a school board member in Suffolk County, Virginia (2018-2022). With over 40 years of experience as an educator in the public, private, and homeschooling sectors, she is a dedicated innovator and entrepreneur. After retiring from teaching and completing a four-year term on the public school board, Story co-founded the School Board Member Alliance of Virginia, which promotes a conservative, common-sense approach to school board governance.

Angie Todd – Angie Todd is a member of the Onslow County Board of Education in North Carolina, currently serving her first four-year term, which began in 2023. With a strong commitment to enhancing educational opportunities, she actively engages with the community and advocates for the needs of students and families. As a school board mentor, Angie fosters collaboration and effective governance through her mentorship initiatives. Her passion for education and student success in a vibrant military community positions her as a valuable resource, providing insightful guidance for new school board members and contributing significantly to the educational landscape.

Dedication

To all the moms, dads, and grandparents who have had enough of being silenced at the podium and feeling ignored by those you trusted to advocate for your child's education. This book is dedicated to you! Thank you for stepping up, running for office, and now serving on your school board.

To the devoted parents who once believed they couldn't make a difference in your child's education, remember that your voice matters and your actions can create change. By choosing to run for school board positions and embracing the insights and fundamentals shared within these pages, you can impact your child's educational experience and uplift the entire school district.

Like the authors and contributors of this book, you can be a catalyst for transformation that creates a rippling effect. Your commitment to advocacy and leadership is shaping a successful future for generations to come.

Section 1: **Onboarding**

Objectives for Section 1: Onboarding

1. **Clarify Roles and Responsibilities:** Equip school board members with a comprehensive understanding of their roles, responsibilities, and authority granted under state laws and board policies, enabling them to navigate their duties effectively.

2. **Facilitate a Smooth Transition to Governance:** Support newly elected board members in transitioning from candidate to active decision-maker, celebrating their achievements while preparing them for the governance challenges ahead.

3. **Build a Knowledge Foundation and Historical Context**: Encourage members to research state statutes, review board policies, and gain insights into the historical evolution of K-12 education in the United States, creating a solid knowledge base to inform their decision-making.

4. **Enhance Time Management and Critical Thinking Skills:** Emphasize the importance of effective time management to balance board responsibilities with other commitments while promoting critical thinking and discernment regarding training and information received from various sources.

5. **Encourage Reflective Practice and Adaptability**: Inspire board members to articulate their motivations for serving on the board and provide them with the tools and knowledge necessary to navigate potential shifts in governance structure and educational policy, ensuring they remain proactive and effective leaders.

Welcome to the Onboarding section, where we'll help you to properly understand your role as a school board member. This section is designed to equip you with the knowledge and tools necessary for success in your new position. In Chapter 1, "You Are Elected - Now What?", we will explore the transition from candidate to board member, celebrating your achievement while preparing you for the responsibilities that lie ahead. The excitement of your election is just the beginning; the real work of governance and leadership begins now.

In this chapter, we will address the overwhelming nature of the initial period following your election. Regardless of whether you are a seasoned member or new to the board, it's necessary to have a comprehensive understanding of your responsibilities and the authority granted to you. Familiarizing yourself with state laws and board policies is foundational for your success. This knowledge will build your confidence and enable you to make informed decisions that will have a lasting impact on your educational community. As you settle into this new role, we will underscore the importance of treating your position as a part-time job that requires a full-time commitment.

Moreover, effective time management will be a focal point of our discussion. As a school board member, you will find that flexibility and dedication are paramount. The role's demands can be significant, requiring you to juggle various responsibilities, from attending meetings to engaging with constituents. We will provide insights into how to balance these commitments while ensuring you remain focused on your district's needs. The landscape of school governance is rapidly evolving, and taking a proactive approach to your responsibilities is essential for meeting your constituents' expectations.

In Chapter 2, "Brief History of K-12 Education," we look at the historical context of the educational system in the United States. Understanding the evolution of K-12 education will provide you with valuable insights into the current situation and the challenges you may face as a board member. From the establishment of foundational school finance laws to the increasing federal influence over education, this chapter will highlight key milestones that have shaped public education governance. By grasping the system's historical underpinnings, you'll be better equipped to carry out your role effectively and advocate for responsible governance in your district. Together, these chapters will lay a solid foundation for your effectiveness as a school board member, enabling you to lead with confidence and clarity in your important role.

Chapter 1
You are Elected – Now What?

Congratulations! The election is over, the swearing-in has taken place, the excitement is wearing off, and the real work is beginning. The period between candidate elect to the first school board meeting can be overwhelming.

Whether you are a seasoned school board member or new to the role, it's never too late to deepen your understanding of your responsibilities and authority. Familiarizing yourself with the state laws that govern school boards and the board policies related to your role is foundational for your success. Rest assured, the longer you serve on the board, the more confidence you will gain. This acquired knowledge and confidence will help you make informed decisions and be effective in your position. No one would start a new job without a clear understanding of their job description. For you, this involves knowing the state laws that define your authority, roles, and responsibilities.

With adequate time management and a commitment to learning, you *can* confidently and effectively fulfill your responsibilities. However, it is important to remain mindful of norms and influences with misguided or self-serving intentions. This also means learning to sift through biased perspectives and question their origins. By being cautious and discerning, you can ensure that any professional learning is not influenced by biases that could hinder sound board decision-making.

Step 1 – Time Management

To be a successful school board member, you must approach the responsibility with realistic expectations. While many consider it a volunteer position, it must be treated as a part-time role that demands a full-time commitment. Here are a few specifics:

- Serving on a local school board will require a minimum of approximately ten hours of work per week for small districts, 15 to 20 hours for midsize districts, and 20 to 40 hours for large districts.
- In your first year on the board, you will likely spend considerable time getting acquainted with all aspects of the district, such as visiting schools and facilities. The aim is to gain enough understanding to approve a fiscally responsible budget by understanding the district's needs.
- Due to its unpredictable nature, this job requires flexibility. This is based on the need to attend emergency meetings with the superintendent and respond to constituent phone calls at any time. Votes are conducted during regular board business meetings, special meetings, and routine workshops.
- Spring planning meetings and graduation season are typically the busiest periods for school board members, with numerous graduation ceremonies and budget meetings occurring.

A new generation of school board members is stepping into office, determined to address troubling trends in academic performance, rebuild public trust, and create a competitive educational landscape for parents. To tackle these challenges, board members must actively engage with parents and prioritize their concerns.

This level of understanding requires dedication and a willingness to invest significant time. What was enough in the past is no longer sufficient. School districts have become accustomed to board members taking a hands-off approach, which has proven ineffective. This new wave of board members is increasingly engaging in self-training and ready to challenge the status quo. The shift demands higher expectations and greater involvement from everyone. To move forward, board members must adopt proactive strategies that measure success and lead to tangible improvements in our schools. Effective time management strategies will help board members achieve these goals (see the Board Calendar section).

Step 2 – Build Your Knowledge Foundation

1st: Research State Statutes

Every state differs slightly in terms of the exact parameters of a school board member's role. Still, there are noteworthy constants that all or most states require. Review the relevant constitutional passages, statutes, and local board policies. This vital background knowledge will help ensure a member is not being taken advantage of or misled and won't overstep legal authority. Knowing what authority boards have is probably the most valuable knowledge you as a board member can have.

To be an effective school board member, you must be familiar with the specific guidelines outlined in state statutes. While there may be slight variations in the roles and responsibilities of school board members across states, standard requirements apply to most. Familiarity with constitutional passages, statutes, and local board policies regarding the board's role is crucial for relevant knowledge and protection. ***Check out Appendix to scan the QR codes specific to the authority and roles for school board members unique to your state (Articles, Chapters, or Statutes) laws.***

2nd: Review Board Policies

A later section will provide in-depth policy information. However, members must carefully review the board's governance policies to become familiar with them. You must also conduct research and make any necessary changes that are appropriate for the district.

While you don't need to memorize these policies, you should know where to find them and how to conduct research for meetings and votes. Board members should develop the habit of doing their homework and not accept everything at face value. By investing time and resources into making board policies accessible and transparent to the public, you'll benefit the community and enhance your own efficiency and effectiveness.

SCHOOL BOARD MEMBERS ROLES AND AUTHORITY

STATE	FIRST	ARTICLE OR TITLE	BLAINE AMENDMENT LANGUAGE	STATUTES OR CODE	CONSTITUTION LINK	CODE/STATUTE LINK
Alabama	1819	Article XIV: Sections 256-270	Section 263	Title 16: Chapters 1-67		
Alaska	1959	Article VII: Sections 1-5	Section 1	Title 14: Chapters 3-60		
Arizona	1912	Article 11: Sections 1-11	Section 8	Title 15: Chapters 1-19		
Arkansas	1836	Article 14: Sections 1-4	None	Title 6: Subtitles 1-6		
California	1849	Article IX: Sections 1-16	Section 8	EDC: Titles 1-3		
Colorado	1876	Article IX: Sections 1-17	Section 7	Title 22: Articles 1-98		
Connecticut	1818	Article 8: Sections 1-4	None	Title 10: Chapters 163-184c		
Delaware	1897	Article 10: Sections 1-6	Section 3	Title 14: Chapters 1-94		
Florida	1838	Article IX: Sections 1-8	Section 6	Title XLVIII: Chapters 1000-1013		
Georgia	1777	Article VIII: Sections I-VII	Section VI	Title 20: Chapters 1-18		
Hawaii	1959	Article X: Sections 1-6	Section 1	Title 18: Chapters 296-319		

Technology has made it significantly easier to conduct research and provide information to the public, saving the board time and improving its ability to fulfill its responsibilities. Many school boards utilize BoardDocs or similar systems to manage district policies. This system is highly effective and offers an organized platform for school board members, employees, and the public. There is a cost associated with using it, but it is worth the investment.

3rd: Maintain A Balanced Perspective

State School Board Associations

It is important to note that most state school board associations are affiliated with the National School Boards Association (NSBA). Through these state association affiliates, the NSBA has influenced the training of school board members across the country. However, in recent years, concerns have been raised about the NSBA's ideological alignment and its influence within state-level associations, which some view as politically biased. Guidance and policies have been heavily influenced by the recommendations of superintendents' associations and teachers' unions, leading to a significant shift in control towards special interest groups. As a result, local control of school boards has diminished, and over the decades, the authority has increasingly been transferred to superintendents in particular.

National School Boards Association
1680 Duke St. FL2, Alexandria, VA 22314-3493
Phone: (703) 838.6722 • Fax: (703) 683.7590
www.nsba.org

September 29, 2021

The Honorable Joseph R. Biden
President of the United States
The White House
1600 Pennsylvania Avenue, NW
Washington, DC 20500

Re: *Federal Assistance to Stop Threats and Acts of Violence Against Public Schoolchildren, Public School Board Members, and Other Public School District Officials and Educators*

Dear Mr. President:

America's public schools and its education leaders are under an immediate threat. The National School Boards Association (NSBA) respectfully asks for federal law enforcement and other assistance to deal with the growing number of threats of violence and acts of intimidation occurring across the nation. Local school board members want to hear from their communities on important issues and that must be at the forefront of good school board governance and promotion of free speech. However, there also must be safeguards in place to protect public schools and dedicated education leaders as they do their jobs.

NSBA believes immediate assistance is required to protect our students, school board members, and educators who are susceptible to acts of violence affecting interstate commerce because of threats to their districts, families, and personal safety. As our school boards continue coronavirus recovery operations within their respective districts, they are also persevering against other challenges that could impede this progress in a number of communities. Coupled with attacks against school board members and educators for approving policies for masks to protect the health and safety of students and school employees, many public school officials are also facing physical threats because of propaganda purporting the false inclusion of critical race theory within classroom instruction and curricula.[1] This propaganda continues despite the fact that critical race theory is not taught in public schools and remains a complex law school and graduate school subject well beyond the scope of a K-12 class.

On behalf of our state associations and the more than 90,000 school board members who govern our country's 14,000 local public school districts educating more than 50 million schoolchildren, NSBA appreciates your leadership to end the proliferation of COVID-19 in our communities and our school districts. We also appreciate recent discussions with White House and U.S. Department of Education staff on many critical issues facing public schools, including threats school officials are receiving.

---

[1] The Armed Conflict Location & Event Data Project (ACLED), "Fact Sheet: Demonstrations over Critical Race Theory in the United States," July 14, 2021, https://acleddata.com/acleddatanew/wp-content/uploads/2021/07/ACLED_Fact-Sheet_CRT-Demos_2021.pdf.

The leading advocate for public education

Best In Ed is on a course to correct years of misguided training. Through this book and other supplemental resources, we intend to help members get back on track regarding the school board's proper roles and authority as prescribed by law. This involves offering guidance to operate outside the filter of superintendents and other associations that have skewed board abilities and created obstacles. Being a school board member is tough enough, but knowing where these associations come from will provide a clearer view of balancing all the information.

In recent years, it's become clear some organizations, such as the NSBA, held a monopoly on power and influence, which has led to an outcry from taxpayers and board members. This led to demands to separate from the NSBA. Some states did separate; some did not, and some even went as far as to cut ties with state school board associations. Even though the NSBA has recognized its missteps, alternative organizations have launched across the states out of a need for balance in school board training and mentorship.

So, what was the straw that broke the camel's back? Why is there distrust among some of the NSBA and State School Board Associations? You can find it on Page 2 of the NSBA letter to President Biden dated September 29, 2021.

Page 2 of this 6 page letter has been criticized for the NSBA's political bias and an exaggerated portrayal of parental concerns. In particular, the paragraph that compares the actions of outspoken parents at board meetings to an act of domestic terrorism, sparking controversy and drawing unexpected attention.

> As these acts of malice, violence, and threats against public school officials have increased, the classification of these heinous actions could be the equivalent to a form of domestic terrorism and hate crimes. As such, NSBA requests a joint expedited review by the U.S. Departments of Justice, Education, and Homeland Security, along with the appropriate training, coordination, investigations, and enforcement mechanisms from the FBI, including any technical assistance necessary from, and state and local coordination with, its National Security Branch and Counterterrorism Division, as well as any other federal agency with relevant jurisdictional authority and oversight. Additionally, NSBA requests that such review examine appropriate enforceable actions against these crimes and acts of violence under the Gun-Free School Zones Act, the PATRIOT Act in regards to domestic terrorism, the Matthew Shepard and James Byrd Jr. Hate Crimes Prevention Act, the Violent Interference with Federally Protected Rights statute, the Conspiracy Against Rights statute, an Executive Order to enforce all applicable federal laws for the
>
> *Page 2 of 9/29/2021 NSBA Letter to President Biden*

Source: www.DocumentCloud.org

State associations have become an NSBA conduit for talking points, political agendas, and board governance practices, typically provided during the annual convention or conference. This gathering is where members commonly hear updates on legislation, gain awareness of current topics/issues, and receive recommendations for adapting to the current environment. This annual event also allows school districts to introduce programs or initiatives they seek to promote. Other trainings such as Superintendent Evaluations, Legislative Days, Chair & Vice Chair training, and more vary by state and depend on how active state associations are.

Familiarity with board policies and recognizing consistencies across the states helps to identify some of these broad-brush policies that get adopted. For example, the three-minute public speaking rule for general business meetings is a practice seen only in school board policy. Why is the 3-minute rule found in other local government meetings, such as county commissions and city councils? These rules stem from school board training on best practices and recommendations that have stuck. The good news is that policies can be revised! As you read through the 1st Amendment, there are descriptions in law that have been passed down through norms where the public is becoming more vocal in court challenges and winning. The excuse "this is the way we have always done it" can change with a board majority and understanding of the governing laws.

Our best advice is to go into training sessions fully aware that delivery will be agenda-driven and biased. Find a balance. Always question who the person delivering the content is. Are they politically motivated? What is their experience? Even if training is from a former or current school board member, where are they coming from? Are they retired administrators, professors, or superintendents? We are not advising you not to attend state association meetings; our purpose is to prepare members for the bias and help them bring balance to the discussion. The biggest takeaway from attending association meetings is not the training, rather, it is the collaboration and camaraderie gained from being with other board members and learning from them. Alternative training opportunities will help members face upcoming challenges and decision-making.

Every school board has an opportunity to champion legislation that would strip away the monopoly and allow for choice regarding access to professional learning. For example, Florida passed a bill in 2016 that gives school board members more autonomy. The bill amended state statutes to allow a school board member to choose whether to pay membership association dues. This example could benefit other states regarding association memberships and encourage members to lobby their legislators to champion similar legislation.

More detailed information about the NSBA, including its mission and priorities, particularly legislative, can be found at *www.NSBA.org*, on its "about me" page.

Alternative to State School Board Associations

Over the past several years, the education system has undergone significant changes and challenges, especially during the implementation of lockdowns and distance learning. These circumstances have illuminated various aspects of the education system and made them more transparent about the need for good school board members.

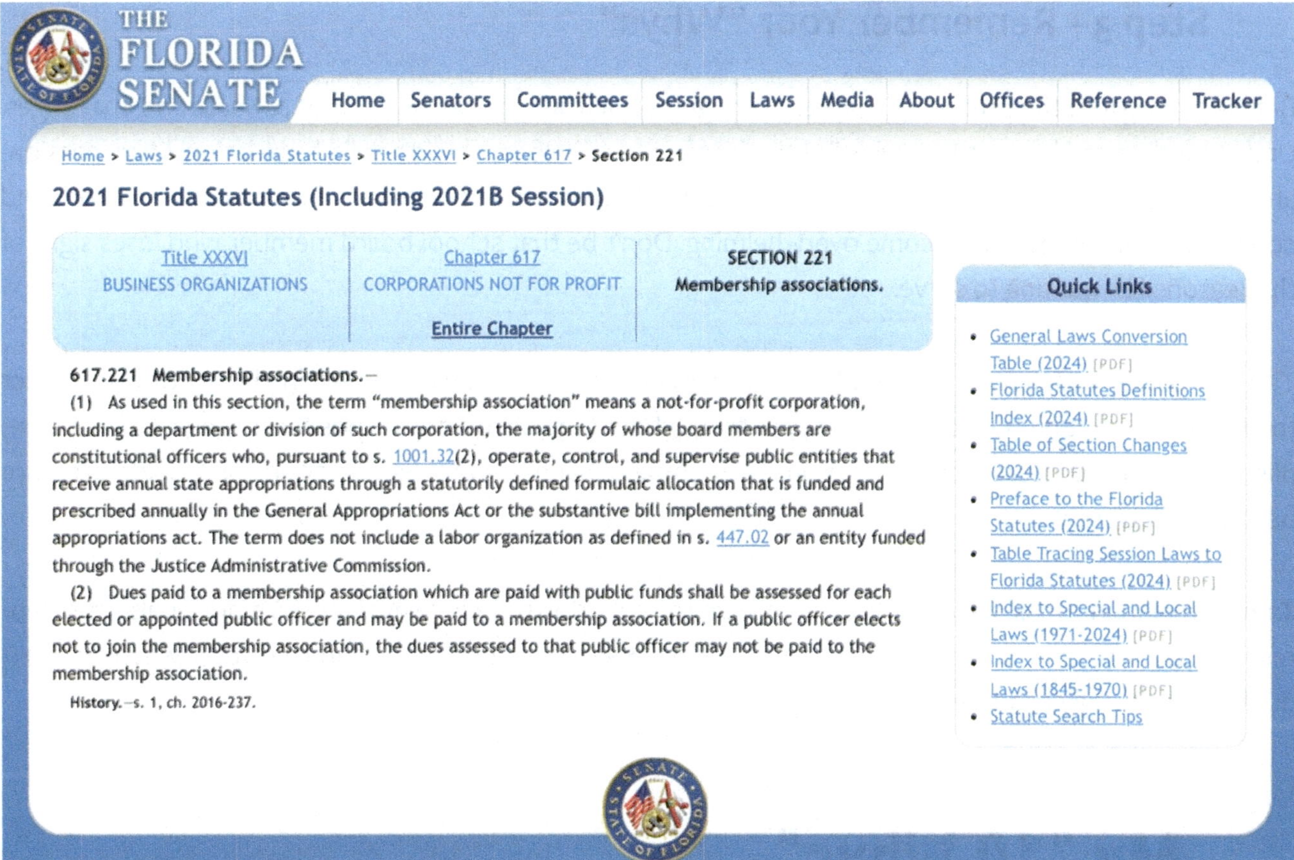

THE FLORIDA SENATE

Home | Senators | Committees | Session | Laws | Media | About | Offices | Reference | Tracker

Home > Laws > 2021 Florida Statutes > Title XXXVI > Chapter 617 > Section 221

2021 Florida Statutes (Including 2021B Session)

Title XXXVI	Chapter 617	SECTION 221
BUSINESS ORGANIZATIONS	CORPORATIONS NOT FOR PROFIT	Membership associations.
	Entire Chapter	

617.221 Membership associations.—

(1) As used in this section, the term "membership association" means a not-for-profit corporation, including a department or division of such corporation, the majority of whose board members are constitutional officers who, pursuant to s. 1001.32(2), operate, control, and supervise public entities that receive annual state appropriations through a statutorily defined formulaic allocation that is funded and prescribed annually in the General Appropriations Act or the substantive bill implementing the annual appropriations act. The term does not include a labor organization as defined in s. 447.02 or an entity funded through the Justice Administrative Commission.

(2) Dues paid to a membership association which are paid with public funds shall be assessed for each elected or appointed public officer and may be paid to a membership association. If a public officer elects not to join the membership association, the dues assessed to that public officer may not be paid to the membership association.

History.—s. 1, ch. 2016-237.

Quick Links

- General Laws Conversion Table (2024) [PDF]
- Florida Statutes Definitions Index (2024) [PDF]
- Table of Section Changes (2024) [PDF]
- Preface to the Florida Statutes (2024) [PDF]
- Table Tracing Session Laws to Florida Statutes (2024) [PDF]
- Index to Special and Local Laws (1971-2024) [PDF]
- Index to Special and Local Laws (1845-1970) [PDF]
- Statute Search Tips

Source: www.flsenate.gov

One notable outcome of the 2020 focus on school boards is the emergence of new school board associations. These associations are alternatives to the union-backed, Superintendent-sanctioned associations. They have been initiated mainly by current and former school board members who recognize the need for different perspectives and approaches in education and take the initiative to create alliances or coalitions.

The Arizona Coalition of School Board Members, School Board Member Alliance of Virginia, Carolina Academic Leadership Network, Kansas School Board Resource Center, Pennsylvania School Directors Coalition, and Florida Coalition of School Board Members are just a few alternatives trying to right the wrongs of the past. They aim to provide alternative viewpoints and solutions for board members in their respective states.

In addition to the state organizations, national organizations like ***Best In Ed*** have been recruiting and training school board candidates since 2020 to help candidates get elected and realize success. This has become the go-to source through books like this, as well as online and in-person leadership training for individuals, groups, and organizations. ***Scan the QR code to learn more about Best In Ed's resources***

Step 3 - Remember Your "Whys"

Before getting into the preceding chapters, recognize that this role can be a mix of rewards and challenges. Understanding and keeping the "whys" at the forefront will help you build a solid foundation. Many passionate elected officials launch their campaigns for the right reasons, but once they face the role's realities and complexities, it can quickly become overwhelming. Don't be that school board member who loses sight of the reasons for wanting to serve.

The role comes with a hefty workload that will demand serious commitment. As an elected official, expect to encounter scrutiny and criticism, but your focus should remain on driving positive change within a complicated system. Success ultimately lies in the members' hands—don't let self-doubt or outside pressure become a deterrent.

To help maintain focus, we encourage members to write down their "whys." They're not goals; they represent your motivations to run for the school board. Keep this note handy and refer to it whenever self-doubt rears its ugly head.

1. **My "10 Whys"**

Why am I here? What is my purpose for being here?

1. ______________________________
2. ______________________________
3. ______________________________
4. ______________________________
5. ______________________________
6. ______________________________
7. ______________________________
8. ______________________________
9. ______________________________
10. ______________________________

Board Member's Exercises **Exercise 1**

Chapter 2
Brief History of K-12 Education

From the earliest days of American colonial governance, education has been held in high esteem, leading to the establishment of foundational school finance laws aimed at supporting educational funding. These legislative efforts can be traced back to the Massachusetts Act of 1642, which emphasized the responsibility of parents and heads of households to ensure children's education. As property was viewed as a reflection of wealth, it became the basis for local education taxation, thereby establishing the state's initial authority to create and maintain schools. This was indeed a significant milestone in the evolution of public education.

Massachusetts's example quickly resonated with other states, prompting the adoption of similar laws utilizing property taxes to finance education. Connecticut followed suit in 1650, implementing even more stringent requirements. To this day, property taxes remain the predominant source of local school budgets.

As time progressed, notably in the wake of the Declaration of Independence in 1776 and the establishment of the Articles of Confederation, governance in the United States transitioned from having a federal focus to an emphasis on state constitutions. During this period, leaders vigorously debated whether governance should occur at the national or state level. The compromise reached in these discussions resulted in the exclusion of "education" from the Tenth Amendment, which means that matters not explicitly addressed by the federal government would default to the states' authority. Consequently, the Tenth Amendment is understood to designate educational powers to state governments.

The framers of the U.S. Constitution recognized the significance of education for the nation's future and democratic integrity. While the Constitution does not explicitly address education, the founders believed that many aspects of life should be managed by those closest to home—specifically parents, businesses, and state and local governments. This perspective continues to shape the dialogue around education policy today.

The Beginning of Federal Education Influence

1785

Although the framers suggested leaving education to the states and local communities, Congress could not help themselves and began passing legislation that forced funding through various mechanisms, such as the Land Ordinance of 1785 and the Northwest Ordinance of 1787. These laws illustrate how Congress started getting into the weeds of state and local governance by providing guidance and imposing restrictions on establishing territories.

Over the years, more mandates and intrusions continued. Congress passed federal legislation regarding education in 1802, 1845, 1868, 1876, 1890, 1936, and 1954, among other years.

1965

Over time, a state-centric approach was replaced by broader federal legislation. As long as federal requirements were adhered to, the creation of more federal laws increased the attachment to State, Student, and School funding (also referred to as the 3S's)

The money set aside by Congress for the 3S's now became interwoven with the ability to provide programs and services through these federal dollars. Fast forward to 1965, when President Lyndon Johnson's leadership led Congress to pass Public Law 89-10, known as the Elementary and Secondary Education Act (ESEA). (This Act laid the groundwork for today's Titles and was reauthorized through No Child Left Behind [NCLB] legislation enacted in 2001 under President George W. Bush.) The ESEA arguably catalyzes the establishment of the U.S. Department of Education (USDOE), providing federal funding for educational programs through USDOE. It originally included five titles that created categorical aid programs designed to address specific academic needs at the federal level. ***Scan the QR code to read the 1965 32 page act.***

The Birth of the First Five Titles

Title I, Supplemental program "grants" for economically disadvantaged communities.

Title II. consolidated nearly 30 categories at the time, including Americans with Disabilities Act (ADA), the Civil Rights Act of 1964, Social Security services, Part A, and other programs that are seen to support and provide funding through formulas and subgrants.

Title III, provides funds for supplemental education services for private and public schools. This includes block grants to address various special needs, including the creation of programs to teach non-English speaking students and the Jobs Act for universities with high rates of minority students,

Title IV, allocated funds for educational research and training laboratories. A key beneficiary of these funds is leading researcher Robert Marzano, who gained recognition in the early 2000s for his publications and research on classroom teaching. His work is now known for contributing to the debatable shift of teaching strategies to improve student learning. This work ultimately led to the widely used Marzano Teacher Evaluation Rubrics.

Title V provides funding to strengthen state education departments, commonly called State Education Agencies (SEAs). Before this legislation was enacted, approximately 15,000 school districts reported to a federal agency. School districts now go through their SEA, which reports to the federal agency. While other states chose to use the term "State Department of Education," Texas opted to align with the terminology used in the statute and named itself the Texas Education Agency.

1979

In 1979, Congress passed the Department of Education Organizational Act (Public Law 96-88) to consolidate several federal agencies into one department. This new department began operations in May 1980 after President Jimmy Carter signed legislation establishing the Federal Department of Education to manage the Title programs and federal funding to states and school districts. ***Scan the QR Code to read the full Department of Education Organization Act.***

Department of Education Organization Act

[Public Law 96–88, Approved Oct. 17, 1979, 93 Stat 669]

[As Amended Through P.L. 117–286, Enacted December 27, 2022]

【Currency: This publication is a compilation of the text of Public Law 96–88. It was last amended by the public law listed in the As Amended Through note above and below at the bottom of each page of the pdf version and reflects current law through the date of the enactment of the public law listed at https://www.govinfo.gov/app/collection/comps/】

【Note: While this publication does not represent an official version of any Federal statute, substantial efforts have been made to ensure the accuracy of its contents. The official version of Federal law is found in the United States Statutes at Large and in the United States Code. The legal effect to be given to the Statutes at Large and the United States Code is established by statute (1 U.S.C. 112, 204).】

SHORT TITLE; TABLE OF CONTENTS

SECTION 1. 【20 U.S.C. 3401 note】 This Act may be cited as the "Department of Education Organization Act".

TABLE OF CONTENTS

TITLE III—TRANSFERS OF AGENCIES AND FUNCTIONS

TITLE IV—ADMINISTRATIVE PROVISIONS

PART A—PERSONNEL PROVISIONS

PART B—GENERAL ADMINISTRATIVE PROVISIONS

TITLE V—TRANSITIONAL, SAVINGS, AND CONFORMING PROVISIONS

TITLE VI—EFFECTIVE DATE AND INTERIM APPOINTMENTS

TITLE I—GENERAL PROVISIONS

FINDINGS

SEC. 101. [20 U.S.C. 3401] The Congress finds that—

(1) education is fundamental to the development of individual citizens and the progress of the Nation;

(2) there is a continuing need to ensure equal access for all Americans to educational opportunities of a high quality, and such educational opportunities should not be denied because of race, creed, color, national origin, or sex;

(3) parents have the primary responsibility for the education of their children, and States, localities, and private insti-

February 2, 2023 As Amended Through P.L. 117-286, Enacted December 27, 2022

Source: www.govinfo.gov

2024
The USDOE website (www.ed.gov) states education is primarily responsibility of the state and local governments. *"It is states and communities, as well as public and private organizations of all kinds, that establish schools and colleges, develop curricula, and determine requirements for enrollment and graduation."* But is that truly the current situation?

The current structure does not reflect the aim of being an *"emergency response system"* that assists states and local communities during critical needs. It sounds like they see themselves as the "FEMA" of education. However, that is not the current model. The existing approach has become overreaching and often holds funding hostage for states and communities that do not comply with federal regulations and political whims.

In 2008, the federally-funded Race to the Top Grant (RTTT) incentivized states to adopt a unified set of educational standards, the Common Core State Standards, the sole national standards available at that time. Is it merely a coincidence that this alignment occurred?

and,

2022 USDOE established rule changes to enforce new regulations and stipulations under Title IX that, if not followed, could result in districts losing federal funding.

The Future of Education Is in Your Hands

The question is, board members, are you up for the challenge?

History is about to be made as President Donald J. Trump (47) aims to make significant changes by dismantling the U.S. Department of Education (USDOE). With a strong majority in both the U.S. Senate and Congress during his second term, starting January 20, 2025, we can expect rapid changes. The Trump Administration will focus on reversing federal control over local education. All members serving from 2025 to 2029 will have a front-row seat to witness these transformations.

As we have discussed, the U.S. Constitution suggests that education should be managed by those closest to it—specifically, you, as school board members. Board members are responsible for upholding their duties in accordance with their oaths. The Federal Department of Education was established nearly 45 years ago, and moving towards less federal oversight is a natural progression for education in America. The founding fathers never intended for education to be controlled by a distant bureaucracy that creates rules and laws based on a one-size-fits-all approach.

Communities and states have the best understanding of their students and parents—this is a fact. Board members, it is your job to educate yourselves! By studying and understanding the authority granted to you through your state's articles, codes, and statutes, you will realize you have everything needed to support your community without federal intervention. Furthermore, if challenges arise regarding governance, it is your responsibility to advocate for changes on behalf of all school board members in your state to modify existing laws.

This is not a time for fear; instead, it is a significant moment in history for board members to engage in the long-overdue return of educational control to local communities. Each state, with its unique characteristics, has the right to establish laws and board established policies that give you authority over your students' educational outcomes, with or without the Federal Department of Education. You will be able to chart this course.

Regardless of whether you govern with liberal or conservative principles, you were elected because your constituents align with your goals and beliefs. No matter who is sitting in the presidency or controlling the House and Senate, local communities can maintain their own governance model by returning funds and power to the states. These facts should alleviate any anxiety that may come from the potential dismantling of the federal Department of Education.

The Constitution's intent cannot be fulfilled if board members do not grasp their roles, authority, and responsibilities. It will take a commitment to invest time in understanding the relevant laws. There's a saying, "If I can't trust you with the small things, how can I trust you with the big ones?" In our lifetime, when it comes to education, there is nothing more significant than the dismantling of the USDOE.

Are you ready? Are you prepared and capable of exercising your authority according to existing state laws? Suppose the Trump Administration (47) successfully dissolves the federal department and returns control to the states. Can you catapult your local education system through good governance and strategic planning? Setting priorities and meticulously monitoring the funds in and out of your district? Or are you going to be unprepared, resist the change, or delegate your authority to the Superintendent and the internal bureaucracy and undermine the fundamental principle outlined in the U.S. Constitution that communities should manage education through elected representatives at all levels?

Often, one does not know what is needed until it is required. That is why this resource is not a one-time read. It is a guide to help members with the various issues or questions that will arise. The future can be forecasted but cannot be predicted.

This book will help you take a proactive approach rather than always being reactive. While it's impossible to predict every situation you may encounter, the fundamental principles and foundational components shared by current and former school board members will ensure you have support along the way.

The following section will help you understand all aspects of board governance. By gaining this knowledge, you will be better prepared to face the everyday challenges board members encounter and become an emerging leader on the board.

Notes

Section 2: **Board Governance**

Objectives for Section 2: Board Governance

1. **Establish a Framework for Effective Governance:** Provide school board members with a structured understanding of governance principles, emphasizing the importance of a clear organizational framework to enable effective oversight and decision-making.

2. **Promote Ethical Decision-Making:** Equip members with knowledge and tools necessary to manage ethical dilemmas and manage conflicts of interest, ensuring decisions align with the best interests of students and the community.

3. **Enhance Meeting Effectiveness:** Guide board members in the importance of structured meetings and well-prepared agendas, promoting productive discussions and informed decision-making that adheres to best practices in governance.

4. **Build Collaborative Relationships:** Emphasize the significance of professional trust and collaboration among board members, the superintendent, and staff to create a healthy board dynamic to support student success.

5. **Master Parliamentary Procedures:** Familiarize school board members with Robert's Rules of Order to ensure meetings are conducted fairly, efficiently, and effectively, allowing all members to participate equally in discussions and decision-making.

Governance, as defined by the Merriam-Webster online dictionary, refers to the act or process of overseeing and directing an organization, such as a school district. For school board members, this concept translates into a structured framework for exercising their authority and responsibilities.

Effective governance and respected ethical practices establish a clear set of rules and regulations that enable school board members to express their opinions and hold one another accountable. This framework ensures each member understands their role and the parameters within which they operate. While state constitutions and statutes provide legal foundations for school board governance, board members should also pursue additional learning to better serve their communities. By studying resources such as Robert's Rules of Order, Sunshine law, and educational law, members can tackle complex issues, shape policies, and engage meaningfully in local governance. School board members must approach their roles intentionally, recognizing the significant influence they wield in transforming education from a leadership position within local government.

Successful governance extends beyond structuring work; it also relies on professional and collaborative relationships. Key elements that contribute to effective school governance include preparation and differentiation, positional empathy, the development of professional trust, and the promotion of leadership through meaningful professional development (Eubanks, Goldson, & Callahan, 2024).

The Corporate Body of the School Board

A school board's authority operates as a corporate body, meaning that its power and oversight derive from the collective Board rather than individual members. Each member has one vote, and decisions regarding policies, recommendations, and other matters are made by majority vote. This collective approach underscores that authority resides with the board as a whole, not with individual members.

A healthy board dynamic is characterized by mutual respect among the superintendent, staff, and board members. Every board member's input, whether shared in one-on-one discussions or during publicly advertised meetings, contributes to the decision-making process.

Foundation of Board Governance Includes:

1. **Structured Framework:** Governance provides a clear organizational structure for school board operations.

2. **Legal Compliance:** State statutes establish essential governance elements.

3. **Intentionality and Organization:** Understanding governance principles strengthens leadership skills, enabling leaders to guide and support student success effectively.

The role and significance of school board governance are important in shaping student outcomes, as lackluster leadership among board members often results in equally disappointing results for students. Conversely, when boards actively seek improvement, they advance a culture of high expectations and mutual accountability that drives enhanced performance. While the focus often falls on the superintendent to spearhead success, effective governance is equally important for student achievement through a comprehensive strategy encompassing several key components. At its core is "clear accountability," which establishes the roles of board members and school administrators, creating a culture of excellence that inspires staff and reinforces their commitment to student success. This structured approach ensures educational initiatives are meticulously tailored to address the specific needs of their communities, ultimately leading to better outcomes for students.

In Chapter 3, we will examine the subject of "Ethical Decision-Making and Conflicts of Interest," exploring the principles and practices that form the foundation of effective governance. This chapter aims to equip school board members with a solid understanding of ethical dilemmas they may encounter and the frameworks for resolving their responsibilities

Chapter 4 takes an in-depth look at "The School Board's Master Calendar," highlighting its importance in strategic planning. We will discuss how a well-structured calendar ensures all board activities are systematically organized, facilitating a proactive approach to governance and ensuring important deadlines and events are not overlooked.

In Chapter 5, the focus shifts to the significance of "Meetings and Agendas." We will examine the importance of structured meetings in promoting meaningful discussions, encouraging collaboration, and facilitating informed decision-making. This chapter will provide practical strategies for developing effective agendas that help maximize each meeting's productivity.

Finally, Chapter 6 will guide readers through the intricacies of "Parliamentary Procedures: Robert's Rules of Order". This chapter aims to furnish board members with essential tools and techniques to maintain order and efficiency during meetings, ensuring that everyone has a voice and discussions remain focused and constructive.

Collectively, these chapters will provide valuable insights and practical guidance, enabling school board members to refine their governance practices and make a lasting, positive impact on their educational communities.

Chapter 3

Ethical Decision-Making and Conflicts of Interest

As a school board member, your primary responsibility is to act in the best interests of students, educators, and the community you serve. However, this ideal can sometimes be challenged when personal, financial, or political interests intersect with your duties. Ethical decision-making is vital for maintaining trust within the community and ensuring the integrity of school governance. One of the first trainings a board member should take is "Ethics."

Violating ethics laws in your role could result in losing your position, facing fines and penalties, and in some states, ethical violations can be considered criminal offenses. Members should be aware of the ethics training requirements in their state and use this chapter as a guide to understanding ethical decision-making and effectively managing any conflicts of interest.

The Importance of Ethical Decision-Making

Ethical decision-making in the context of school board governance involves ensuring personal beliefs, biases, and external pressures do not cloud your judgment or interfere with your responsibilities as a public servant. School board members are entrusted with significant responsibilities, including setting policies, overseeing budgets, and making decisions that impact the lives of students, staff, and families. Therefore, it is essential that every decision made aligns with the public good and is grounded in fairness, transparency, and accountability.

Ethical decision-making requires a clear understanding of personal values and the ability to prioritize the interests of the community over personal or political agendas. Upholding ethical standards ensures school boards function with integrity and build public trust, which is vital for achieving long-term educational success and strengthening a positive school culture.

Key Principles of Ethical Decision-Making

1 **Transparency**: Always be open about your decision-making process and the factors that influence your choices. Transparency builds trust and ensures the public can review and hold you accountable.

2. **Accountability**: Take responsibility for your decisions and actions. When making decisions, be mindful of the consequences and ensure your choices align with your obligations to the community and the students you serve.

3. **Fairness**: Strive to treat all individuals equally, considering the needs of all students and families in the community. Ethical decision-making involves balancing competing interests in a way that promotes fairness and impartiality for all stakeholders.

4. **Objectivity**: Avoid making decisions based on personal preferences, external pressures, or political motivations. Ensure all decisions are made based on facts, research, and in the best interests of the educational system as a whole.

Dealing with Conflicts of Interest

Conflicts of interest arise when a school board member's personal interests—whether financial, familial, or political—compete with their public duty. These conflicts can undermine the decision-making process and erode public trust. Identifying, disclosing, and managing conflicts of interest ensures ethical governance and avoids situations where board members may be perceived as acting in their own interest rather than in the best interest of the students and community.

Types of Conflicts of Interest

1. **Financial**: These occur when a school board member stands to personally gain from decisions made by the board. For example, a board member who was previously employed by a contractor that participated in discussions for specific technical services may face a conflict of interest. These types of conflicts are particularly sensitive and must be handled with transparency and caution.

2. **Family and Personal Relationships**: Conflicts can arise if a board member has personal relationships that could influence their decisions. For example, if a board member's relative is up for a teaching position or seeking a contract with the district, it could present a conflict of interest, as the board member may be inclined to influence decisions to benefit their family member.

3. **Political**: School board members may face pressure from political parties or interest groups that have a stake in educational decisions. These political influences can create conflicts when board members' political views or affiliations influence their votes rather than making impartial decisions that benefit students and the community.

Managing Conflicts of Interest Best Practices

1. **Disclosure**: Full disclosure of any potential conflicts of interest is essential. When a board member has a conflict, they must openly disclose it before participating in relevant discussions or voting on related matters. Disclosure should be made during public meetings; written statements may be required to ensure transparency.

2. **Recusal**: In situations where a board member has a conflict of interest, they must recuse themselves from participating in the discussion or vote. Recusal helps protect the integrity of the decision-making process and prevents any undue influence from personal interests.

3. **Avoiding the Appearance of a Conflict**: Even if a conflict of interest does not exist in a legal sense, it's important to consider the appearance of a conflict. School board members should act in ways that avoid even the perception of impropriety. This helps maintain public trust and confidence in the board's work.

4. **Establishing Clear Policies**: School boards should develop clear policies outlining how conflicts of interest should be handled. These include procedures for disclosure, recusal, and reporting and are reviewed regularly to ensure compliance with local laws and regulations. Adopting a formal policy also provides a consistent framework for addressing conflicts and helps prevent potential ethical lapses and violations.

5. **Independent Oversight**: In certain cases, especially when conflicts of interest are complex, it may be appropriate to seek guidance from an independent third party, such as the board's legal counsel or an ethics commission. Independent oversight ensures conflicts are handled impartially and in accordance with the law.

Avoiding Ethical Pitfalls

In addition to managing conflicts of interest, school board members must be vigilant against other ethical pitfalls, such as bias, favoritism, and undue influence from external sources. Here are some tips for avoiding common ethical challenges.

Be Aware of Personal Bias: Recognize your biases and actively work to ensure these do not influence your decisions. This includes biases related to political affiliation, personal relationships, or past experiences. Strive to make decisions based on objective criteria rather than personal preferences.

Maintain Professionalism: Always approach your role with professionalism and integrity. Avoid behaviors that could be perceived as unethical, such as accepting gifts or favors from vendors, contractors, or individuals who have business with the school district.

Engage in Ethical Reflection: Regularly engage in ethical reflection, considering how your decisions align with your values, your responsibilities to the community, and the students' best interests. Ethical decision-making is not always clear-cut, and regularly reflecting on your actions can help ensure decisions are made in good faith.

Establish Open Communication Channels: Encourage open and honest communication among board members, staff, and the public. Transparency and dialogue help ensure that all perspectives are considered and the board remains accountable to the community.

Seek Training on Ethics: Many school districts provide training programs on ethics, governance, and conflict management for their staff. By participating in these programs, you can enhance your understanding of the ethical standards expected of you and gain resources for addressing ethical dilemmas.

Ethical decision-making and managing conflicts of interest are integral to the effective governance of school districts. School board members must prioritize the public good above personal interests, maintain transparency, and adhere to the highest ethical standards in their decision-making. School boards need to govern with integrity to maintain trust in the educational system and ensure board members fulfill their duties in a manner that benefits all students, staff, and the community at large.

Chapter 4

The School Board's Master Calendar

It's important to differentiate between the board calendar and the district calendar. The district calendar is closely tied to instructional time and staff needs for the school year and follows a defined academic schedule (e.g., 2025-2026). In contrast, the board calendar operates on a continuous yearly cycle.

If the board lacks a calendar, this presents an opportunity for positive change. Collaborating with the board to establish and maintain a functioning calendar can significantly enhance effectiveness and mitigate the risk of being caught off guard regarding time management. Ideally, this calendar should be regularly updated throughout the year, with the board clerk in charge. All assistant superintendents and the superintendent should feel encouraged to contribute important dates, ensuring comprehensive coverage.

Throughout the year, the board will engage in budget hearings, budget approvals, state legislative sessions, organizational meetings, superintendent evaluations, contract reviews, school start and end dates, days off, graduations, performances, and committee meetings. Having all these events on the board calendar can relieve some stress of staying organized and prepared.

The calendar will require regular adjustments and asking the clerk to create calendar invites can be a simple yet effective way to ensure everyone is on the same page. This way, all relevant information will be readily available, making it easier to manage time, location, and agendas.

A well-structured calendar will help you stay organized and prepared for upcoming meetings. For instance, if there's an upcoming budget review; knowing about it in advance will allow you time to review the materials thoroughly rather than rushing in at the last minute.

Attending Committee Meetings

As a board member, attending committee meetings is a way to gain valuable insights into their ongoing work. Staying connected to these discussions is a part of the monitoring role for understanding the process and learning who the individuals are involved in making recommendations to the superintendent, which will ultimately be presented to the board for approval. Even if there is no formal invitation, attending as a citizen observer can keep one aware of processes.

If holding back thoughts during the meeting is challenging, it might be wise to reconsider attending. As an observer, the role is to learn and absorb information without influencing the committee's dynamics. This respect for the process is essential for maintaining the integrity of their work, allowing other board members to rely on the committee's recommendations without another board member's influence.

School District Activities

Attending school events offers one of the most rewarding ways to support the district. Whether it's graduations, science fairs, or music concerts, being present reflects your commitment. It shows students, teachers, and parents that you have a genuine concern for the impact on their lives and an eagerness to learn about what happens in their school.

To build trust as a board member, you must stay actively engaged throughout your term of office rather than only during campaign season. By being present and participating in community activities, you'll gain valuable insight that will enhance the board's perspective when the budget season arrives. Engaging with the students, parents, and staff allows for understanding educational needs and making informed and thoughtful decisions rather than viewing budget items merely as numbers. Ongoing involvement will enrich your contributions and strengthen the connection between the board and the community.

Being actively involved in school visits and community events doesn't just show support; it can also be gratifying. Witnessing firsthand the positive impact of the board's dedication to students and families can invigorate your enthusiasm and be a reminder of your "whys" rooted in reasons for serving. It can be discouraging at times, but take advantage of the opportunities to see the impact the board is making.

To sum up, understand that serving as a board member is a significant commitment. The reward comes with the responsibility to participate and be visible within the community. Try to adhere to the calendar commitments, stay engaged, attend various activities, and be alert to district and community needs.

Important Dates to Remember

- Board business meetings and work sessions
- Superintendent evaluation due
- Superintendent contract renewal
- Budget workshops
- Legislative education committee hearing start
- Legislative session begin and end
- District office is closed
- Committee meetings
- Graduations
- First day of school year
- Last day of school year
- Public hearings
- Board clerk's vacation days
- Annual state required professional development completion dates

Chapter 5

Meetings and Agendas

School boards typically hold various types of meetings to manage school districts' governance. These meetings are essential for setting policies, making decisions regarding educational programs, and overseeing the district's budget and administration. As you spend more time on the board, you will become more familiar with each type of meeting. Below is a description of the common types of meetings held by school boards, from the most common to the least frequently used.

Before we discuss the various types of meetings and their characteristics, it's important to know what is essential for all meetings. Each meeting should have proper notice, a posted agenda, supporting documentation, and minutes recorded. Additionally, the meeting should be open to the public unless it is an executive session.

Regular Business Meetings

Scheduled meetings are held consistently, either monthly or bi-monthly, and are open to the public. They constitute the school board's business sessions. They focus on overseeing budgets that range from millions to billions of dollars, as well as policies and learning initiatives that impact hundreds to thousands of students and employees. Acknowledging the complexity of this institution is essential, and this should be the primary focus.

Attendees need to receive constant updates on various issues, including employee vacancies, quarterly budget expenditures, safety concerns, adherence to policies and regulations, compliance of the superintendent with state report submissions, student attendance updates, public concerns, and, most importantly, ongoing monitoring of student achievement progress. (This is not an exhaustive list.)

The meetings should be a transparent process for the public. Regular meetings are not the appropriate setting for promotional activities or to showcase presentations by the school district. While different forums may be established for such public displays, they should not occur during the school board's business meetings. Time is valuable for board members, employees, and the parents attending these meetings. Parents expect a board meeting that responsibly addresses all aspects of the district and operates efficiently rather than delegating these responsibilities solely to the superintendent.

School boards must fully embrace their accountability for student learning progress. They must ensure they have created and maintained a safe teaching environment while demonstrating their collective authority over the school division.

The Agenda

The agenda for each meeting must be prepared well in advance to meet posting requirements and comply with the Sunshine Laws and the Freedom of Information Act (FOIA). The responsibility for preparing the agenda may vary by board and state. Many boards will have a policy that states the superintendent will prepare the agenda with consultation by the board chair/president. The agenda sets the tone for all the meetings and requires thorough preparation from the superintendent and their staff. Depending on board policies and state laws, the chair relies on the superintendent to manage these details effectively. The presiding chairman will use the agenda to guide the meetings. ***Scan the QR code that refers to the illustration below as a guide of a well organized and prepared business meeting agenda, complete with supporting information.***

Understanding Agendas

Many categories on the agenda are referred to as agenda items. How the board will vote and discuss the items will be determined depending on how they are categorized.

Action Agenda

An action item for a school board is a specific task that requires discussion and action from board members. Unlike routine items, an action item signifies a defined task that requires careful deliberation and decision-making by the board.

These items demand open discussion and an explanation from the superintendent regarding the recommendation.

- Budget revisions and new contracts are examples of such items. During meetings, board members can propose action items by expressing their interests or through committee recommendations.

It's important not to underestimate the significance of moving an item from consent to action if you believe it warrants further debate or explanation. Remember that most people have jobs and may not be aware of what was discussed in a work session that led to the item.

Consent Agenda

Consent items typically include ministerial or routine matters, such as renewed contracts for budgeted positions and preparations for the new school year. The purpose of the consent agenda is to streamline meetings, allowing the board to focus on its primary business. This agenda usually contains multiple items that require board approval but generally does not necessitate a whole discussion at every meeting.

The standard procedure is to make a motion to approve the consent agenda. However, it is best practice not to include financial items or policy changes here. Therefore, reviewing the consent agenda items carefully before the meeting is essential. As mentioned previously, any board member may request the removal of an item for further clarification or discussion before the vote, and the chair should honor this request.

Be mindful of potential transparency issues. A superintendent, unfortunately, could try to include controversial items in the consent agenda to bypass discussion or scrutiny. Remembering your authority and responsibility to monitor and govern effectively is important here. Treat consent items with the same level of diligence as any action item, as there is no such thing as a routine item that doesn't require a thorough examination before you cast your vote.

Typically, appropriate items for a consent agenda include routine procedural decisions and those that are unlikely to be controversial. Examples of these are approval of meeting minutes; final approval of proposals or reports the board has been discussing for some time and with which all members are familiar; routine matters such as committee appointments; staff appointments that require Board confirmation; reports provided for informational purposes only; and correspondence that requires no action.

Although meeting minutes may seem mundane, they ensure consistency and oversight. The board's attorney should review them before each meeting. If the board clerk falls behind on transcription and preparation, the district may violate board policy and state laws regarding meeting minutes. Minutes should be created consistently to ensure compliance after Board approval. This can be achieved if the clerk is organized and adequately trained. It is important not to overlook this responsibility; always remain vigilant and ask questions if any minutes are missing.

Public Comments

Public comment is a standard aspect of all regular business meetings. The guidelines for this portion of the meeting vary significantly depending on each board's policies. While school boards often adopt a three-minute speaking limit for public comments, this practice is less common in city council, commission, and other city government meetings. Your board can modify this speaking time or maintain the current practice, which may or may not be effective for your district.

Speaking at a public meeting can be incredibly daunting. For many individuals, it often represents the last resort to voice frustrations over issues that may have been overlooked or mishandled, ultimately leading them to present their concerns at a school board meeting. Acknowledging the feelings behind these frustrations and treating all community members with the utmost respect is vital. Their willingness to engage with and advocate for their children in the public school system deserves sincere appreciation. This level of involvement is what helps create a supportive and collaborative educational environment.

The chair ensures the superintendent provides detailed updates to the board about parents' concerns. These concerns are often deeply personal and tied to the daily lives of families within the school district. Addressing this feedback in future board meetings demonstrates these individuals' voices are heard and valued.

SCHOOL BOARD MEETING
Minnetonka I.S.D. #276
5621 County Road 101
Minnetonka, Minnesota

www.minnetonkaschools.org

January 7, 2025

The mission of the Minnetonka School District, a community that transcends traditional definitions of excellence and where dreams set sail, is to ensure all students envision and pursue their highest aspirations while serving the greater good, through teaching and learning which

- *Value and nurture each individual,*
- *Inspire in everyone a passion to excel with confidence and hope, and*
- *Instill expectations that stimulate extraordinary achievement in the classroom and in life.*

(All times are approximate)

6:35 Recognitions: Tonka District Select Choir State Conference Performers; Football 6A State Runners-up; Bowling State Qualifiers; and 2024 AP Scholars

7:00 I. Call to Order

II. Pledge to the Flag

III. Adoption of the Agenda

7:00 IV. Election of School Board Officers for 2025
A. Chair
B. Vice-Chair
C. Treasurer
D. Clerk
E. Deputy Clerk/Deputy Treasurer

7:05 V. School Report: SAIL

7:20 VI. Community Comments
Community Comments is an opportunity for the public to address the School Board on an item included in this agenda in accordance with the guidelines printed at the end of this agenda.

7:25 VII. Organization of the School Board
A. Fixing the Time, Day and Place of Each Regular Board Meeting
B. Fixing the Time, Day and Place of Board Study Sessions
C. Setting of Salaries: Chairperson; Vice Chairperson; Treasurer; Clerk and Board Directors
D. Resolution Designating Depositories
E. Designation of Official Newspaper

F. Designation of Official Radio Station for Emergency Announcements
G. Appointment of Auditor
H. Setting of Superintendent's Evaluation Dates
I. Setting of Mileage Allowance for Business Purposes
J. Determination of Board Committee Assignments

7:30 VIII. Approval of FY26 Budget Adjustments

7:50 IX. Presentation on Draft of 2025-26 School Board Goals

8:00 X. CONSENT AGENDA
a. Minutes of December 5, 2024 Regular Meeting
b. Study Session Summary of December 19, 2024
c. Payment of Bills
d. Recommended Personnel Items
e. Gifts and Donations
f. Electronic Fund Transfers
g. Course Addition

8:00 XI. Board Reports

8:05 XII. Superintendent's Report

8:10 XIII. Announcements

8:10 XIV. Adjournment

GUIDELINES FOR *COMMUNITY COMMENTS*

Welcome to the Minnetonka Schools Board Meeting! In the interest of open communications, the Minnetonka School District wishes to provide an opportunity for the public to address the School Board. That opportunity is provided at every regular School Board meeting during *Community Comments*.

1. Anyone indicating a desire to speak to an item included in the meeting agenda—except for the Consent Agenda and/or information that personally identifies or violates the privacy rights of an individual—during *Community Comments* will be acknowledged by the Board Chair. When called upon to speak, please state your name, connection to the District, and topic. All remarks shall be addressed to the Board as a whole, not to any specific member(s) or to any person who is not a member of the Board.
2. If there are a number of individuals present to speak on the same topic, please designate a spokesperson who can summarize the issue.
3. Please limit your comments to three minutes. Longer time may be granted at the discretion of the Board Chair. If you have written comments, the Board would like to have a copy, which will help them better understand, investigate and respond to your concern.
4. During *Community Comments* the Board and administration listen to comments. Board members or the Superintendent may ask clarifying questions of you in order to gain a thorough understanding of your concern, suggestion or request. If there is any response or follow-up to your comment or suggestion, you will be contacted via email or phone by a member of the Board or administration in a timely manner.
5. Please be aware that disrespectful comments or comments of a personal nature, directed at an individual either by name or inference, will not be allowed. Personnel concerns should be directed first to a principal or executive director of the department, then to the Executive Director of Human Resources, then to the Superintendent and finally in writing to the Board.

School Board meetings are rebroadcast via a local cable provider.
Please visit the "District/Leadership/School Board" page on our website for a current schedule.

Source: www.minnetonkaschools.org

Acknowledging citizens' concerns is not only courteous but also a fundamental aspect of honoring their contributions, primarily because their hard-earned taxpayer money supports many operations within the public education system. Unfortunately, following up on parent and citizen concerns is often missing in school board meetings. For school boards that aspire to be responsive and accountable to their parents and constituents, recognizing and addressing these critical concerns should be seen as a best practice and an essential part of facilitating a supportive and transparent educational community.

To avoid legal issues, refer to the First Amendment chapter to understand the expected legal challenges school boards have faced in recent years due to practices and policies deemed not allowable according to recent court cases.

The Superintendent Report

The report needs to be a business report to the school board. As the most highly paid employee of the district and the one directly accountable to the school board, superintendents must be ready and able to give these important reports at most business meetings:

- Follow-up to concerns from the public at the previous meeting
- Follow-up to requests from board members
- Reporting on student achievement progress as requested by the board
- Reporting on employee concerns, employee vacancies, employee hires, and retirements (this may also be submitted to the board as a document each month)
- Reporting on budget expenditures to date (budget update)
- Explain and share the reports submitted to the State and the Federal Government on behalf of the board during the past month.
- A brief report of upcoming reports to be submitted to the State and Federal Government on behalf of the board next month.
- Any request from the administration for needed action, study, or policy to be done by the board in the near future.
- Any personal leave from the district in the past month regarding presentations and/or professional development (of the superintendent and other administrators as requested by the board)

School Board Member Discussion

Most school board meetings allow members to contribute during a member "discussion time" before closing the meeting. Depending on the board's traditions and policies, this discussion time may occur at the beginning or the end of the meeting and may or may not have limited time frames. Typically, board members are free to discuss any item of celebration or concern of their choosing. Use this time strategically and purposefully.

It may be a time to discuss your reasoning behind a particular sensitive vote or to respond to concerns you have received via emails or texts. It may be used to make a special request for information from the superintendent or request public input on a topic before the next meeting. It may be a time to inform the public of your particular interests in improving the district or to complement improvements made within the district.

Other Meetings

Organizational Meeting

The organizational meeting will be your first meeting as a new board member for the calendar year. This meeting will include voting for the new board chairman and vice chairman. Once the new presiding chairman is in place, the board may take a recess to allow the new chairman a minute to review the agenda in order to proceed. The board should vote on the year's business meeting schedule during the organizational meeting. For example, "Meet 1st Tuesday and 4th Tuesday of the month at 6 pm." The business meetings should be set and consistent.

Secondly, the board chairman will assign committee appointments during the organizational meeting. Every district has relationships and various board liaisons with government entities, and some of these positions are voting positions. The clerk should have prepared the board with the details of these appointments and they should be equally divided among all. These are outside school district meetings and committees. For example, legislative liaison, health advisory committee, tri-county local government meetings, and workforce development.

Work/Study Sessions

Although work sessions may be less formal than regular meetings, they are still legal board meetings and are subject to all public records requests and Sunshine law requirements. To be productive, work sessions require strategic planning so a focused and purposeful agenda with minimal topics should be followed. These sessions may or may not occur regularly. To call a session a "work" session, all board members should be asked for suggested input.

These work sessions may be used for boards to receive professional development. These are also open meetings to the public. Again, the time, date, location, and agenda publication must meet legal requirements for a work session. The clerk may need to provide various documents and reports to the board relevant to the "work" to be done by the board. Ideally, this occurs before the meeting, giving time for the board members to come prepared to work. The board may also require a special presentation from the administration for their information on a specific topic. In short, work sessions are not to be just another "regular" board meeting.

Special Meetings

Special meetings are called as needed, outside the regular meeting schedule, to address urgent or specific issues that cannot wait until the next meeting. These meetings must be publicly announced in advance, and they typically focus on a single topic, such as a pressing budgetary decision or an emergency.

Executive Sessions or Closed Meetings

This type of meeting is closed to the public and is held to discuss confidential matters such as personnel issues, legal advice on potential litigation, contract negotiations, and security issues. Although decisions cannot be made in executive session, the board may discuss matters privately and then return to an open session to vote or take action. See your state laws to understand what must be in a motion for the board to go into a closed or an executive session. The public must know why they are not hearing the business of the board. For instance, the Virginia FOIA law requires explicitly three components to be in every motion: 1) the subject, 2) the purpose of the subject being discussed, and 3) the specific *exemption number* of the FOIA law being used to validate the use of the closed meeting.

Emergency Meetings

Emergency meetings may be convened with minimal notice during emergencies requiring immediate attention. However, these meetings are subject to specific legal requirements regarding notice and the nature of the emergency being addressed.

Public Hearings

Public hearings are specially designated meetings that gather public input on specific issues, such as budget proposals, boundary changes, or policy revisions. They provide a formal opportunity for community members to present their views and comments directly to the board.

Retreats

First of all, can we call these something other than "board retreats?" It creates the wrong image in your constituents' minds – members enjoying a vacation on the taxpayers' dime, and we know this is not and should not be the case. These board working sessions are less formal gatherings where board members and district leadership can engage in extended discussions about long-term goals, monitor strategic planning progress, and engage in team-building activities.

Just like all meetings, proper laws govern public notification, including an off-site board training day. If the board chooses an "off-site" location, it should not be so far that the public is inhibited from attending if they so choose. Minutes should also be recorded of all activities that occur at these retreats. Ideally, the retreat should be broadcast live, the same as any meeting of the district school board.

Each type of meeting plays a distinct role in the governance of a school district, allowing school boards to fulfill their responsibilities transparently and effectively while engaging with the community they serve.

Notes

SCHOOL BOARD MEMBERS'

uide to Common Parliamentary Procedures and Language

erstanding primary proceedings as a board member requires familiarization with parliamentary procedures and language, specifically Robert's Rules of Order, ch outline the framework for conducting meetings. These rules enable board members to actively participate by asking questions, proposing limits on debate, redirecting discussions that stray from the agenda. With a solid understanding of these procedures, you can advocate for fairness, guarantee equal speaking e for all members, and spot inconsistencies in how rules are applied. This knowledge not only enhances your effectiveness on the board but also makes a e structured and respectful atmosphere during meetings.

BASIC RULES

Only one subject may be before a group at one time Each item is proposed as a motion, requires a "second," and is restated by the chair before voting.

"Negative" motions are generally not permitted Motions should propose positive actions. If the action is undesired, vote it down unless denial needs justification.

Only one person may speak at any given time Robert's Rules dictate a speaker order. The mover speaks first and last for clarity and rebuttal.

All members have equal rights Each speaker must be recognized by the chairman prior to speaking. Each speaker should make clear his or her intent by stating, "I wish to speak for/against the motion" prior to stating an argument.

Full and free debate Everyone has the chance to speak once before anyone speaks twice.

Rights of minority, will of majority Minority views are heard, but decisions reflect the majority's will.

IOTIONS

iness is brought before the school board by motions, a formal procedure for taking actions. To e a motion, a member must first be recognized by the chairman or president of the board. After member has made a motion (and after the motion is seconded if required), the chair must then tate it or rule it out of order, then call for discussion. Most motions require a second, although re are a few exceptions.

portant to note exact wording of motions and amendments is important for clarity and recording in minutes. If it's complex, the motion should be written down for the chair to read.

bert's Rules of Order provides for four general types of motions: main motions, subsidiary tions, incidental motions, and renewal motions.

lain Motions

e most important are main motions, which bring before the board, for its action, any particular oject. Main motions cannot be made when any other motions are before the group.

ubsidiary Motions

Tabling Postpones discussion until a majority vote resumes it. Requires a second and is not debatable or amendable.

Previous question or close debate Ends debate and moves to a vote. Requires a second, is not debatable, and needs a two-thirds majority.

Limit/extend debate Sets or adjusts time limits for discussion as needed.

Postpone to a definite time Delays discussion to a specific date and time.

Refer to committee Assigns the matter to a committee for further study and reporting.

Amendment Modifies a motion to make it more acceptable. Requires a second, is debatable, and is voted on before the main motion.

Postpone indefinitely Defeats a motion without direct rejection. Requires a two-thirds vote to reconsider later.

Incidental Motions

Incidental motions are housekeeping motions which are in order at any time, taking precedence over main motions and subsidiary motions. These motions include:

- **Point of order** Highlights rule violations. Requires the chair to rule on immediate consideration.
- **Appeal from the decision of the chair** Allows the board to overrule the chair's decision. Requires a second, limited debate, and a majority vote.
- **Parliamentary inquiry** Asks if an action is in order. Not a motion. Point of information Offers relevant information to the group without debate.
- **Division of assembly** Requests precise vote counting (e.g., hand-raising). Requires no second, vote, or debate.
- **Request to withdraw a motion** Mover needs majority approval to withdraw a motion.
- **Suspension of the rules** Allows exceptions to formal rules with a two-thirds vote. Requires a second but is not debatable or amendable.
- **Object to consideration of a question** Blocks an improper motion. Requires a two-thirds vote if not ruled out by the chair.

Renewal Motions

Once the board has taken action, renewal motions require the group to further discuss or dispose of a motion. The motions include:

- **Reconsider** When the board needs to discuss further a motion that has already been defeated at the same meeting. A majority of the board must approve taking additional time to debate the motion again. The motion can be made only by a person who previously voted on the prevailing side. Contrary to another popular misconception, the motion may be brought up again at a subsequent meeting. If the moderator does not believe the group's wishes have changed, however, the motion can be ruled out of order, subject to an appeal from the decision of the chair.
- **Take from the table** Unless the original motion to table directed that the motion be brought back at a specific date and time, a majority of the board must pass a motion to take from the table. Such a motion is non-debatable.
- **Rescind** When the board wishes to annul an action, a motion to rescind is in order at any time. If prior notice has been given to the board that this action will be considered, the motion to rescind can pass with a simple majority vote; however, if no prior notice has been given, the vote requires a two-thirds majority.

QUESTIONS OF PRIVILEGE

Finally, there are a few questions of privilege that are in order at any time and must be disposed of prior to resuming discussion on the matter at hand:

- **Fix the time for next meeting** This is in order at any time, including when a motion to adjourn is pending. Second required, not debatable, and amendable.
- **Adjourn** To bring the meeting to a halt. Second required, not debatable, and not amendable. Alternatively, instead of a motion, the chair can ask if there is any further business. If there is no response, the chair can say, "Since there is no further business, the meeting is adjourned."
- **Recess** A temporary break in the meeting; should state a time at which the meeting will resume. Second required, not debatable, and not amendable.
- **Point of privilege** A matter that concerns the welfare of the board. Can be raised even when another person is speaking. No second, not debatable, and no vote required.
- **Call for the orders of the day** A demand that the board return to the agenda. Can be taken when another person is speaking, no second required, not debatable, and no vote required.

SCHOOL BOARD MEMBERS'

Guide to Common Parliamentary Procedures and Language

Common School Board Meeting Proceedings	Board Member's Statements	Requires Second?	Motion Oper for Debate?
Adjourn a meeting before the business is completed	"I move that we adjourn."	✓	✗
Recess the meeting	"I move that we recess until..."	✓	✗
Table an item / suspend further consideration of an issue until later in the meeting	"I move we table _____until... (specifically state when later in the meeting)."	✓	✗
Take up a previously tabled matter	"I move; we take from the table ... (specifically name the item that was tabled)."	✓	✗
End debate on any issue	"I move the question." **Or** " I move the previous question."	✓	✓
Study an issue further	"I move we refer this matter to a committee." **Or** "I move the superintendent to study this issue further and provide the Board with a thorough report on said study."	✓	✓
Introduce business / make a primary motion	"I move that..." **Or** "I make a motion to..."	✓	✓
Amend a motion	"I move that this motion be amended by..." **Or** I make a motion to amend ______ by... (be specific)."	✗	✗
Object to procedure/object to how something is being conducted / object to misuse of Robert's Rules of Order	"Point of order... (be specific with your objection)."	✗	✗
Postponing a motion	"I move; we postpone until ..."	✓	✓

Disclaimer: Best In Ed, School Board Leadership: The Right Way is a resource meant to offer general guidance to local school boards. It is intended solely for informational purposes and should not be viewed as legal advice or a replacement for the counsel of your board attorney. If you have questions regarding your legal rights or any other legal matters, please reach out to your own legal counsel.

Sources: The National Association of Parliamentarians (NAP) provides education and resources to facilitate efficient and democratic decision-making processes through the effective use of parliamentary procedure **https://www.parliamentarians.org** and *Municipal Research and Services Center (MRSC)*

Chapter 6
Parliamentary Procedures: Robert's Rules of Order

Parliamentary procedures are used by organizations of all sizes, from the federal government to social club board meetings, to ensure meetings are run efficiently and effectively and that all board members have equal voices to ensure fairness. These rules help you NOT feel railroaded or overwhelmed. The value of parliamentary procedures is they allow organizations to work out satisfactory solutions to the most significant number of questions in the least amount of time. In some form, Robert's are most commonly used by school boards across the United States, with some modifications.

Robert's Rules of Order

Robert's Rules of Order is the name of the rules that manage the parliamentary procedure used in legislative bodies. It is a standard for facilitating discussion and group decision-making using parliamentary procedures that govern most government or organizational meetings with the board of directors or board members.

Robert's Rules set the basic guidelines for board meetings. The meetings are run according to the rules by a person, usually the chair or president of the board. A parliamentarian, usually the school district attorney, is the reference point for questions about the rules, the order, and how individuals on the board can be "recognized" to speak.

The basic operating principle is to ensure every member is treated equally and fairly, the **majority rules**, and the **minority has rights**. All members have equal standing, privileges, and obligations.

What Are Robert's Rules?
Robert's Rules primarily function on two principles: making motions/inquiries and majority votes. The main tenets allow everyone to participate in a discussion or debate uninterrupted. Everyone has the right to know what is going on at all times. A speaker can be interrupted for urgent matters only. Finally, only one motion can be discussed at a time.

According to the rules, you must establish a quorum to run a meeting and vote on an issue. A **quorum** protects against unrepresentative actions by a minority of members by stipulating that a quorum be obtained and an item advanced in a meeting. In other words, you must have a majority of board members present. Other non-present members may participate via telephone or video conference. Once a quorum has been established, its continued presence is **presumed** until the chair or any other member **alerts its loss**. Any member noticing the absence of another member counted as part of the quorum can and should make a motion such as a "Point of Order."

A **motion** is the topic under discussion (e.g., "I move we add a coffee break to this meeting"). After being recognized by the board chair, any member can introduce a motion when no other motion is on the table (has been made). A motion requires a second to be considered. If there is no second, the matter is not considered. Each motion must be passed by formal action (vote), defeated, tabled, referred to committee, or postponed indefinitely. The motion is the primary tool for getting things done, from proposing a new rule to changing the wording of something being considered to requesting a bathroom break. To make a motion, simply use the phrase, "I move that ..." and state what you want.

Main Motions are any proposals that need to be discussed and voted upon, such as adopting a new rule, raising dues, amending the constitution or by-laws, etc. **Secondary Motions** occur during the discussion of main motions and are generally about amending the main motion. **Privileged Motions** can be made at any time. The most common Privileged Motion is a motion for a recess, i.e., a bathroom break. Robert's Rules also have provisions for **Inquiries** and **Points of Privilege**, among other actions a member can take.

How Do I Use Robert's Rules?

Robert's Rules of Order guides every interaction with fellow board members from the dais. If you want to move a board item to a debate and then a vote, you utilize a **Main Motion** to start that process. If you support someone else's main motion, you can **Second** it to move to debate. Once the debate begins, you can discuss why you **Second** the item. Note: Even if you second a main motion, that does not mean you support it with your vote. Out of courtesy to board members who want to bring an item up for discussion, a member will second an item to allow for the debate/discussion. Finally, after the debate has been exhausted, the item is put to a vote. For most matters, most members who have achieved and maintained a quorum take a proposition into an adopted policy.

Making a main motion, for example,

1. Main Motion by board member
    "I move the school district to buy 10 televisions for classroom use."
2. Needs a second
3. Second made
    "I second the motion to buy 10 televisions for classroom use."
4. The chair re-states the question.
    "It's been moved and seconded that the school district buy 10 televisions for classroom use."
5. The chair opens up the floor for debate.
    Debate begins on the question; the chair recognizes members
6. If there is no second, the chair must declare the motion failed for lack of a second.

In the above example, you can see many aspects of Robert's Rules. The strict procedure and language are part of what makes Robert's Rules unique in guiding parliamentary debate.

However, Robert's Rules doesn't only manage how debate is conducted in board meetings. Indeed, it orders every interaction on the dais. This is where points of privilege and/or inquiry become relevant.

Voting

The board chair/president will ask any variation of the following questions:

- "Are you ready for the question?"
- "Is there any further debate?"
- "Are you ready to vote?"

Chairman: All those in favor say, "Aye." Those opposed say, "No." The motion the school district buy 10 televisions for classrooms carries in favor 3-2 (or failed 3-2)

May I Abstain?

If you are present in a meeting, there can be no "abstention vote" except for conflicts of interest.

- An abstention vote is a "NO" vote.
- A silent vote is not an abstention vote. Silent vote is a "YES".

Parliamentary Motions

1. Main motion
2. Debate
3. Amend
4. Vote
5. Postpone indefinitely
6. Postpone definitely (to a certain time)
7. Previous question (call for the question)
8. Point of order
9. Appeal
10. Withdraw

Using Robert's Rules to Your Advantage

Individuals with a firm understanding of Robert's Rules are well prepared to utilize them. If you face hostility from your board chair, for whatever reason, you can use Robert's Rules to protect your right to voice your opinion during meetings.

For example, you can ensure your ability to speak to any motion, including those you disagree with, by providing you can always move it to a vote. Expert use of Robert's Rules and a deep understanding of them also puts you in the position to probe the chairman/president with points of inquiry or privilege.

A complete examination of Robert's Rules could be a book of its own. There are references to where you can purchase and access that in our glossary and information section. Still, there are a few basics we can help you get familiar with.

Common Motions

Robert's Rules allow board members to ask questions, move to limit debate, register a complaint, return to the agenda when the discussion goes off-topic, and much more. Understanding Robert's Rules before you step onto the dais will allow you to hold your ground, identify inconsistent enforcement of parliamentary rules, ensure equal speaking time for all members, and ensure impartial treatment.

3

Section 3: **Transparency**

Objectives for Section 3: Transparency

1. **Understand Public Records Obligations:** Educate school board members on their responsibilities as custodians of public records, including compliance with state and federal laws, to promote transparency and accountability in governance.

2. **Understand Sunshine and Open Meetings Laws:** Familiarize board members with the legal requirements of Sunshine and open meetings laws to ensure all board activities are conducted transparently and in the public interest.

3. **Protect First Amendment Rights:** Enhance board members' understanding of First Amendment rights as they relate to governance, ensuring they can advocate for free speech and transparency while fulfilling their duties.

4. **Implement Effective Communication Strategies:** Equip board members with practical tools for engaging with constituents and the media, promoting proactive communication, and maintaining transparency in their interactions.

5. **Build a Culture of Transparency:** Encourage school boards to adopt policies and practices to reinforce a culture of transparency, ensuring all stakeholders have access to information and feel welcomed to participate in the educational governance process.

Transparency is a fundamental component of effective governance, particularly within the educational arena. In this section, we will thoroughly examine the multiple dimensions of transparency concerning school boards and their vital responsibilities to the public. Each chapter will offer insightful perspectives on how transparency can be achieved and sustained, fostering a robust sense of trust and accountability between school boards and their constituents.

Beginning in Chapter 7, "Public Records" initiates our exploration by looking closely at the role public records laws play in promoting governmental openness. These laws empower citizens to scrutinize the actions and decisions of their elected officials, reinforcing the principle that public entities exist primarily for the community's benefit. This chapter will outline school boards' specific obligations as custodians of these records, along with the processes for ensuring public access to vital information. It will also discuss the potential consequences of failing to comply with public records laws, highlighting the importance of transparency in ensuring public trust.

Chapter 8, "Sunshine and Open Meetings Laws," analyzes the legal requirements governing public meetings and the disclosure of governmental activities. Sunshine laws serve to promote ethical standards and deter corruption by mandating school boards transparently conduct their business. This chapter will emphasize the critical importance of public participation in the decision-making process and the legal frameworks support open governance. Furthermore, it will cover the exceptions to open meetings, ensuring that board members understand when confidentiality is warranted and how to tackle those situations while still prioritizing transparency.

Chapter 9, "First Amendment Rights," will focus on the intersection of free speech and the responsibilities borne by school board members. A thorough understanding of these rights is vital for cultivating a culture of open dialogue, allowing diverse perspectives to be heard and respected within the educational setting. This chapter will highlight key legal precedents and recent court cases that affirm First Amendment protections for board members and the public alike. It will also address common misconceptions about free speech within the context of school governance, enabling you as a board member to advocate for these essential rights effectively.

Lastly, Chapter 10, "Communications with Constituents and Media," underscores the significance of proactive and transparent communication strategies. This chapter will equip you with practical tools and techniques for engaging effectively with your community, handle media inquiries, and maintain an open dialogue with various stakeholders. It will also cover the importance of clear messaging, the role of social media in modern governance, and strategies for addressing public concerns while remaining compliant with legal obligations.

These chapters, combined, will provide you with a comprehensive understanding of how transparency is the bedrock of responsible governance. By embracing the principles discussed in this section, school boards can enhance their accountability, build lasting trust with their constituents, and ensure they fulfill their role in the educational landscape.

Chapter 7

Public Records

The school board is entrusted with the essential role of custodian of public records, a responsibility that underpins our commitment to transparency and public accountability. Adhering to state public records laws is a legal obligation that reinforces your dedication to ensuring the activities of public entities, including educational institutions, are open for public scrutiny. The public has a fundamental right to know what their government— including school boards—is doing, as the US Supreme Court affirmed.

The purpose of state public records laws is to ensure that public activities are open to public review so that, as the US Supreme Court put it in the context of the FOIA, citizens in a free nation "are permitted to know what their government is up to."

– Envtl. Prot. Agency v. Mink, 410 US 73, 105 (1973)

As government entities, school districts are bound by these public records laws. Now that you are an elected official, you must diligently uphold these requests. Many of us campaigned on transparency and accountability, making it imperative that we not only profess these ideals but also actively embrace them in our conduct.

Familiarize yourself with state and federal laws regarding public records and open meetings. For example, North Carolina's open meetings law emphasizes that the government exists "solely to conduct the people's business," making it clear that public policy mandates transparency in hearings, deliberations, and actions. Similarly, the state's public records law states government documents are "the property of the people," allowing citizens to access copies at minimal or no cost unless specifically restricted by law. Remember, our role is to serve the public, and it is essential we treat records as people's property, reinforcing their right to access information freely.

The Nature of Public Records Requests

Public records laws vary from state to state, yet they share a common goal: transparency. Each state, alongside federal regulations like the Freedom of Information Act (FOIA), established its own rules governing access to public documents. This encompasses many entities, including school districts, that receive taxpayer funding. The term "public entities" refers to any organization or institution funded by the public and, therefore, accountable to them. The laws generally promote openness, presuming that records should be disclosed unless the government provides a compelling reason for withholding them.

Now You are Subject to Records Request

As an elected official, you have assumed a significant responsibility within the government's framework. That role comes with stringent rules and regulations that apply specifically to you. It is essential to recognize that these rules often carry more significant consequences and require a higher level of transparency than those that may pertain to the general public.

As a public servant, you must facilitate and ensure transparent policies that resonate with your constituents. This means promoting open communication and being prepared to comply with numerous information requests. These requests may pertain to a wide range of your communications, including emails, text messages, phone call records, and social media activity.

Moreover, with your new status as an elected official, it is of utmost importance to practice due diligence in your correspondence. Whenever you send or receive messages, be mindful of initialing and documenting these interactions, understanding that they could be subject to scrutiny or requests for disclosure at any time. The request will stem from various sources, including formal inquiries, media investigations, or even interested individuals who may have personal biases against you. Such requests can be particularly prevalent if you intend to seek re-election, as opponents and critics may intensify their efforts to unearth any potential controversies.

Adhere to these principles and be proactive about maintaining transparency. You will safeguard your position, build trust with your constituents, and uphold the integrity of your office.

Email

Email communication is straightforward; keep all correspondence for your records. Most school districts have internal systems to capture and save emails, which can be retrieved using keywords to fulfill requests without your involvement. However, you must also comply with requests that involve emails sent to and from your email account.

Sometimes, situations may appear deceptive and are treated as such. A pertinent example is from 2017, when three former county commissioners were charged with violating public records law. The case, prosecuted by the State Attorney's Office, was filed with the Martin County Clerk of Courts on January 15, 2013. The documentation indicated that one of the commissioners failed to promptly acknowledge a request to inspect or copy public records in good faith, which violated Florida Statutes 119.10(1)(a) and 119.07(1).

The charges against her originated from a lawsuit filed in 2013 by the rock mining company Lake Point, which alleged she and former Martin County commissioners had either destroyed or failed to produce relevant emails. Her legal expenses, which included a $5,000 flat fee for her initial attorney, $408,489 in billable hours, and $36,873 in additional costs, helped her avoid severe consequences. After a lengthy jury trial, the commissioner was acquitted; however, had she avoided the appearance of hiding information, she might have avoided this situation entirely.

Text

Know your laws, and don't rely solely on hearsay. Text messages are considered public records, even if they are sent from your personal phone. When you conduct business as a board member, privacy is not the same as an individual right. No matter which device or email account you use, all communications related to your official duties are subject to scrutiny.

Some members may believe using their private phone instead of their district-issued phone exempts them from these regulations. However, that is not the case. Even your cell phone records are subject to public records requests.

It is the legal right of media members and community citizens to request these cell phone records, and officials are required by law to maintain and provide them upon request. In Florida, an informal opinion by former Attorney General Bill McCollum clarified that the same public record rules for emails also apply to text messages and social media instant messages.

Some may think they can cleverly delete a text message to evade record requests, but phone records can reveal if a message has been deleted in a thread. Intentionally deleting messages to avoid public scrutiny can lead to severe consequences. Remember, every text you send is traceable, and attempting to delete or hide messages is not worth violating the law.

Texting during meetings can lead to public records requests since the video timestamps your actions. If you want to keep your thoughts private, making a phone call is better. Stay professional and avoid texting, emailing, or messaging anything you do not wish to be broadcast on the 6 o'clock news.

Social Media

What to remember about social media is you must keep your private messages and social media posts separate from your school board member social media accounts when communicating about board business. It is similar to your text and phone records, which means when making any post, IMs, and answering questions from constituents, it becomes subject to public records requests. You mustn't delete these messages because once sent, they are now open to a records request. Capturing data is not a fun way to spend your day, so let this be a forewarning that you will get requests, especially during a time you are running for reelection from your opponent or during a time you are making a controversial decision on a matter. Understanding this now can help you make wise choices in keeping your social media accounts separate from board business to avoid accidentally deleting original posts or messages. Under the First Amendment chapter, we discuss a board member's rights and how to avoid negative situations.

Members Set the Example

School board members are the frontline defense and advocates for transparency. They are tasked with ensuring their districts comply with public records laws. Your role is vital in prioritizing education on these laws and empowering yourself and your colleagues to reinforce a culture of openness. By understanding their obligations and the rights of citizens, board members can help ensure public trust is maintained and the school district operates as a responsible steward of public resource

To enhance compliance and transparency, several reforms can be considered:

- Internal Policies and Procedures – You should seek to review Board policies and ask the superintendent to review the procedures established by policies and state laws.
- Establishing methods for requesters to appeal decisions without hiring legal counsel can make the process more accessible and efficient. This could lead to quicker resolutions and a more positive experience for all parties involved.
- *Mandatory Training* – Regular training for all public record stewards can help prevent violations before they occur.

Boards Can Set Policies and Expectations

Now that you understand your obligation to compile public records, you should know that your role does not stop there. By setting policies that align with laws and training everyone, you are protecting your school district's integrity and complying with the spirit of transparency and accountability.

Responsibilities and Processes

When a citizen, even in worst-case scenarios, or a board member submits a public information request, the school board-appointed representative must respond promptly and thoroughly. The district must maintain comprehensive records and ensure its staff is adequately trained to handle inquiries. If a request is denied, the board must communicate the reason; ideally, a formal appeals process should be in place. This process encourages accountability and helps avoid legal disputes arising from improper denials.

Legal and Financial Implications of Non-Compliance

Failure to comply with public records laws can lead to significant legal repercussions for school boards. If a request for information is unjustly denied, the school district may be liable for legal costs incurred by the requester and potential restitution for any harm caused. In many jurisdictions, the laws also include provisions for fee-shifting, a legal concept where the prevailing party in a dispute may recover attorney's fees from the losing party. This incentivizes compliance, as boards may face financial penalties if they do not uphold transparency standards.

To learn the specific public information laws and penalties for noncompliance in your state, ***Scan the QR code to view the Open My Government: A Citizen's Guide to Public Records Request.***

Takeaways

In conclusion, school boards are essential for transparent governance and promoting a culture of openness. By adhering to public records laws and promoting this culture, school boards meet legal requirements and standards with the communities they serve. Through education, robust processes, and a commitment to accountability, school boards can ensure they remain responsive and responsible stewards of access to public information.

Notes

Chapter 8

Sunshine and Open Meetings Laws

Sunshine laws mandate the public disclosure of meetings and records from government agencies. These regulations compel government agencies or organizations to uphold transparency and inform the public about their activities. The main goal of Sunshine laws is to deter corruption and inequality while ensuring high ethical standards. All 50 states and the District of Columbia have Sunshine laws (also referred to as open meetings laws).

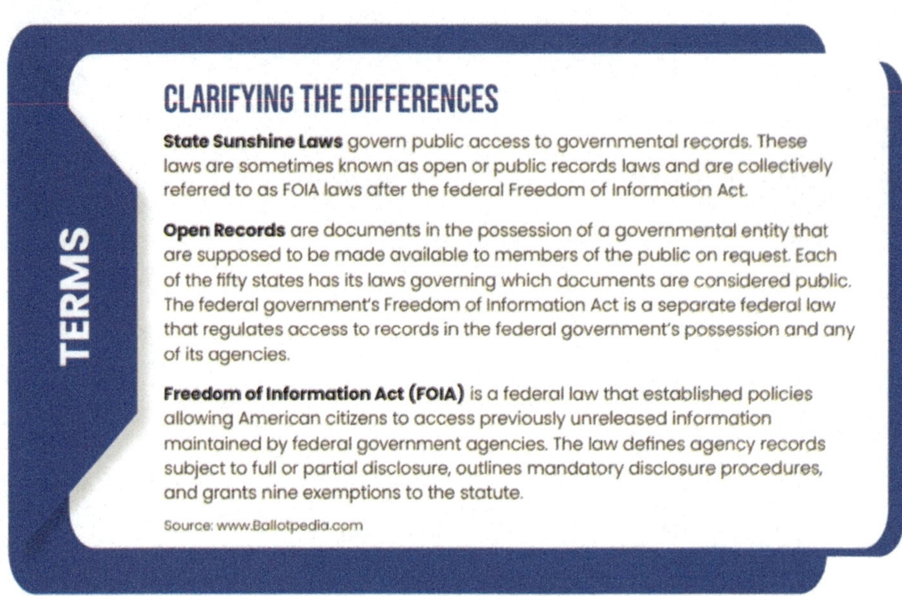

Sunshine laws outline how to request records and attend meetings held by elected officials. They are intended to ensure the government is open and honest with its citizens.

Board business should always be in the public interest, so board meetings should always be held publicly. Of course, there are statutory exceptions, including disciplinary reviews under investigation, open litigation, safety and security measures, and even union negotiations.

Sunshine laws per state explicitly explain the topics allowable for closed executive sessions.. All other business will be conducted in open meetings, with public notification and discussion. Each state has its laws and statutes regarding transparency.

Understanding these laws will enable you as a board member to uphold the intent of public transparency. This knowledge can also be advantageous when certain board members attempt to keep others uninformed, as illustrated in the ruling of Story vs. Suffolk School Board, reviewed in the First Amendment chapter. ***Scan the QR code to explore a comprehensive list of state open meetings laws.This resource can help you understand the regulations that ensure public access to government meetings.***

Chapter 9

First Amendment Rights

A Vital Component of Governance

As a board member, understanding First Amendment rights as they intersect in your governing role will make for a better board. These rights impact the ability to exercise authority at meetings, promote transparency with constituents, and ensure policies respect the board's rights, students, and the public.

This section provides examples of recent court cases that set important legal precedents that support being an informed board member. The takeaways will be highlighted in recent rulings that have increasingly prioritized public rights over the interests of school boards, airing on the side of the public. Having practical knowledge will help you identify potential issues and mistakes to avoid. Before jumping into the court cases, let's first look at the 1st Amendment and the protected freedom of speech.

Freedom of Speech

The First Amendment to the US Constitution guarantees the freedoms many consider to be the essence of America. The five freedoms guaranteed under the 1st Amendment are **religion**, **speech**, **press**, **assembly,** and **petition**. Collectively, these are referred to as **freedom of expression** or, in legal terms, the **Establishment Clause**.

School board members play a major role in shaping public opinion. Freedom of speech, the cornerstone of all other First Amendment freedoms, ensures the existence of these rights. Its purpose is to protect minority, often unpopular, viewpoints from being overshadowed by the majority or government. Over the years, the courts have clarified when and how the government can and cannot restrict speech.

For example, threats and obscenity are **not protected speech,** but provocative or offensive political opinions are. The government can only regulate protected speech in particular instances, such as when protecting public safety or national security.

Board Rights Protected by the First Amendment

Great news! When board members understand their rights, it becomes easier for them to carry out their elected responsibilities. Under governing law, all elected officials have rights protected by the US Constitution, specifically the First Amendment. These rights are not waived due to others' expectations or board policies, including local documents such as norms and protocols.

Once elected and actively participating in board business, some individuals or organizations may try to limit freedom of expression. They might assert that members cannot speak independently of the board, give interviews, or communicate with the press about issues or concerns. They may even suggest that addressing constituent questions must be done through the superintendent or the board chair, or they may try to limit the ability to communicate with constituents through social media.

Sometimes, the protocols established by the board stem from a lack of understanding of the law and are passed down through tradition. As a board member, being knowledgeable about the First Amendment, information requests such as the Freedom of Information Act (FOIA), public records request (PRR), and open meetings laws is important for you. These act as a guide to advocate for free speech and prevent silencing others with opposing views. Do not rely solely on what you're told. Conduct research, ask questions, and seek advice from experienced school board members in other districts when in doubt. While adhering to tradition, outdated norms, protocols, or state association training may seem appropriate, it is not always the most suitable course of action.

Let's be frank! Your thoughts on votes, policies, issues, actions, and inactions are essential to serving as an elected official. Various communication channels must be utilized to ensure constituents' voices are heard. Whether supporting or opposing a specific agenda item, you can and should express your opinion.

The primary point to remember is that board members' opinions are protected. Sometimes, board members find themselves on the dissenting side of a vote, but the right to express views does not diminish. The majority of the board may set the direction on specific issues, but individual perspectives are important for the public to hear.

Be cautious of training that reinforces unfounded norms established by the board, as this can create a misleading expectation that members must act in a specific manner. Also, be wary of training that is not grounded in the laws of governing boards; these laws are not merely suggestions for training sessions but should be the basis of board governance practices.

Finally, "the vote is the vote" is often repeated, implying the board's decisions must be accepted without question. However, this is not accurate! Board members are responsible for being honest with the public about their decisions—the reasons for their actions. There are several effective ways to communicate the rationale behind a decision, and it is the board's absolute duty to uphold the Constitution of the United States, which also applies to students and the public. In the final section of this chapter, listen to the 30-minute court argument in the case of Ison vs. Madison School Board for insights into a common violation school boards are known to commit.

Meetings: When discussing agenda items in business meetings, communicate your thoughts on the issues. Do not be intimidated or bullied into not speaking up when you disagree or if something is relevant to a decision.

Press: Regarding an issue to address, consider writing an op-ed and submitting it to a local newspaper. Hold a press conference as a board member for a more urgent call to action.

Public Platforms: Organizing town hall meetings or creating social media accounts, blogs, or email updates can be beneficial.

As an elected school board member, it is appropriate and essential for you to communicate with constituents. While it may be easier to conform to maintain harmony, the best practice is to prioritize transparency. This approach helps build trust and confidence while ensuring sensitive, inappropriate, or unlawful information is not disclosed.

Board, Student, and Public Case Scenarios

Rights of Individual Board Members Protected in Court

Case Scenario: Story vs. Suffolk County School Board (2022)

Sherri Story, a school board member, filed a case against her fellow board members for violating the Freedom of Information Act. The case highlighted the significance of First Amendment rights and FOIA with five claims.

First Motion Addressed: The board's motion to enter a closed session was not specific enough for the citizens or Story to understand what topics would be discussed. This meeting involved the board privately discussing and issuing "violations" against Story. Neither the board members nor the public was adequately informed about the closed session concerning "public officials." Story felt ambushed by the board for her willingness to express her opinions and comments about board actions on social media. In this meeting, the board scrutinized her for speaking freely with the press. Ultimately, Story won this claim based on Virginia law, which states the motion must explicitly state the subject, purpose, and FOIA exemption.

- The violations issued to Story during the closed session were based on "norms and protocols." They were never presented in court, as they have no legal standing. Ultimately, the board member had the First Amendment right to speak freely. After receiving these violations in the closed session, Story had the right to publish them on social media, exercising her First Amendment right to share these "violations."

This situation is an essential lesson for board members– always double-check state laws! Still, here, Story can discuss anything related to herself and share her personal experiences, regardless of whether it occured in a closed session. She was thus able to expose bullying behind closed doors.

Second Motion: Story won this motion regarding the meeting invitation extended to the chair and vice-chair by another entity, in this case, the city mayor and their team. Story argued this meeting had to be considered an "open meeting" because the chair and vice-chair were part of two of the board's standing committees. Therefore, when these two board members attended the meeting, it had to be publicly noticed.

Story emphasized, but the board ignored the law that if two members from a standing committee meet to conduct any business, it constitutes a committee meeting and must be advertised. Essentially, you cannot simply *"de-commit"* yourselves. The board member won this claim, highlighting the board had been meeting privately with the city council frequently, and neither the public nor the rest of the board knew what was discussed in those meetings.

Both of these claims were upheld at the VA Supreme Court level.

Suffolk City School Board, et al., against Record No. 201334 Circuit Court No. CL20-1263 Sherri D. Story. (2022, January 20). Supreme Court of Virginia. ***Scan the QR code to read the Story Court Decision.***

Case Scenario: US Supreme Court Creates Legal Test for School Boards Social Media Accounts Private vs Public Use

O'Connor-Ratcliff v. Garnier (2024)

Two school board members in Poway (Calif.) Unified School District created public Facebook pages to promote their campaigns. After they won, they used those pages to post information related to the school district (e.g., what happened at school board meetings, public safety updates, and local budget plans). They also used Facebook to dialogue with community members. The pages described the two as "Government Official[s]" and stated their official positions. One of the members also created a Twitter page to use similarly. These two board members, Michelle O'Connor-Ratcliff and T.J. Zane kept separate personal Facebook pages that they shared with friends and family.

Christopher and Kimberly Garnier were a couple with children in the district. They began posting lengthy and repetitive comments on the board members' public pages. The board members first deleted the comments but then blocked the couple from being able to make any comments. The Garniers alleged a violation of their First Amendment rights.

Case Summary

The Free Speech Clause of the First Amendment prohibits governmental curtailment of speech. This can lead to litigation when citizens feel school board members or other public officials have blocked them unlawfully from commenting on their social media posts.

In 2024, the US Supreme Court established a two-part test to determine whether a public official's social media activity is considered government action:

The tests were the results of two US Supreme Court cases; a unanimous court provided a test to determine whether a public official engages in state action when posting job-related topics on social media. *Lindke v.*

Freed concerned the Facebook page of a city manager in Michigan, and *O'Connor-Ratcliff v. Garnier* concerned the Facebook pages of two school board members in California. This test is important for you to understand as it determines whether your social media activity can be considered government action, which has legal implications for their freedom of speech.

- Part 1: The official must have the authority to speak on behalf of the government.
- Part 2: The official must appear to be exercising that authority when speaking on social media. ***Scan the QR code to read the Supreme Court Opinion.***

Other First Amendment Right Case Scenarios Applicable

Other considerations besides the board's First Amendment Rights include issues and actions involving students, parents, and the general public.

Rights of Students Protected in Court

Case Scenario: Student's First Amendment Rights on Campus

***Tinker v. Des Moines* (1969)**

The *Tinker* case is the most significant in upholding student free speech rights. After school officials suspended Mary Beth Tinker, her brother John, and her brother's friend Chris Eckhardt for wearing black armbands to school to protest the Vietnam War, the Supreme Court held that students do not "shed their constitutional rights to freedom of speech or expression at the schoolhouse gate." School officials may not punish or prohibit student speech unless they can demonstrate it will result in a material and substantial disruption of normal school activities or invade the rights of others. ***Scan the QR code to read about the SPLC: Student Free Speech.***

Case Scenario: Student's First Amendment Rights Off-Campus

***Mahanoy v. B.L.* (2021)**

High school student Brandi Levy failed to make the varsity cheerleading team and was frustrated. So, one Saturday afternoon, using her phone and her private Snapchat account while at an off-campus convenience store, she posted a photo extending her middle finger and saying, "F*** school f*** softball f*** cheer f*** everything."

After viewing the video, the cheerleading coach kicked Levy off the team. The Supreme Court held that the school violated Levy's First Amendment rights, but the court didn't provide a broad rule defining when schools can restrict off-campus speech.

Rights of Constituents Protected in Court

Case Scenario: Olathe Public Schools, Kansas First Amendment Lawsuit (2022)

In January 2022, a former school board candidate, Jennifer Gilmore, was removed from an Olathe Public Schools board meeting after voicing allegations that family connections had influenced the elections. Gilmore insinuated her opponent Julie Steele's father, former Olathe City Council member Jim Randall, had helped "buy" the election. School board president Joe Beveridge, Steele's brother-in-law, interrupted Gilmore's remarks and called for her removal, asserting her comments violated the board's public comment policy. This policy prohibits personal attacks or defamatory statements about anyone associated with the district.

Gilmore subsequently filed a lawsuit, arguing her First Amendment rights were violated by her ejection from the meeting. A federal judge ruled in her favor on April 4, 2024, ordering the school district to pay $259,233 in legal fees. According to Gilmore's attorney, Beveridge's actions were influenced by personal interest, not by the need to maintain order, which the court found as arbitrary enforcement of the board's policy. The judge deemed the board's policy unconstitutional, suggesting it allowed it to censor remarks based on subjective interpretation of "rudeness," which infringes on free speech rights under the First Amendment.

Case Scenario: *Ison v. Madison Local School District* at the 6th Circuit (2021)

In July 2021, The 6th U.S. Circuit Court of Appeals ruled in *Ison v. Madison Local School District Board of Education* that a school board's policy restricting "personally directed," "abusive," and "antagonistic" comments during public meetings violated First Amendment free speech protections. This case began after Billy Ison, a local Madison, Ohio, resident critical of the board's pro-gun stance following a school shooting, was removed from a meeting by a security officer. The board president claimed that Ison's "hostile" demeanor and objections from other attendees justified his removal. Ison and three others sued the board, arguing its public meeting policy allowed the presiding officer to unfairly limit speech deemed critical or offensive.

The court found the board's policy unconstitutional, as it restricted speech based on viewpoint. It ruled that terms like "antagonistic" and "abusive" were vague and suppressed dissenting opinions, constituting viewpoint discrimination under the First Amendment. Although the district court initially dismissed Ison's case, the appellate court reversed this, emphasizing the government cannot prohibit speech merely because it is critical

or offensive. The court clarified that while regulations against personal attacks could be permissible, and opposition to ideas—even if offensive—cannot be conflated with personal attacks, upholding Ison's right to challenge the board's policies openly.

[The court cited U.S. Supreme Court decisions *Matal v. Tam* (2017) and *Ianacu v. Brunetti* (2019) and its own decision in *American Freedom Defense Initiative v. Suburban Mobility Authority for Regional Transportation* (2020.)] ***Scan the QR codes to listen to the (1) June 9, 2021 oral arguments in Ison v. Madison Local School District at the 6th Circuit, and read the (2) court's July 7, 2021 opinion.***

Notes

Chapter 10
Communications with Constituents and Media

Now that we have discussed your rights as a board member regarding communication, particularly concerning your First Amendment rights and the relevant laws, be prepared for some pushback when invoking your rights to communicate with your constituents and the media. Bypassing the norms established by your board and previous boards may lead to a sense of loss of control over communications, which is typically managed by the superintendent, who approves information released from the district.

However, it is important to remember you are not an employee of the district or the superintendent. Your district's organizational chart should reflect that you work for your constituents. You owe it to them to provide transparent communication without the district's filter, and utilizing the media can help you in this process.

Legal considerations regarding privacy and protecting sensitive information during closed-door meetings remain. Adherence to these regulations is essential. Nevertheless, as discussed previously, there are ways to maintain open communication with your community through earned media, which must comply with FOIA and open records laws.

Legal Considerations

As with everything concerning an elected official, legal considerations should be considered when communicating with constituents. You must know and follow board policies that manage or limit your communication with constituents. state statutes, FOIA, Sunshine laws, and other state policies also become relevant.

As a general rule, you should never share information that is explicitly and reasonably not meant to be made public. Information that should be public by board policy and state law but is being de-emphasized, hidden, or outright controlled is another matter. You need to demonstrate good and well-researched judgment when handling sensitive information, as it will do nothing to further your role or the cause of parental rights for you to land yourself in legal trouble.

The most important things to consider when preparing to address an issue publicly are the medium you will use (i.e., social media, local news, podcasts, etc.) and who your audience is (typically your constituents or some segment of them).

Making an Impact with Earned Media

"Earned media" is any media or press coverage generated without you purchasing it. In other words, earned media is free exposure for you to communicate and stay transparent with constituents. It's an excellent way to share insight on issues outside your typical network.

How to Tap Into Earned Media

Be Involved

- To earn media, as a school board member, you must understand the issues the community cares about
- What are upcoming issue awareness you need community feedback on?
- What are the issues being asked about?

Drafting a Press Statement

For emerging or urgent issues, consider writing a press statement to raise community awareness as a mayday alert about upcoming votes and to attract media attention. This should be used very sparingly. Be prepared for the possibility that the media may not share your perspective on the issues, but generating awareness is still worthwhile.

It is important to note the subtle difference between a press release and a statement in response, as these terms are often used interchangeably. A press release generally conveys new information, such as announcements or updates. A response statement is intended for situations that require a reaction or explanation.

When sending a press release or statement in response, remember everything is on record as soon as you hit *send*. Be ready to respond to media inquiries and receive pushback. Here are a few key points to remember when working with the media.

Be Prepared to Push Send

1. Always have someone proofread your statement for clarity and accuracy.
2. Double-check the address, dates, and times of location.
3. Always BCC reporters.
4. Monitor for responses.
5. Keep track of press interactions.
6. Know that it is okay only to answer questions you feel comfortable answering. It's okay to say, "I want to give an accurate response; I will need to get back to you on that."

Write Letters to the Editor

Letters to the editor can be a compelling resource. It's a way to reach a large audience, bring attention to issues or information not addressed in news articles, and capture the attention of constituents and news editors. Fortunately, writing a letter to the editor is easier than you think.

Tips on Writing a Letter to the Editor

1. Keep it short and address only one subject. Generally, 250 words or less is most effective.

2. Know the maximum word count allowed and do not exceed it. Many newspapers have strict limits on the length of letters and have limited space to publish them.
3. Carefully highlight the key takeaways the reader should remember.

How to Submit a Letter to the Editor

1. To submit a letter, send it directly via email to the editor. Begin your email with a summary of your letter, followed by the entire text in the body of the email. Avoid submitting your letter as an attachment.
2. Alternatively, some publications require you to submit your letter online. These forms may ask for your full name, city, daytime telephone number, and email address in addition to the text of your letter.

Publication Requirements to Keep in Mind

- The letter should address current issues and not sound like a commercial pitch.
- The letter should be originally written.
- Editors usually only publish letters from writers inside the paper's circulation area. Therefore, it is best to submit to local papers.
- If your letter is published, editors usually prefer that you, as an individual, wait 30-60 days before submitting another letter for publication.

Blocking and Bridging

Prepare for Criticism

Attacks against you are inevitable, mainly when you express dissenting views or expose issues being suppressed from the public. Once your opinions are publicly recognized, negative attacks will likely follow. Mentally prepare yourself, as the forces protecting the status quo are very real.

You should consider the individuals and groups in your district that control the school district's budget and the school board's decision-making process. Often, the opposition will come from local political parties, current or former school board members, union/association leaders, and candidates hopeful for election.

Preparing for lies or innuendos that might be malicious and based on falsehoods can be challenging. Your response to this negativity can make or break your momentum. Avoid engaging in or overreacting to hostile exchanges; instead, focus on the issues and consistently present the facts and data that support your viewpoints.

There may be times when you need to respond to set the record straight. If that happens, clarify the facts and then move on!

✗ WHAT NOT TO DO:

1. Do not become defensive, regardless of whether the claims are true or false.
2. Avoid focusing on the negative by discussing it publicly or with your supporters.
3. Do not repeat negative information in public settings, such as forums or media interviews. Be prepared to address the accusations without reiterating the negative details.

✓ WHAT TO DO:

Use this as an opportunity to show your knowledge and expertise. This is called "blocking and bridging."

The classic block-and-bridge technique can steer the conversation toward more favorable and often mutually beneficial topics. You can use this technique to regain control over the topic. Blocking and bridging are helpful when a discussion forum occurs during meetings with other members and / or media interviews that may be confrontational.

Block First

Blocking doesn't mean completely ignoring the allegation or attack and jumping into defensive mode, as this can damage your credibility. Remember the adage, "If you are explaining, you're losing."

A successful block starts with acknowledging the question. A brief acknowledgement signals to the audience that you heard and understand what they are asking. However, be careful not to repeat the adverse claim. Acknowledging the question and repeating it have two different meanings.

After acknowledging the question, use an appropriate transition to steer the conversation differently. This technique will allow you to maintain a positive rapport while regaining control over the conversation.

A few tried-and-true blocking options include sticking to the facts.

1. "Thank you for bringing that up; however, it's also important to emphasize ..."
2. "That is an important point, and it also speaks to a bigger issue, which is ..." And for outrageous statements or false information
3. "Unfortunately, that is a fabricated misinformation campaign started by my XYZ, but I can tell you this ..." and keep repeating the facts.

Follow a successful block with a bridge.

Instead of fumbling through an excuse in response to an allegation or misinformation, view it as an opportunity to present your perspective and highlight positive solutions.

Anticipate and prepare for tough questions before every public forum or media interview. It can be beneficial to sit down with someone you trust to review the key messages you want to emphasize. This exercise will help you stay focused and avoid distractions.

Be the Solution

When speaking to constituents, remember your goal as a board member is to solve the district's problems. Avoid getting caught up in discussing all the minutiae of the issues. Instead, focus on directly addressing these challenges by intentionally spending most of your time presenting solutions. A helpful approach is to examine the issues in bullet points while elaborating on your solutions in paragraph form. This will help you stay on track without overwhelming your audience.

Notes

Notes

Section 4: **Authority and Roles**

Objectives for Section 4: Authority and Roles

1. **Understand Board Authority:** Explore the various powers and responsibilities conferred upon school board members, including legislative, executive, and quasi-judicial authorities, to ensure effective governance and informed decision-making.

2. **Recognize the Superintendent's Role:** Examine the relationship between the school board and the superintendent, understanding the dual responsibilities of the superintendent as both a manager and an advisor, and the importance of communication and collaboration in achieving district goals.

3. **Utilize Legal Counsel Effectively:** Gain insights into the role of legal counsel in supporting school boards, including the distinction between board and in-house counsel, and the importance of having independent legal representation to safeguard the board's interests.

4. **Appreciate the Clerk's Functions:** Identify the functions of the school board clerk or executive assistant, recognizing their role in maintaining efficient operations, facilitating communication, and ensuring compliance with administrative responsibilities.

5. **Engage Parents and Guardians**: Understand the legal rights of parents and guardians, emphasizing the board's obligation to uphold these rights and create a collaborative environment to encourage parental involvement in education.

The responsibilities of school board members play a role in shaping the educational landscape within their communities. This section is devoted to an in-depth exploration of the authorities and duties assigned to these elected officials, providing a comprehensive perspective on the numerous responsibilities they undertake. As a board member, you need a deep understanding of these duties as you govern and advocate effectively for the educational needs of students and their families.

In Chapter 11, we'll look at the "The School Board" illuminating the various powers conferred upon them. This chapter underscores the importance of board members possessing a thorough understanding of their responsibilities, as their authority spans legislative, executive, and quasi-judicial realms. Legislative authority enables boards to create policies and approve budgets, while executive authority is primarily held by the superintendent, who manages day-to-day operations. Moreover, quasi-judicial authority allows boards to make determinations in specific disciplinary matters. The chapter emphasizes knowledge is indeed power; without a solid grasp of their roles, board members risk making ill-informed decisions may not serve the best interests of their district or the students they represent.

Transitioning into Chapter 12, we focus on "The Superintendent," highlighting the intricate relationship between the school board and the district's chief executive officer. The chapter articulates the superintendent's dual role as a manager overseeing daily operations and an advisor providing strategic insights on educational matters. It stresses the importance of effective communication and collaboration between the board and the superintendent, as this relationship is essential for achieving the district's goals and ensuring accountability. Furthermore, the chapter discusses the need for board members to hold the superintendent accountable while recognizing the importance of delegating authority appropriately for effective governance.

Chapter 13 brings to light "Legal Counsel." This chapter discusses the indispensable support legal advisors provide to school boards, aiding them in untangling the complex web of federal and state laws and regulations that govern school operations. Legal counsel ensures compliance with educational laws while safeguarding the district and its stakeholders' interests. The chapter also explores the distinction between board counsel and in-house counsel, emphasizing the importance of having independent legal representation to advocate for the board's interests without undue influence from the administration.

In Chapter 14, we introduce the essential functions of the "School Board Clerk/Executive Assistant." This chapter emphasizes the vital administrative support necessary for effective governance, outlining the key responsibilities of the board clerk, which include preparing meeting agendas, recording minutes, and ensuring compliance with open meetings laws. The chapter underscores the importance of professionalism, impartiality, and discretion in this role, as the board clerk often serves as the first point of contact for constituents and plays a crucial role in maintaining the integrity of board operations.

Lastly, Chapter 15 highlights "Parents and Guardians" in the educational framework. It emphasizes the legal rights afforded to parents and guardians, reinforcing the obligation of board members to uphold these rights as mandated by federal and state legislation. This chapter advocates for the development of a collaborative environment between parents, guardians, and the school board, recognizing active parental involvement is essential for student success. By providing open communication and transparency, board members can create a supportive atmosphere that encourages parental engagement in their children's education.

The aim of this section is to equip school board members with the essential insights and tools necessary to fulfill their duties effectively. By enhancing their governance capabilities and understanding the complexities of their role, board members can significantly contribute to the success and advancement of their educational institutions, ultimately generating an environment conducive to student achievement and community trust.

Chapter 11
The School Board

The authority vested in school board members is fundamental to their capacity to effect meaningful change and contribute positively within the school district. A comprehensive understanding of your powers and responsibilities is vital for maximizing achievements during your limited term. If you bear in mind that time is a big factor, every meeting, workshop, and discussion will suddenly take on immense significance. When board members lack essential knowledge, the repercussions can be severe, impacting not only district governance but also the educational experiences of students and the community's trust in their leadership. An inadequate grasp of their roles often leads to difficulties in making informed decisions regarding policies, budgets, and overall governance. This lack of knowledge can result in choices that do not serve the best interests of students or the broader community, potentially resulting in ineffective or harmful policies.

Moreover, uninformed board members may find themselves vulnerable to manipulation by school district administrators, who can present information in ways that further their own agendas rather than genuinely addressing the needs of the district. Such situations can culminate in decisions prioritizing administrative interests over students' welfare. Additionally, without a solid understanding of their role, board members may struggle to hold the superintendent and other administrative leaders accountable. This lack of clarity can obstruct their ability to provide necessary oversight, leading to mismanagement, improper fund allocation, and unresolved urgent issues.

Elected officials are often evaluated based on their ability to fulfill campaign promises, but the process of implementing change can be gradual and met with resistance from other board members or administrative staff. Do recognize the role of a school board member comes with authority—authority that must be wielded effectively. School board members carry the responsibility to champion the educational needs of students and their families. Without a thorough understanding of their responsibilities, they may struggle to secure the essential resources, programs, and policies needed for fostering student success. Misunderstandings about their role can also lead to conflicts and discord among board members, resulting in a dysfunctional governance structure that hinders effective collaboration and decision-making.

Being uninformed opens the door to unintended violations of laws, regulations, or ethical standards governing educational governance. Such breaches can expose the board and the district to potential legal challenges and loss of community trust. In essence, a lack of knowledge can significantly undermine the effectiveness of you as a school board member and jeopardize the overall governance of the school district. Therefore, you must actively pursue ongoing education about responsibilities, seek training opportunities, and engage in meaningful discussions to enhance your understanding of role. And, we can not stress it enough to understand your powers and duties found in your state law. ***The illustration will give an understanding of key takeaways to look for when scon the state specific QR code in Appendix A.***

EVERY STATE HOLDS DISTINCT POWERS AND RESPONSIBILITIES

TEXAS EDUCATION CODE
TITLE 2. PUBLIC EDUCATION
SUBTITLE C. LOCAL ORGANIZATION AND GOVERNANCE
CHAPTER 11. SCHOOL DISTRICTS
SUBCHAPTER B

SEC. 11.1511. SPECIFIC POWERS AND DUTIES OF BOARD. (A) IN ADDITION TO POWERS AND DUTIES UNDER SECTION 11.151 OR OTHER LAW, THE BOARD OF TRUSTEES OF AN INDEPENDENT SCHOOL DISTRICT HAS THE POWERS AND DUTIES PROVIDED BY SUBSECTION (B), EXCEPT AS OTHERWISE PROVIDED BY SECTIONS 39A.201 AND 39A.202.

(B) THE BOARD SHALL:
(1) SEEK TO ESTABLISH WORKING RELATIONSHIPS WITH OTHER PUBLIC ENTITIES TO MAKE EFFECTIVE USE OF COMMUNITY RESOURCES AND TO SERVE THE NEEDS OF PUBLIC SCHOOL STUDENTS IN THE COMMUNITY;
(2) ADOPT A VISION STATEMENT AND COMPREHENSIVE GOALS FOR THE DISTRICT AND THE SUPERINTENDENT AND MONITOR PROGRESS TOWARD THOSE GOALS;
(3) ESTABLISH PERFORMANCE GOALS FOR THE DISTRICT CONCERNING:

- (A) THE ACADEMIC AND FISCAL PERFORMANCE INDICATORS UNDER SUBCHAPTERS C, D, AND J, CHAPTER 39; AND
- (B) ANY PERFORMANCE INDICATORS ADOPTED BY THE DISTRICT;

(4) ENSURE THAT THE SUPERINTENDENT:

- (A) IS ACCOUNTABLE FOR ACHIEVING PERFORMANCE RESULTS; (B)
- RECOGNIZES PERFORMANCE ACCOMPLISHMENTS; AND (C) TAKES
- ACTION AS NECESSARY TO MEET PERFORMANCE GOALS;

(5) ADOPT A POLICY TO ESTABLISH A DISTRICT- AND CAMPUS-LEVEL PLANNING AND DECISION-MAKING PROCESS AS REQUIRED UNDER SECTION 11.251;
(6) PUBLISH AN ANNUAL EDUCATIONAL PERFORMANCE REPORT AS REQUIRED UNDER SECTION 39.306;
(7) ADOPT AN ANNUAL BUDGET FOR THE DISTRICT AS REQUIRED UNDER SECTION 44.004;
(8) ADOPT A TAX RATE EACH FISCAL YEAR AS REQUIRED UNDER SECTION 26.05, TAX CODE;
(9) MONITOR DISTRICT FINANCES TO ENSURE THAT THE SUPERINTENDENT IS PROPERLY MAINTAINING THE DISTRICT'S FINANCIAL PROCEDURES AND RECORDS;
(10) ENSURE THAT DISTRICT FISCAL ACCOUNTS ARE AUDITED ANNUALLY AS REQUIRED UNDER SECTION 44.008; (11) PUBLISH AN END-OF-YEAR FINANCIAL REPORT FOR DISTRIBUTION TO THE COMMUNITY;

The Board's Authority

The authority of school boards primarily resides in three key areas:

1. **Legislative Authority:** This is where the bulk of the board's power lies. As the legislative body of their respective districts, school boards create rules by establishing policies and approving budgets. In certain states, boards may have the power to levy taxes, issue bonds, and incur other forms of debt. For instance, a school board might vote on implementing a new dress code policy for all students.

2. **Executive Authority:** This authority is primarily vested in the district superintendent, who manages day-to-day operations. This authority is either outlined in statutes or granted by the board itself. However, the school board oversees the superintendent and their administration. For example, the board may delegate authority to the superintendent to enforce disciplinary actions based on established policies and the approved code of conduct.

3. **Quasi-Judicial Authority:** Not all boards possess quasi-judicial authority, but some do for specific matters requiring the determination of facts, drawing conclusions, applying laws, and taking official action. In this capacity, a board functions as a neutral party, similar to a judge, particularly in decisions related to disciplinary actions involving staff and students. For example, a hearing may be conducted to assess whether a student's expulsion is justified according to the code of conduct. Additionally, during an impasse hearing, the board may address personnel-related issues, such as disputes over labor contract items that were not resolved during negotiations

Board Member Roles and Responsibilities

Across the nation, power-driven school district administrators often rely on school board members remaining uninformed or unaware of their roles and responsibilities. This leaves uninformed board members vulnerable to manipulation, misinformation, or becoming mere rubber stamps for the recommendations of the superintendent and other administrators. Consequently, as an elected school board member committed to faithfully representing your constituents, you must rapidly develop an understanding of your authority, role, and responsibilities.

SCHOOL BOARD'S MOST IMPORTANT RESPONSIBILITY

STUDENT ACADEMIC SUCCESS

While state statutes and board policies provide many details about your functions, there are common constants that apply to school board members nationwide. In subsequent chapters, we will explore each aspect in depth. Generally, the role of school board members can be summarized as follows:

#1 Student Academic Success: The Board's Most Important Responsibility

Simply put, your chief responsibility is to work with your superintendent, fellow board members, and the community to ensure children progress from kindergarten to graduation proficient in math, reading, and other core subjects.

The COVID-19 pandemic revealed and exacerbated the collapse in the quality of our education. Compounded by school closures, which produced a significant decrease in proficiency, schools continued the decades-long trend towards stagnation of academic proficiency across the country, in every state. Though the general plateau and downward trend in academic proficiency predate the pandemic and are profound, the trend continues despite the pandemic catch-up efforts in the preceding years. School districts, state education departments, and the federal Department of Education fail to deliver high-quality, factual, and retained education for our students.

#2 Adopt Goals, Set Priorities, Monitor Success

The school board's adopted goals and priorities set the tone for the entire district. By paying positive attention to maintaining high standards and offering quality opportunities for students and employees, the board can see ongoing growth that builds a stronger community of learners. The board conducts regular meetings during which members review updates from administrators on the state of the district's services, facilities, and goals. The board has a vision statement shared with all stakeholders to guide them when setting goals.

Examples of goals to support the vision to improve achievement for all students:

- Support faculty and staff to be leaders and innovators of learning and build relationships between the district and community for student success
- Improve technology as a means of supporting staff and students

#3 Adopt Policies

School boards are responsible for determining how the district functions because they consider and adopt the policies that are followed. The policies they approve must comply with federal and state laws so all decisions made within the district are compliant as well. Once district policy is determined, school leaders are able to make decisions within the scope of what is allowed. We will discuss this process in detail later.

4 Hire, Fire, and Evaluate the Superintendent of Schools

The school board's decision on whom to appoint or hire as superintendent or director of schools is one of the most critical actions they take. Having the right person in place to carry out the approved policies with leadership that fits all stakeholders makes the educational system work effectively and efficiently. While the board ensures the district operates within the law in the best interest of the community, the superintendent is the face of the school system. The board should work carefully to make the best selection for all involved. Each year, as part of its responsibility to keep the district's direction positive and practical, the board evaluates the superintendent's work toward achieving the district's goals.

#5 Adopt a Budget

The superintendent and their leadership team prepare and submit a school district budget to the board for approval. The board reviews the submission and, based on the available funds, accepts, rejects, or recommends revisions. The superintendent then makes any necessary changes and the board then reviews the budget and adopts it if no further changes are needed.

#6 Communication with the Community

Because board members are not school district employees, they better serve the public's interests in school-related issues. Thus, they are critical to communication between schools and the community. They build this link by reporting district actions and progress to the public, conveying messages of support and concern to the superintendent.

Most board meetings are open for the public to attend. Members of the public may submit a request to speak before the board about topics related to the district and schools.

Individual board members are responsible for making time for taxpayers and parents. As an elected official, you are responsible for meeting with your constituents in person for one-on-one meetings when appropriate, responding to emails, and returning telephone calls. Many superintendents and like-minded board members will try to convince you that all matters must be addressed through the superintendent and you should not communicate with constituents. At the same time, we have seen members try to convince new board members that all communications go through the chair/president. You will need to know your board's adopted policy on this matter. You are the elected official and should never hand over your authority to the superintendent or one board member. The chair works with the superintendent to set the agenda and preside over the board meetings. No one board member has more authority than another. Because of lingering practices and the "we've always done it this way" mindset, you should expect pushback if you are trying to change the status quo. (Revisit Chapter 9: 1st Amendment)

Notes

Chapter 12
The Superintendent

The Superintendent's Role

The superintendent is the chief executive officer of the school district. Tasked with running the day-to-day operations, the position is of paramount importance. The board and the superintendent both have leadership roles and responsibilities. As discussed previously, the board's role is through governance, and the superintendent's through management.

The superintendent's role is to advise and give counsel on educational matters. Their recommendations made to the school board are not just matters to be voted on but necessary decisions that significantly shape the district's future. Their role as a trusted advisor should instill a sense of reassurance and confidence.

Superintendent's Authority

The school board delegates authority to the superintendent through policy-making if not prescribed in state law. The superintendent is managed by the board's overarching policies, strategic plan, capital plan, and annual budget. These management tools are the superintendent's blueprint to fulfill their role. Through clear policy, the implementation of a strategic plan, capital plan, and annual budget, the board provides the superintendent with directives that drive their planned outcomes.

The board has the authority to hire the superintendent and hold them accountable through the superintendent evaluation process and job duties outlined in the superintendent's contract.

While specifics of a superintendent's authority can be found in state statutes and board policies, there are responsibilities for superintendents across the nation, including:

1. Management, control, operation, administration, and supervision
2. Day-to-day operations
3. Responsibility for district personnel
4. Serves as the executive officer of the school board
5. Prepare, distribute, and publish meeting agendas

Management Opportunities for Improvement

There are typically areas where improvements can be made:

1. Last-minute agenda items
2. An agenda without adequate backup information to make an informed decision
3. Lacks consistency of when the agenda is posted
4. Posting the agenda a week before the scheduled meeting

If the superintendent struggles with any of these issues, they must be addressed with the board as a discussion item or during a workshop. A good leader will provide all necessary information and documentation. However, policies and expectations must be implemented if the superintendent struggles with the above mentioned four issues.

Agenda Planning

An agenda is a tool to guide the board's work through governance, not to manage it. It reflects the superintendent's capacity to lead. The agenda needs to encapsulate a structured process that includes transparency and clear communication with the individual board members. If the agenda and meetings are riddled with dysfunction, lack of clarity, and backup information, it's a sign of management concerns. By default, the board will want to start getting more involved by advising and giving input on operations and management issues.

Poor delivery of an agenda can lead to conflict amongst board members. For instance, suppose Board Member A typically approves everything that comes their way without much consideration, but Board Member B likes to invest time and read everything before voting. Board Member A gets annoyed with Board Member B during the meeting, making snarky comments because they have different governing styles. Board Member A has a "trust everything mindset." After all, that is what they hire the superintendent to worry about. On the other hand, Board Member B has a "trust but verify" mindset for whatever is being formally voted on. These differing perspectives typically cause conflict.

Something that seems simple can cause havoc among board members and hinder the board's relationship when one board member continuously comes to the superintendent's "defense." This leads other board members to believe they are being shut down from doing their jobs. The good news is the board and superintendent can avoid these distractions through adequate planning by the chair, superintendent, and their team.

If sufficient structure is in place, last-minute agenda items should never occur. These usually happen due to the absence of planning and structure, which causes failure when there is no proper plan. Either way, the superintendent must hold the district's management team accountable for adequate planning.

Last Minute Agenda Items

Last-minute agenda items are unacceptable and should be rare. Proper planning and a support structure help all parties meet deadlines and updates. The superintendent must hold their management team accountable when adding to or modifying an agenda at the last minute.

Once the agenda is posted and the superintendent has reviewed agenda items with the board members in advance, there should not be last-minute surprises. The chair should hold the superintendent accountable for meeting these expectations. However, if the chair does not, another board member can bring it up for discussion, and if need be, the board can draft a policy to reinforce expectations. Last-minute agenda items can disrupt the meeting flow, limit the board's ability to thoroughly review and discuss items, and potentially lead to hasty or uninformed decisions. Therefore, it is vital to avoid such situations by planning and communicating effectively in advance.

Backup Information

We have dedicated an entire chapter to information because it is that important. It is simple: boards cannot govern and make informed decisions if insufficient information is provided to make an informed vote. Every item being voted on by a board member should have supporting documents. Every recommendation is from someone within the administration, and should have been adequately vetted and researched before being placed on the agenda. There should be evidence of their decision for the superintendent to recommend the item to the Board. Even for routine items, there should be backup. Never approve anything that raises questions. If no research supports it, ask how a recommendation can be made. Either way, blind voting is not a good practice and often results from poor management.

Posting Agendas

Posting the agenda should be consistent and not a last-minute afterthought. Many board members have part-time jobs, and consistency in when the agenda is published will help them manage their time to be prepared for meetings.

School board meetings are set unless a special meeting is called. There should be limited reasons for the superintendent to not adhere to the deadline for posting the agenda. Many states have transparency laws with parameters regarding posting or publishing requirements. For states that do not have laws, a board policy is suggested to require a minimum of seven business days before the business meeting. The superintendent is required to post and publish the agenda with backup.

Minimum requirements should not be an anomaly. They are the norm in many states and are a good practice to have in place for several reasons. Transparency with the public and the board is the primary reason. Posting an agenda on a Friday before the Monday meeting does not give sufficient time to read and vet agenda items. It is an unfair expectation of the board and lacks respect for them and the public. In addition, it's a sign the superintendent is not running a tight ship among their management team.

Superintendent Communication with the Board

When a new board comes together, the communication standard should be made clear at the first board meeting, the Annual Organizational Meeting. This is where expectations regarding communications, agenda timelines, requests for information, and so forth are decided.

It is incumbent upon the superintendent to communicate with all board members regularly. Board members should never be surprised about actions, incidents, or concerns that compromise their ability to do their job. Equally important, board members should communicate with the superintendent and schedule time to meet routinely. Even if there is no agenda item to review, board members are in the public and should share feedback and questions that are more suitable for a more informal setting. These meetings make for better school board members.

New board members should meet privately with the superintendent to discuss goals, priorities, and preferred communication methods. Many board members have jobs and other commitments. For some members, phone calls might not be the best form of communication, but text and email might be. It is up to the member to prioritize setting the meeting and beginning the dialogue!

Collaborative Relationship with the Superintendent

The policies, strategic plan, capital plan, and annual budget established by the board provide the framework that supports the superintendent. These documents are necessary to set clear goals and expectations. Their development must involve meaningful collaboration, ensuring the superintendent consults with the board before making decisions about hiring consultants or directing staff in the drafting process. This collaborative approach emphasizes aligning the superintendent's educational insights with the board's priorities and objectives.

For example, the annual budget serves as a financial plan and a key management tool for the superintendent. Careful thought and consideration must be given to these plans. By collaborating on developing the budget, the superintendent can effectively lead initiatives that embody the mission and vision outlined by the board in the early planning stages. This collaborative process respects the board's final authority and guides the superintendent in achieving the board's goals because, ultimately, this document must garner the board's endorsement and support.

Collaborative Relationship vs. Partnership

Does the board and superintendent have a collaborative relationship or a partnership?
Board members are not on equal footing with the superintendent; therefore, it is not a partnership!

This relationship can be compared to the relationship between an architect and a contractor. The architects' customers hire them for their vision, and architects employ general contractors for their talent and skills. In this analogy, the board acts as the architect, and the superintendent is the general contractor responsible for bringing the architect's vision to life by managing the project and hiring qualified personnel. Each role is vital to the project's success; however, the customer/constituents and the architect/board members have the final say and authority.

Nevertheless, the board and superintendent dynamic is often framed as a partnership. Authors and trainers in education leadership frequently propagate this concept. Our examination reveals that a significant portion of training content derives from materials authored by superintendents, so they would want members to comply with that. However, this is a misconception.

While partnership typically implies a 50/50 relationship, you should recognize the board and the superintendent do not operate with equal authority. As an employee of the board, the superintendent bears ultimate accountability. Thus, when discussing roles, try to avoid terminology suggesting equal authority is essential. The board should consider the superintendent's recommendations within the context of this accountability.

Establishing a foundation of mutual respect will determine the caliber of the relationship and progress toward the board's objectives. The concept of equal partnership does not apply to this relationship. However, pursuing a collaborative approach grounded in trust and respect is vital. By emphasizing these elements and effective communication, the board can ensure accountability and create a constructive environment that ultimately benefits the school district.

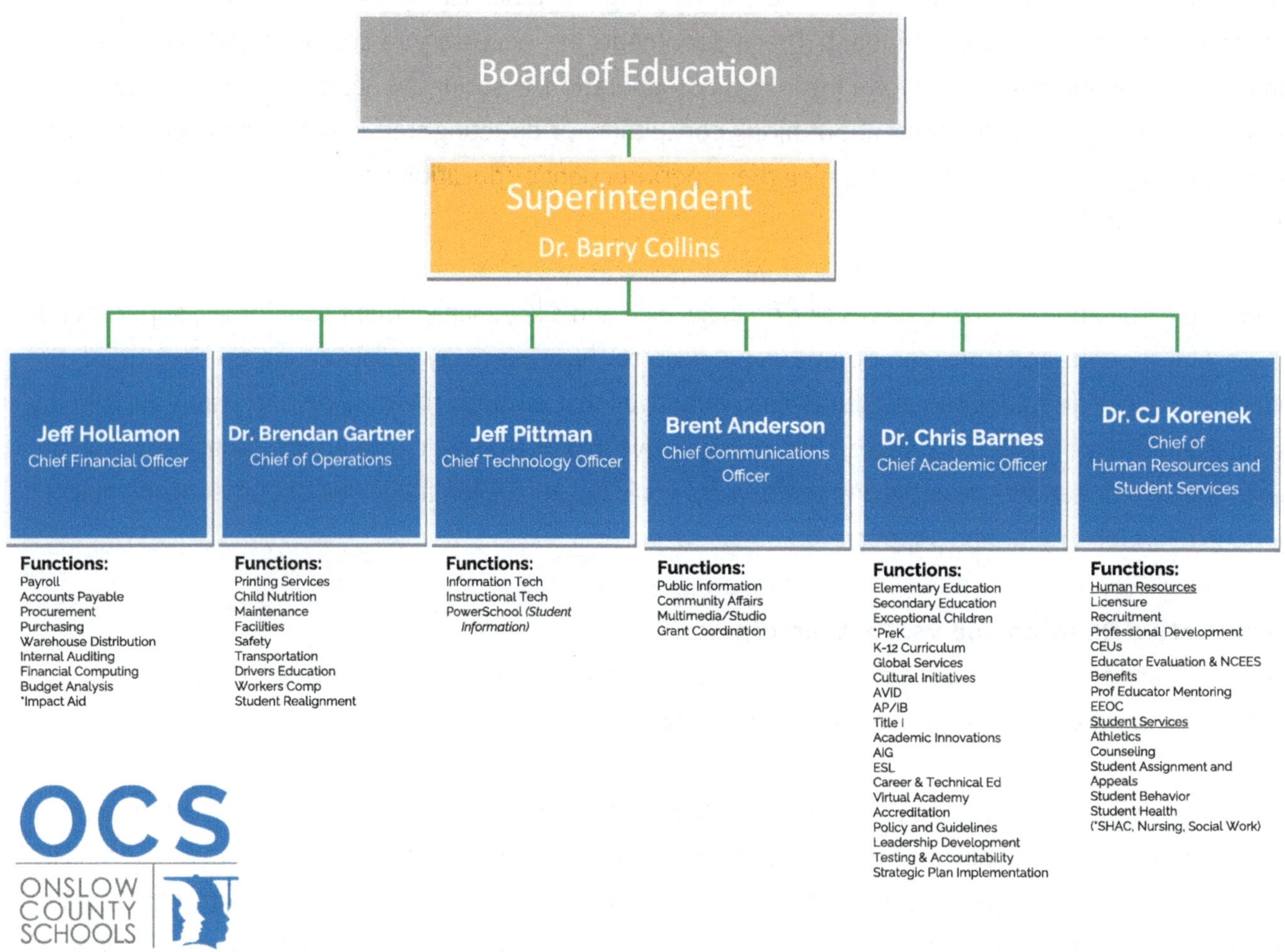

Source: www.onslow.k12.nc.us

Separation of Duties: Governance vs. Management

Now that we recognize the board's ultimate authority in the case of the annual budget, let's examine governance vs. management in a practical setting. We will use this as an example to highlight how governance and management can work together effectively but in separate roles.

Case Scenario: Application of Separation of Duties: Governance vs. Management

Board's Role: The board has the final authority to approve the budget.

Superintendent's Role: The superintendent takes charge of the preparation and presentation. to the board in the form of work sessions.

Board's Role: In this collaborative session, the board provides clear direction regarding any key priorities for the superintendent to consider while creating the draft budget.

Superintendent's Role: The superintendent ensures the budget aligns seamlessly with strategic and capital plans and that board priorities beyond operational funding are incorporated into budget planning.

Board's Role: The board votes to approve and amend the annual budget. Once the budget has been approved, the board will hold the superintendent accountable and receive quarterly updates on yearly goals.

Notes

Chapter 13
Legal Counsel

The Role of Legal Counsel

Many state and federal laws and regulations govern virtually every detail of school operations, and these laws are constantly changing. The average public school district often requires the assistance of legal counsel to stay informed and compliant. This chapter addresses how to work with a school district attorney, including finding legal information and advice, hiring a school attorney, considering in-house counsel, and communicating with the attorney.

Board Counsel

Does the board have legal representation or access to legal opinions? Board counsel is distinct from in-house or superintendent counsel. Typically, board counsel is hired through a contractual relationship to represent the board's interests. They may also collaborate with the superintendent on day-to-day legal matters and attend board meetings at the board's discretion.

In-House General Counsel

The general counsel's role in a school district is multifaceted. This legal professional primarily represents the superintendent and oversees the district's day-to-day operational aspects. The general counsel ensures district adheres to legal statutes and regulations while managing administrative functions. Although the general counsel provides invaluable legal advice and insight to the board during meetings, it's important to note they do not officially act as the board's legal representative. Their primary allegiance is to the superintendent, which creates a distinct separation in their responsibilities.

The decision to hire in-house counsel carries advantages and disadvantages, making it challenging for school boards to weigh their options carefully. Large school districts frequently employ "in-house counsel," which refers to lawyers who are directly on the district's payroll rather than operating as part of a consortium or as external, contracted legal representatives.

In-house counsel in a school district handles various legal matters. They determine fault and negotiate settlements in cases like slip-and-fall incidents. They also work on Individualized Education Programs (IEPs) for students with disabilities and ensure the district follows federal and state laws.

However, there are drawbacks, such as possible conflicts of interest and less access to specialized legal knowledge than external lawyers. Therefore, choosing between in-house and outside legal help should be based on the district's needs and goals.

Consortium Counsel

It is not uncommon for school districts to engage multiple forms of outside legal counsel. They frequently face litigation over various issues, such as an employee slipping in the cafeteria or a parent suing for a child's injury on the playground. Many districts are turning to consortiums – pools of attorneys representing school districts, to manage legal costs and settlements.

The legal fees incurred with these consortiums are typically based on usage. These groups negotiate on behalf of the school board and provide final recommendations on whether to settle a case or proceed to court if an agreement cannot be reached.

While consortiums have advantages and disadvantages, one notable benefit is in-house legal counsel or board attorneys can focus on the board's core business and delegate other legal matters to a group of legal experts within the consortium.

However, a downside is consortiums can be compromised. They are typically hired and paid by the district, meaning as boards change, district superintendents continue to influence the reputation of consortium attorneys. Consequently, these attorneys may feel pressured to please the superintendent, which can lead to inherent conflicts of interest.

Specialty Counsel

Legal counsel specializing in collective bargaining is essential when the board encounters an impasse with unions or associations. In the context of collective bargaining, the board will need an attorney, while superintendent will also require separate legal representation on behalf of the district. It is important to note both parties cannot use the same attorney.

This area of law requires expertise not all attorneys possess. Other specialized fields may include real estate and civil rights law.

Who Is the Client?

The term "client" refers to the individual who signed the contract, the individual to whom this attorney reports, and the person responsible for evaluating the attorney's performance. To understand the relationship between the board and their attorney, one must review either the contract or the job description, particularly in the context of in-house counsel.

The optimal situation for the board is when the attorney is engaged or appointed directly by the board and maintains loyalty and accountability to that board. However, the role of a school board member can become increasingly complex and problematic when the superintendent exerts authority over the legal counsel. In such circumstances, the attorney, who is expected to attend all board meetings to provide legal advice before and during those meetings, may inadvertently serve as a conduit for the superintendent's directives. As a result, the attorney's allegiance may lean more toward the superintendent, leading to the presentation of information that reflects the superintendent's stance rather than offering the board independent legal counsel.

Due to the increasing challenges board members face because of strenuous relationships with general counsel, some, in particular, are having increasing issues with condescending and argumentative attorneys who are quick to defend the superintendents' agenda items when board members seek legal opinions. If members encounter this, they are not alone; the best practice is always to stay in control of board representation.

Board Representation

Investing in legal counsel for the board is an important step toward empowering the decision-making process. As responsible guardians of taxpayer funds, it's natural to be cautious about legal expenditures. However, when the board's legal representation is directly linked to the district, it can place the board in a subordinate position regarding legal matters, interpretations of law, and school board policies. This dynamic can limit the ability to advocate for the best interests of the board. Securing legal representation prevents this.

If the board you're on lacks legal representation, now is the time to prioritize hiring legal counsel. Building this into the budget can significantly enhance the board's position. With counsel, the board can negotiate with the superintendent's legal representative to reduce their hours and fees. For instance, if the board spends 10 hours a month communicating with legal counsel, those costs can be effectively reallocated to support legal efforts, thus optimizing the board's resources.

While this approach may differ from current practices in a district, having board representation is vital for the board to do their job and maintain a healthy governance structure

Counsel Communication

Communication with the board's counsel should be accessible to all board members regardless of whether the council reports to the superintendent or is a direct hire of the board. Some school boards establish policies stating counsel only communicates with the superintendent and the board chairman. This is not a good policy, and here's why. As it has been emphasized multiple times, the board chairman does not have more authority than any other board member. While they may serve as a point person on various issues, individual board members should be able to seek clarification or counsel on how to propose discussion items without having to filter through the superintendent or another board member.

A communication protocol should be established for personal matters and non-governance issues involving all other counsel, but best practices should be followed. Board members should not be limited in their ability to perform their duties.

2. **Legal Overview**

Understanding Your Legal Representation and Open Litigation

If you don't know, ask the superintendent for a list of all the board's attorneys under a counsel contract and retainer.

Ask the superintendent or board attorney for a comprehensive list of all pending litigation cases. This will give a clear picture of the legal issues the district is currently facing and allow the boards to be prepared for any potential developments.

The board/superintendent's attorney may be a salaried or contracted employee. Review the job description and responsibilities to understand better the scope of work and who the employee reports to.

Board Member's Exercises — Exercise 2

Notes

Chapter 14

School Board Clerk/Executive Assistant

Your board clerk, superintendent, and board attorney will play instrumental roles in your time on the school board. Not every school board has a dedicated board clerk or executive assistant. No matter who this person is, the board clerk or executive assistant must have high professionalism and excellent customer service skills from the time this person answers the phone; they represent you as the board. First impressions with constituents, knowledge, and following through are essential attributes.

Most likely, you will inherit the person already in the position. You should expect them to be unbiased, remain neutral, refrain from gossip, professionally conduct themselves, and not share individual board matters with other board members, externally or internally, unless given permission. This person must be able to multitask, be meticulous with details, and be reliable and willing to go above and beyond to ensure the board has everything needed to stay organized and ready to perform its duties. It is a big pair of shoes to fill. Still, this position cannot be underappreciated because they are your representative and should look out for your best interests with transparency and integrity.

A discussion and decision concerning your board clerks role is critical for boards aiming for transparent and accountable operations. Many state laws may give a minimal job description for the school board clerk. If your state does not have this in code, then it is up to the school board to discuss and set this job description. However, remember job descriptions can not be altered until the end of the contract or unless negotiated. For example, if you have an executive assistant and decide to start having this person collect bids but that is not in the job description, be mindful when it is a significant alteration to the original responsibilities that at the appropriate time you will have to approve the new job description and the person will have to sign a new or amended employment contract in some states. If unsure, talk to your district attorney to confirm. ***In the meantime, here is an example from the Virginia Code that outlines the job duties of a school board clerk.***

Legal

VA §22.1-77, their responsibilities encompass a range of administrative tasks: scheduling and managing board member training, preparing agendas and documents for all meetings, recording all meeting minutes, and saving bid submissions on any building, material, supplies, work or project to be let to contract by the school board. These documents, maintainable in electronic formats, may be periodically reviewed by the Board of Education. In compliance with VA §22.1-67, the board clerk may be tasked by the board to oversee that a detailed record of the Superintendent's office and travel expenses are being kept as required by law and available to the Board for review periodically.

In addition to the requirements set by state law, board clerks can take on additional duties as assigned by the entire board or at the request of individual members, as long as these tasks are reasonable and relate to board matters. ***Below is a non-exhaustive list of duties for a school board clerk.***

DUTIES OF THE SCHOOL BOARD CLERK

- Collect and gather necessary documents to ensure the board makes informed decisions.
- Ensure that all board meetings are publicly posted in complete compliance with all open meetings laws, i.e., Freedom of Information Act or Sunshine laws.
- Participate in forming agendas, distributing them to board members, and posting them publicly according to state requirements. This includes preparing essential documents needed before board workshops and meetings.
- Work collaboratively with the school board chair (and or vice chair) and administrative delegate to create a unique, dedicated school board meeting and reports calendar.
- Conduct essential historical research for board members regarding past motions, documents, etc.
- Attend all school board workshops and meetings as described in the contract.
- Create minutes for legal records during any or all board-related meetings (which may include standing committee meetings, work meetings, and closed-session meetings)
- Coordinate and organize logistics for members to attend school board professional learning and conferences, keeping records of all financial transactions for such.
- Keep detailed records of school board members' professional learning certificates as may be required by state law (FOIA, COI, professional learning topic requirements).
- Organize any public task force meetings for particular board purposes.
- Organize the logistics for the public to speak at each open meeting, ensuring board policy and all pertaining laws are being followed.
- Direct school board inquiries, electronic or otherwise, to the appropriate party or parties.
- May be required to become a notary, take Freedom of Information Act (FOIA) and Certificate of Insurance (COI) training, etc., as dictated by individual state laws.
- When directed by the board, act as a liaison with the school board attorney.
- Manage and oversee the administrative activities and operations assigned to the school board office by the school board.
- Demonstrate a pleasant and professional demeanor with all board members, the administration, and the public.
- Maintain a detailed record of the superintendent's travel expenses, professional development, absences, daily whereabouts, office expenses, and accruing of vacation days.
- Maintain a detailed record of the board's travel expenses, professional development, and monthly P-card records.
- Be the point person to answer the incoming calls into the board offices.

Conflict of Interest

The board clerk's contract must indicate they serve at the pleasure of the school board and board members, not the administration. Suppose the school board clerk is the same person as the superintendent's executive assistant, which has too often become the case. In that case, a conflict of interest usually results in unnecessary tension between all parties. In the meantime, the clerk is in a position they should not be in. The two roles are very different; therefore, the board clerk should be a separate hire if at all financially feasible. Common sense would conclude that working for both the employer and the employee is difficult, if not impossible. Do not be surprised if this generates a fair amount of pushback from superintendents. Such pushback emphasizes the need for the job to be separate from the executive assistant.

The board must evaluate the board clerk annually in conjunction with the decision to renew their annual contract. For this person to serve you at their best, board members must allow time for professional learning. Serving in this position is highly stressful, and continuity in this role will be paramount to their success. The longer this person has been in this position, the more historical knowledge they bring to a board that cycles through new members every two years, depending on election outcomes.

Notes

Chapter 15

Parents and Guardians

The Role of the Parent or Guardian

The parents' role is firmly established by law, and board members must uphold their rights as mandated by federal and state legislation. District staff and board members have no authority to override the rights granted to parents concerning things like acceptable curriculum, transparency discussions, and health and mental care. U.S. Supreme Court case law and state laws unequivocally support parents' rights, and these rights must be respected and enforced.

Numerous laws and court cases exist, and this section highlights that boards need to familiarize themselves with these laws when passing policies that may infringe on parental rights. Regardless of board policy, the law takes precedence, and ignorance could lead to costly court expenses that will likely favor the parents. ***Scan the QR code to check out An Overview of Federal Parental Rights Protections.***

Knowing the laws will help you be an informed school board member, for instance did you know?

Legal

The Department of Education Organization Act (1979) established the Department of Education. The act begins with congressional findings, asserting that ***"parents have the primary responsibility for the education of their children, and states, localities, and private institutions have the primary responsibility for supporting that parental role." It also emphasizes the principle of American federalism, stating, "the primary public responsibility for education is reserved respectively to the states and the local school."***

Legal

The parents' primary role in raising their children is now established beyond debate as an enduring American tradition." - **Wisconsin v. Yoder, 406 US 205 (1972)**

Parents' Rights Are Afforded Through the Protection of Pupil Rights Amendment (PPRA)

Federal law protects parents' right to review curricula and opt their children out of student surveys. According to the Protection of Pupil Rights Amendment (PPRA), these surveys may include information that is not permitted.

STUDENT SURVEYS

PPRA also requires schools to inform parents about any surveys given to their students and allow them to opt their children out. The PPRA explicitly indicates surveys should not include questions about Personally Protected Information (PPI) including:

- Political or religious affiliations
- Psychological problems
- Illegal, anti-social, self-incriminating, demeaning details on family members or their income level
- Sexual behaviors or attitudes

CONSENT TO DISCLOSURE OF PERSONALLY IDENTIFIABLE INFORMATION

Schools collect information from students, and PPRA limits their use.

PPRA requires boards to develop and adopt policies to protect student privacy and parents' rights. **Important to note that schools must directly notify parents of these policies or annual changes to them.**

Request to Inspect Child's Curriculum. Rights of Parents Afforded Through the Individuals with Disabilities Education Act

The Individuals With Disabilities Education Act (IDEA) was signed into law in 1975. If a parent believes their child has a disability or problems in school, the child's teacher should be contacted to discuss these concerns. Parents play a key role in providing important information to schools about their children's needs, particularly for students with disabilities.

An Individualized Education Plan (IEP) is one of the protections given to students. It is developed with the parent. The school is responsible for ensuring the IEP is followed, but many parents have found that schools do not maintain their child's IEP. As a board member you will hear this expressed as one of the biggest issues of parents with an IEP student. ***Scan the QR code for more information about these laws and protections.***

Parental Rights According to State Law

Parents have the fundamental right to guide their children's upbringing, and the education system must support that right. Fifteen states currently have statutes addressing parental rights, including Arizona, Colorado, Florida, Georgia, Idaho, Kansas, Michigan, Montana, Nevada, Oklahoma, Texas, Utah, Virginia, West Virginia, and Wyoming.

Board members are responsible for supporting the academic success of all students and encouraging parental engagement in their children's education.

Recently, many states have highlighted the importance of informing parents about their children's educational progress. By staying aware of relevant laws, board members can promote and enhance family involvement in schools through policies that comply with legal requirements. ***Scan the QR code for additional resources for Parental Rights per state.***

Legal Disclaimer

The information provided is intended for informational purposes only and should not be interpreted as legal advice. It is always best to consult with legal experts licensed to practice in the specific state, such as school board counsel.

Notes

Section 5: **Board Responsibilities**

Objectives for Section 5: Board Responsibilities

1. **Set Strategic Priorities:** Learn how to identify and establish key objectives that align the board's vision and mission with actionable goals, emphasizing the importance of strategic planning for student success.

2. **Draft and Adopt Effective Policies:** Understand the significance of creating robust school board policies to promote academic excellence, ensure accountability, and meet the needs of a changing educational landscape.

3. **Hire, Fire, and Evaluate the Superintendent:** Gain insights into the processes involved in hiring, terminating, and evaluating the superintendent, ensuring these actions align with the board's goals and the district's mission.

4. **Monitor and Oversee Information Flow:** Explore the importance of accessing relevant and timely information to facilitate effective governance, enabling board members to make informed decisions and hold the administration accountable.

5. **Fulfill Fiduciary Responsibilities:** Comprehend the fiduciary duties of school board members, including the duty of care, loyalty, and obedience, and the implications of neglecting these responsibilities on governance and community trust.

SECTION 5, "Board Responsibilities," is this resource's most extended and in-depth section. It is the heart of effective governance, focusing on transitioning authority into meaningful action. Here, we meticulously explore the essential duties board members must embrace to ensure the success and integrity of their school district.

This section is organized into five subsections, each containing detailed chapters that break down board members' responsibilities into categories. This structured approach allows for a clear understanding of each duty.

SUBSECTION 5.1: "Setting Priorities" focuses on identifying key objectives, which is essential for aligning the board's vision and mission with actionable goals. Within this subsection, Chapter 16, "Strategic Planning," discusses the development of a strategic plan, emphasizing the need for a clear framework that guides decision-making and resource allocation. Chapter 17 addresses "Academic Priorities," highlighting the benchmarks for student success the board must commit to. Finally, Chapter 18 explores "Legislative Priorities," stressing the importance of advocacy and alignment with state and federal educational policies.

SUBSECTION 5.2: "Setting Policy" focuses on the task of establishing guidelines and frameworks for the board. Chapter 19, "Policy," outlines the significance of creating robust school board policies that establish clear expectations and promote academic excellence. This chapter underscores the impact of well-crafted policies on the educational experience. Chapter 20, "Procedure," distinguishes between policy and procedure, emphasizing that while procedures must support policies, they should not deviate without proper authorization. Chapter 21, puts these separation of duties into "Crisis Management." Understanding these distinctions equips board members to effectively draft and adopt policies that nurture a positive educational environment.

SUBSECTION 5.3: "Hire, Fire, and Evaluate The Superintendent" covers the responsibilities related to recruiting, terminating, and assessing the superintendent. Chapter 22, "Hiring a New Superintendent," discusses best practices for hiring a new superintendent, stressing the significance of a thorough search process that identifies candidates who best fit the board's vision and mission. In Chapter 23, "Superintendent's Evaluation," we detail the evaluation process, emphasizing the importance of regular assessments to ensure the superintendent's performance aligns with district goals and objectives.

SUBSECTION 5.4: "Monitoring & Oversight" focuses on the essential aspects of supervision and accountability. Chapter 24 discusses the importance of "Information" as a means of effective governance. Board members must ensure they have access to relevant and timely data to make informed decisions. This chapter highlights the need for transparency and accountability in the flow of information, reinforcing the idea that informed board members are empowered to fulfill their oversight responsibilities effectively.

A solid understanding of state laws, codes, and statutes will guide the work and help maintain focus on responsibilities. By grasping these elements, members will be better equipped to fulfill their role and ensure all parties understand their obligations.

It is equally important to know the possible consequences of challenging situations when performing duties. While avoiding conflicts is ideal and can undoubtedly push comfort boundaries, it's essential to recognize that performing the job requires making informed decisions effectively and casting votes based on comprehensive information. Failing to do so can lead to serious consequences, including a breach of malfeasance, neglect of duties, and fiduciary responsibilities.

Chapter 25, "Fiduciary Responsibilities," encompass the financial oversight required to maintain the district's integrity. And the importance in overseeing financial transactions and ensuring accountability.

Subsection 5.1: Setting Priorities

The board's priorities are the cornerstone that holds up the foundation for achieving successful student learning. While government inefficiencies are often criticized, understand that as the governing body, it is the school board's responsibility to prioritize the district's needs as their authority allows.

This can be accomplished by ensuring all board priorities are complementary and cohesive. Do the school district's mission, vision, and core values focus on student academic success and outcomes? Whether considering the vision, strategic plan, or budget, the board must always ask, "Will this advance student academic outcomes and prepare them for success after graduation?" Or is it a feel-good for adults, and does it have nothing to do with the kids?

Preparedness helps address various demands and distractions and maintains a strong focus on the mission. Although distractions will surface, it's important not to let them redirect the district's goals and objectives. The board's efforts help ensure students are prepared for various paths after graduation, whether in career, college, or military service. Every action taken should reinforce these critical goals.

Who Sets District Priorities?

The answer to this question is simple yet essential: The board and superintendent establish priorities. The superintendent advises the board on these priorities and helps identify opportunities for improvement. The superintendent also shares expertise on education-related matters, statistics, and school district demographics. The board is responsible for determining the school district's priorities based on evidence and advice from the superintendent.

Priorities manifest themselves in several forms, such as:

1. Strategic plan that articulates the district's academic goals and priorities.
2. Budgetary priorities determine the funding for the vision, mission, goals, and priorities established by the board.
3. Academic priorities, which must be integrated into all plans.
4. Legislative priorities are designed to support initiatives while tackling challenges based on underlying state laws, mandates, and funding priorities.
5. A capital plan provides a budgetary framework addressing board priorities and long-term needs, including transportation, maintenance and improvements, growth, and the strategic opening or closing of buildings based on demographic shifts.

The board must actively maintain and monitor priorities through rigorous planning and coordination with the capital budget, which provides the necessary funding. Without adequate funding, plans will remain mere aspirations, and achieving them will be exceedingly difficult.

SUBSECTION 5.1: SETTING PRIORITIES

Being mindful of the time a board spends together will help drive the agreed-upon priorities. In addition, the processes implemented by the superintendent will help the board achieve its desired outcomes.

It's easy to get distracted. Be cognizant of the rabbit hole that sucks up valuable time and energy over petty disagreements like "What lighting company should we contract with because Company A can finish the lighting for the football field before the practice season?" or "How will transitioning to contractor services for trash collection save thousands in general operations for additional math tutors?"

As a board member, it's important for you to understand and effectively use governance tools as this improves decision-making and drives positive outcomes. When board members understand their roles and responsibilities, it supports their success, and ultimately, the board's success. Successful boards have a direct, positive impact on students.

The following chapters contain information that will set a board up for success. It will help the board lean into effective planning and goal-setting. The section will help solidify priorities and the important questions to be asking before casting a vote:

1. Does it align with the district's mission and vision?
2. Does it support student learning?
3. Does it align with the goals and objectives outlined in your 5-year strategic plan?
4. Does the budget item reinforce the mission, vision, goals, and objectives specified in the strategic plan?
5. Does the item align with one of the board's priorities or plans?
6. Is the conversation focused on student learning or personal disagreements?

Chapter 16

Strategic Planning

As previously discussed, a school board's primary function is to ensure the district provides quality education for all children. The strategic plan is one of the most robust tools a school board has in pursuing its goals. Such plans put school boards in the driver's seat of a school district over the long term, so let's learn a little more about them.

What Is a Strategic Plan?

This plan is the school district's primary document and serves as the blueprint for achieving its self-determined education and improvement goals. The timeline for a strategic plan can range from 3 to 5 years or more.

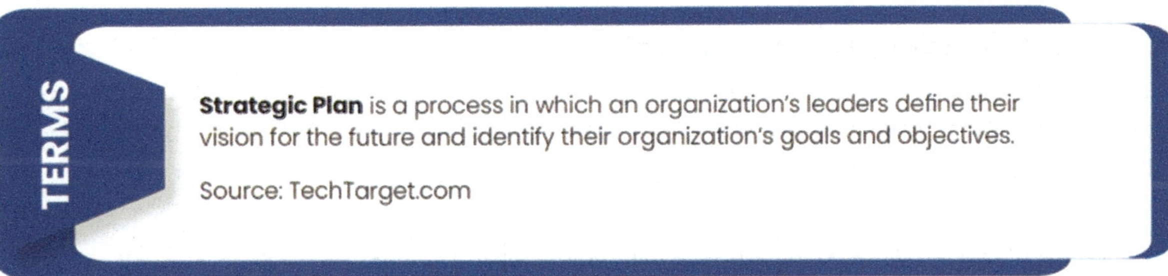

A successful strategic plan has three major components:

1. **Vision**
2. **Goals or Objectives**
3. **Measurable results**

The **vision** is embedded in the strategic plan based on the identified overarching prescriptive outcomes. The **goals or objectives**, and yes, there should be multiple, will be the pursuit of aligning them with the established vision. Finally, **measurable results** based on the vision and goals determine the district's success in implementing the strategic plan. The measurables must be realistic and be measured against identified results.

Purpose of a Strategic Plan

A strategic plan is a tool with an intentional purpose for the district and its school board. It is a document for the public and administrators/educators that focuses on the goals and measures expected results over a set period. This clarity empowers good administrators to act accordingly and directs district resources toward the stated objectives in accordance with the fiscal year's budget. The plan also gives stakeholders a template for what to expect in the future.

The strategic plan allows for continuity over periods and between elections. Since it encompasses a specific period, the approved strategic plan allows districts to organize around something other than individual administrators or boards, which often change from election to election. This is why crafting a well-thought-out, implementable, and measurable strategic plan is important, as these plans will continue beyond the current school board's tenure.

STRATEGIC PLANS INCLUDE

1. Goals and objectives
2. Funding expectations
3. Deadlines
4. Responsible parties
5. Data & measurable benchmarks

How Can School Boards Use Strategic Plans?

Strategic plans provide the opportunity for school boards to focus on their vision and put it into action. The school board leads the writing, adopting, and overseeing of the plan. Not that the board will physically write the plan, but they will be the force driving the strategy.

Others will typically be involved, but the board will decide who. The superintendent is usually a participant, as they are responsible for oversight, tasking administrators with implementation, and ensuring progress is tracked against measurable results.

The process of adopting a strategic plan must be transparent and accountable. Before the final plan is adopted, the public must be informed of the process, including the development and review meetings, the participants, and other activities.

Once a plan has been adopted, the district will focus on determining the tools to measure achievement. The school board oversees the superintendent and administration to measure the progress of the stated goals regularly. The plan should review the cycle with documented changes or updates. Should the district fail to meet the stated objectives, the board should be provided with data and information to help them understand why and what corrective actions need to be taken. Additionally, if the superintendent fails to lead the district toward achieving these goals, this is relevant information for the board's annual superintendent evaluation.

Reviewing and Adopting a Strategic Plan Involving Community Input

Once a strategic plan has been formulated and documented, it will not be finalized until it is voted on and adopted at a public business meeting.

When the district begins creating a strategic plan, inviting the community and/or stakeholders for input is one aspect to consider. This can be done by utilizing an existing committee or forming a special committee and holding public meetings. However, there are pros and cons to including various interested parties to review and discuss the district's expected goals and objectives.

When involving the community, consider having a list of key issues so discussions can be focused. This will help inform the public of the priorities and significant elements to be considered. Managing expectations is vital. This demands that the public be informed of the constraints, which often include the student population, staffing needs, available funds, and operational and facility limitations.

Districts frequently contract with consultants for professional services. Including them throughout the entire process, from development to adoption, would be wise. Using an outside source for objectivity can give the process credibility and provide continuity and consistency.

Each district has unique elements. Some prefer to have community input, while others may choose to keep it within the scope of the board and administration. Either way, the objective is to ensure a realistic strategic plan can be implemented and measured to achieve attainable outcomes.

Strategic Plan Example – Vision, Goals, and Measurable Results

You are formulating ideas for a five-year strategic plan for the district. You ran for office on a platform to improve proficiency outcomes in math and reading for students across the district, and you want to make this a significant focus of the strategic plan.

Each school district has its priorities and goals. The following is an example:

Strategic Plan 2024-2029

End-of-Year Measurements
Focus Area 1
ACHIEVEMENT

Goal 1 Improve Reading	Goal 2 Improve Math	Goal 3 Improve CTE
Increase the percentage of All Students scoring at or above benchmark on the end-of-year VALLSS assessment from 80% to 90%.	Increase the percentage of All Students scoring proficient on spring SOL mathematics test from 52% to 70%.	Continue to monitor the percentage of students who are economically disadvantaged.
Increase the percentage of All Students scoring proficient on the 3rd grade spring SOL reading test from 74% to 95%.	Increase the percentage of students with disabilities passing the spring SOL math test from 34% to 45%.	Increase the number of students taking the ASVAB from 15 to 25.
Increase the percentage of All Students passing the spring SOL reading test from 79% to 90%.	Increase the percentage of All Students proficient on the spring SOL math test from: 75% to 80% in grade 3. 63% to 75% in grade 4. 51% to 70% in grade 5. 40% to 60% in grade 6. 48% to 60% in grade 7. 38% to 60% in grade 8.	Increase the number of CTE completers from 22 to 30.
Increase the percentage of Black students passing the spring SOL reading test from 66% to 80%.	Increase the percentage of all students proficient on the spring Algebra I SOL test from 50% to 60%.	Establish a tracking system to determine the pathways students take after high school.
Increase the percentage of students with disabilities passing the spring SOL reading test from 47% to 75%.	Achieve a 25% pass rate for students with disabilities on the spring Algebra 1 test.	Establish a tracking system for post high school data.
Increase the percentage of economically disadvantaged students passing the spring SOL reading test from 75% to 85%.	Increase the percentage of all students proficient on the spring Geometry SOL test from 51% to 65%.	Fully staff the ECON & Personal Finance course.
	Increase the percentage of students with disabilities proficient on the spring Geometry SOL test from 27% to 35%.	Establish a tracking system for ASVAB testing and using data from the results.

Note: Many of the measurements on this chart include those used as part of a school's yearly accreditation.

Chapter 17
Academic Priorities

Every decision you make as a board member should improve student learning outcomes—the primary objective. Therefore, you cannot distance yourself from setting the district's academic priorities. While board members are not expected to be educators, it is wise to seek their sound advice when making decisions regarding classroom needs, typically driven by the need for additional support and the purchase of appropriate curricula. This ensures teachers can effectively educate students at all levels.

The superintendent serves as the district's chief educational advisor; however, the board is responsible for driving outcomes through effective policies, deliberate budgeting, and fiduciary duties. Boards will make decisions regarding curriculum purchases. When that time comes, it's important to be prepared to ask the right questions and consider teachers' opinions. They create the educational experience and should have a say in the tools required to do so effectively.

Understanding the board's statutory authority is part of comprehending the extent of its involvement in selecting curriculum options. Further research may be required to learn more about individual state profiles. These provide an overview of key policymaking roles in K-12 education and a summary of each role's general powers and duties.

Approving Academic-Driven Content in the Curriculum

Teachers are hired to instruct students according to the state standards specific to each course. The curriculum serves as a teacher guide, outlining these standards and the scope and sequence of the material to be covered. It is a tool teachers rely on for daily instruction. To promote individual student achievement, teachers should be able to creatively adapt their lessons to address their students' diverse learning styles. This includes differentiating instruction for students performing below, at, or above grade level.

For students identified with disabilities and English Language Learners, teachers face a severe challenge to meet the individual needs of all their students. As such, the selection of curriculum choices is one of the board's most influential decisions and depends on the statutory authority each state gives the board.

Questions to Ask Before Approving the Curriculum and Learning Resources

- What percentage of the curriculum is academic content, and what percentage is non-academic? This should include SEL (Social Emotional Learning), which is not academic content but is, instead, non-academic.
- What platform will the curriculum be taught to students on: digital, textbook, or both?
- How transparent is the curriculum for parents and caregivers to view?
- How will assessments be administered – on a device or written – or are both options available?
- Will parents be able to see all graded assessments and be given information on the test?

- How will parents be notified of students' graded work for assignments?
- What homework supports are available for parents to help extend learning at home?
- How much will this curriculum cost the district?
- What evidence is available to prove the curriculum's effectiveness? This is a vital question. Ask to be provided with the research studies and any pilot program data.
- What is the time requirement for students in each grade to be on a daily device with this curriculum?
- How about students with disabilities and English Language Learners?

How to Understand Classroom Needs

Board members should listen attentively to educators' feedback to ensure resources are directed toward teaching and learning. This feedback may come up casually, during board meetings, or at workshops. Pay attention and do not overlook their insights. Teachers are professionals who deserve to be treated as such.

As technological advancements continue, teachers' roles are challenged and transformed on many levels. As a result, many educators have felt ignored and powerless to influence how to best educate students in their classrooms, prompting them to leave the profession.

The board must remember that everything happens in the classroom and should aim to help and support teachers directly. There is legitimate, healthy pressure on teachers to improve their work and raise student accountability outcomes. Still, not all mandated initiatives are matched by evidence that they will be either effective in practice or affordable.

The board has an opportunity to learn what teachers need most to improve student achievement and performance. When the board builds positive relationships with teachers, discussions are beneficial in several ways, which include:

- First-hand knowledge about what teachers need to drive high academic achievement for students successfully.
- How realistic are the board's decisions for teachers?
- Teachers must never feel invisible and should have a confidential relationship with board members. In this relationship, teachers can be honest about the problems they see and experience but not be too afraid of retaliation from the school district.

The following will help you develop meaningful connections with teachers that will assist you in understanding the dynamics of the classroom as an insider rather than an outsider when it comes to decision-making that will impact student achievement:

- Asking open-ended questions
- Active listening – see "How to ask teachers, superintendents, and citizens questions that get better results."

Chapter 18
Legislative Priorities

It is the board's responsibility to establish legislative priorities that align with the community's overarching vision and mission. These priorities ensure a consistent legislative approach led by the board rather than the superintendent or district staff. While the district may have its priorities, these must also be approved by the board or must align with the board's priorities. In instances where conflicts arise, the board's priorities will take precedence. Ultimately, the authority to set these priorities rests with the board.

Understanding Legislative Priorities

Local school board members must recognize the significant influence state and federal legislatures wield over education within their jurisdictions. State legislatures dictate standards, regulations, and funding and control a substantial portion of a district's revenue—often between 35% and 50%. Therefore, school board members must grasp the workings of their state legislatures, identify their legislative priorities, and understand the legislative timeline.

Most states operate with a bicameral legislature comprising an upper house (the Senate) and a lower house (the House of Representatives), except for Nebraska, which has a unicameral legislature with a single home. Each year most state legislatures convene to introduce new bills or amend existing laws, typically starting their sessions in January.

To effectively advocate, school board members must familiarize themselves with their state's legislative calendar, understand the dynamics of committee meetings and hearings, and navigate the political landscape in both houses. Effective advocacy may include contacting other districts to collaborate on shared priorities and utilizing phone calls, emails, and testimonies during committee hearings.

The Impact of a School Board Member

As a school board member you're uniquely positioned to influence educational policy and funding based on your firsthand knowledge of your district's needs. By actively engaging in advocacy, board members can emphasize issues impact their schools and communities. Don't restrict your advocacy to local matters; your position now holds significant influence that can benefit the community. Communicating these needs to legislators is essential, ensuring that the board's priorities are articulated effectively. As elected officials, board members must represent their constituents and actively participate in advocacy efforts—citizen lobbying to further advocate for their district's interests.

While the board is collectively responsible for legislative priorities, individual board members can influence them. In collaboration with the superintendent, board members should gather input from staff and the community to identify key issues that require legislative attention. This process can involve surveying staff for their top concerns or aggregating individual board members' priorities to facilitate meaningful discussion and decision-making.

One Pager

A one pager front and back is a must have when lobbying your legislators. You will need this as a leave behind when visiting legislators offices. It should be straightforward and to the point of your board's 3-5 legislative priorities, in addition to a main point of contact. See the Fort Worth ISD draft:

Fort Worth
INDEPENDENT SCHOOL DISTRICT

2025 FORT WORTH ISD

DRAFT

LEGISLATIVE PRIORITIES

For the 89th Session of the Texas Legislature

The Fort Worth ISD Board of Trustees has identified priorities for the 89th Session of the Texas Legislature that address school safety and support student learning.

1. **Increase the basic allotment** and index it to inflation to ensure Texas' investment in public schools remains consistent and allows for long-term solutions to improve education outcomes
   - **Increase the Bilingual Education Weight** to recognize the increase of Emergent Bilingual students in Texas
   - **Increase the Dual Language Immersion Weight** to better match the real cost of dual language education
   - **Increase the Compensatory Education Weight** to support at-risk Texas students and close achievement gaps
   - **Increase the Dyslexia Education Weight** given Texas' increase in students with dyslexia and the unique needs of these students
   - **Expand the Early Education Allotment** to include prekindergarten students to resource the earliest grades and set students up for success
   - **Enact recommendations from the Texas Commission on Special Education Funding** to ensure all learners have the resources necessary to achieve at the highest levels

2. **Create the Permanent State School Safety Fund** to increase per campus funding and provide a safe and supportive environment for all campuses.

3. **Increase Funding for Teacher Compensation and Retention:** Secure new funding for public education in Texas to provide competitive salaries and retention incentives for teachers.
   - **Enhance Teacher Preparation and Support:** Increase funding to expand preparation and mentorship programs to better equip and retain teachers, particularly in response to the growing number of uncertified educators entering the field.

Source: www.fwisd.org

Takeaways

Setting clear priorities and actively engaging with state and federal representatives will ensure your district's needs are addressed, leading to a more effective and responsive education system for all students. While not all members feel comfortable lobbying and advocating, all boards must stay involved.

As a school board member, you should approach legislation like you approached your campaign:

- ✓ By clearly communicating your district's needs and encouraging legislators to be part of the solution.
- ✓ By advocating for education policy and funding, you can create a significant impact beyond your tenure, helping future boards succeed.

3. Lobbying Checklist

When lobbying for legislative priorities, board members should follow a grassroots approach to maximize effectiveness that involves parents and the community.

Here are some vital steps to consider:

Establish Relationships. Cultivate ongoing relationships with elected representatives and individuals on the education committees. Regular engagement will enhance the board's visibility and influence when advocating educational issues.

Organize Collective Advocacy. Consider coordinating advocacy efforts to present a united front in areas with multiple school districts facing similar challenges. This may involve organizing meetings with legislators or hosting community forums to discuss pressing educational issues.

Utilize Grassroots Strategies. You can become a citizen lobbyist, advocating for specific causes or policies using grassroots tactics. These may include writing letters, providing public testimony, or collaborating with community organizations to rally support for educational initiatives.

Communicate Effectively. Clearly articulate the board's legislative priorities and rationale to the community and through earned media channels, such as letters, social media, and public speaking opportunities, to raise awareness and garner support.

Stay Informed. Stay knowledgeable about relevant legislation and current events, actively researching issues that impact their district. This knowledge will empower you to address concerns effectively and propose viable solutions.

Engage in Coalition Building. Collaborate with other activists, organizations, and school board groups with similar goals. By forming coalitions, board members can amplify their voices and increase their chances of success in advocating for educational reforms.

Board Member's Exercises — **Exercise 3**

Notes

Subsection 5.2: Setting Policy

In the preceding chapters, we laid the groundwork for influencing and shaping your district's future in alignment with the vision and mission articulated by the board through its policies. This subsection, Setting Policy, addresses the substantial power and authority school boards wield in guiding the direction of their districts. It emphasizes the transformation of board members from passive observers to active architects of educational policies. Your decisions carry significant weight, potentially furthering your board's objectives or hindering progress. Ultimately, this section aims to empower you to design and implement policies that resonate with your board's vision and mission, thereby reshaping the educational landscape for all students.

In Chapter 19, Policy, we examine the critical role of board members in formulating and adopting educational policies. This chapter provides insights into the profound impact of well-crafted policies on academic excellence and the overall educational experience. It clarifies the vital distinctions between school board policies and district procedures, highlighting how effective policies can reinforce the district's mission while ensuring consistency and accountability. By understanding these dynamics, board members can embrace their responsibilities as policymakers and advocates for educational improvement.

Chapter 20, Procedures, underscore the essential function of procedures as the operational backbone of the policies established by the school board. This chapter explores the intricate relationship between policies and procedures, illustrating how clearly defined procedures facilitate consistent implementation of board decisions. You will learn about the superintendent's responsibilities in managing procedures and the vital role you play as board members to ensure established policies are effectively aligned to promote governance and accountability throughout the district. By mastering these concepts, you will be better equipped to draft, review, and amend policies precisely, enhancing the educational experience for every student within your district.

In Chapter 21, Crisis Management, the dots are connected between policies and procedures, demonstrating how a breakdown in either can negatively affect student success and potentially lead to safety issues. This chapter emphasizes the importance of translating board policies into clear protocols and procedures that are communicated and implemented effectively. After policies are adopted, the board's work is far from over; continual monitoring of their implementation through ongoing communication with the superintendent is essential to ensure policies serve their intended purpose. This proactive engagement helps maintain the integrity of the board's vision and enhances the overall educational environment.

Chapter 19

Policy

As a board member, your role in drafting and adopting school board policy is paramount. The significance of policy in education cannot be overstated in today's world. It has a profound impact on the quality of education provided to students. Well-designed policies are important in promoting academic excellence and equipping students with the necessary skills and knowledge for success in their personal lives and future careers. Conversely, poorly constructed policies can perpetuate limited opportunities and fail to meet all students' needs in your district.

This subsection will guide you through the key elements that will help you understand the distinction between school board policy and district procedures. Recognize that while procedures should complement board policy, they should not deviate without proper coordination with the administration. The procedures aim to align and support the established board policies, ensuring consistency and effectiveness in the education system. By understanding these paramount elements, you will be better equipped to fulfill your role as a board member in drafting and adopting policies that positively impact the education of students.

Good Policy includes:

1. **Focus on Academic Excellence.** The lack of emphasis on funding priorities and policies to support an overarching strategic plan has resulted in many students falling further behind. To ensure academic excellence, the progress of this plan must be measured.

2. **Meet the Needs of a Changing Workforce.** In today's evolving global economy, new technologies are emerging, and the skills and knowledge required for success in the workforce are constantly changing. Education policy is critical in equipping students with the necessary knowledge and skills to thrive in the 21st-century economy.

3. **Ensure Accountability.** It is essential to establish accountability in the education system. Education policy can achieve this by setting standards for student achievement, teacher performance, and school quality. Education policy can significantly improve student outcomes by holding schools and educators accountable for meeting these expectations.

4. **Must Be Clear and Specific.** Avoid ambiguous language.

5. **Align with State Statutes, Department of Education Rules, and the District Strategic Plan.**

What Is Policy?

TERMS

Policy is "a set of ideas or a plan of what to do in particular situations that has been agreed to officially by a group of people, a business organization, a government, or a political party."

Source: Cambridge Dictionary

For school board members, this can be simply defined as documentation adopted by a school district to establish expectations and identify how processes and procedures will be implemented.

Policies relevant to school districts often begin with state legislation. A bill proposing new or additional education-related changes would be introduced, voted on by the House and Senate in a bicameral state, and signed into law by the governor. Individual bills are steps toward an ultimate goal, which can take years to come to fruition. One of the most important factors to consider when analyzing, researching, or voting on policy is the probability of unintended consequences. The policy is meant to be a prescriptive set of actions to respond to a particular situation. Still, broad, overly prescriptive policies, as well as ones attempting to deal with too many issues at once, have the potential to lead to adverse outcomes.

Who Controls Policy?

The policy is the school board's responsibility. Each member must take the time to review, research, and ask the difficult questions before voting to adopt. The state School Board Association or other external organizations often draft proposed policies. Regardless of the origin, the board is the final authority when approving or denying policy via a standard vote. The one exception is when a policy comes from the state board; adoption is not optional. It is also important for school board members to determine if there is redundancy or conflicts with existing board policy. Policy must be discerned and researched effectively so when board members cast their vote, they understand its impact.

Superintendents are a part of the policy process but in an extremely limited way. The superintendent's role as advisor to the board includes policy matters, and their role is to *suggest* policy, not *direct* it.

School board members are local policymakers who should pay attention to legislative changes that drive much of the policy directives within the school district. Policymakers aim to create a world-class education system focusing on the highest student achievement level. With input from a broad range of stakeholders, the state's governor, legislature, the State Board of Education rules, and the district superintendent. According to state laws, school board members must adhere to their lawful authority to write, draft, and pass effective policies that ultimately drive the work to successfully accomplish the goals and missions set forth by the school board.

School Board Policy Implementation Process

The board should consider policy development its chief responsibility. It should strive to reflect the community's values in its policies and commit to an ongoing effort to engage the community regarding policy-level concerns. The board must develop policies and put them in writing to ensure the successful, consistent, and efficient operation of district schools and the high achievement of district students.

It is the board's role to adopt policy. It is the superintendent's responsibility as an advisor to the board to assist with drafting and developing policy. The aim is to implement in a manner promotes continual formation and evaluation of goals and desired results for students.

Many boards use the policy development and codification system of the National Education Policy Network, National School Boards Association, or Neola. However, we believe that you should cautiously review their "recommended" policy language to ensure the policies reflect the spirit of the law they are applying and reflect your foundation and intent.

While this system may be modified to meet needs, it is intended to serve as a general guideline. Tasks include policy research, drafting preliminary policy proposals, reviewing policy drafts with concerned groups, presenting new and revised policies to the board for consideration and action, dissemination, monitoring, and continuous maintenance of the board's policy manual.

The board's policies shall be interpreted per state and federal laws and regulations.

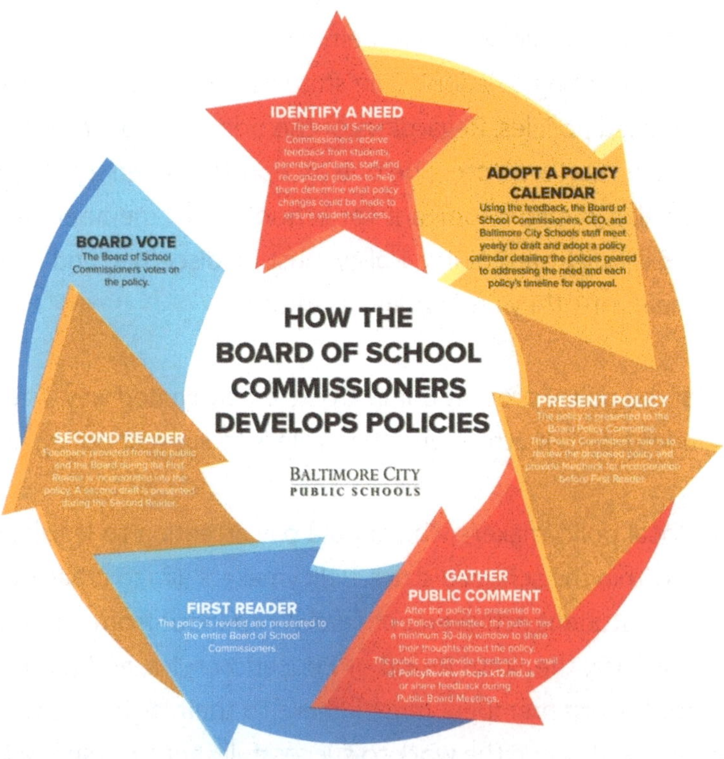

Source: www.baltimorecityschools.org

Policy Adoption

The standard process is the district receives new and/or revised policies after the legislative session concludes, the governor signs them into law, and the state department of education adopts state policies according to the new laws. Once the state-level actions are completed, the state association or external entity sends proposed policies to school districts.

In most states, the statutes govern the adoption process of school board policy. Check with the solicitor or your board attorney for specific laws in your state. In general, the adoption of new policies or the revision or repeal of existing policies is solely the local school board's responsibility. However, policy proposals may originate with a board member, the superintendent, staff members, parents, students, consultants, civic groups, or other district residents. A careful and orderly process shall be used to examine such proposals before action is taken by the board.

The board should adhere to the following procedure when formally considering policy proposals to ensure thoughtful examination of the issues before final adoption:

Sample Policy Adoption Process

- **First meeting:** The proposal shall be presented as an information item.
  - » Brought forward and typically discussed in a superintendent/board workshop.
  - » Seek input and consensus.
  - » Seek a review of the proposal for legal sufficiency (from the board attorney).

- **Second meeting:** The proposal shall be presented for a first reading, discussion, and first vote.
  - » The policy would be moved to the board's business agenda for public discussion and formal action through board consensus. This publicly noticed meeting would serve as a second reading for public awareness and comment.
  - » The policy is placed on public hearings for 28-30 days (depending on the state's requirements for rulemaking procedures).

- **Third meeting:** After the policy is placed on the public hearing, it shall be presented for a third reading, discussion, and final vote.
  - » This meeting is when the final adoption of the policy takes place. Before and during the discussion of a policy proposal, the board shall seek out the views of the community and staff. This should be a transparent and engaging process for the community and give ample time for public input.
  - » Votes are taken.

Policy Amendments

Board members may propose amendments. Amendments do not require the policy to undergo an additional reading except when the board determines further study is needed or would be helpful.

It is not good practice to temporarily approve a policy to meet emergency conditions. Instead of passing a policy, the board should give the superintendent temporary approvals with a sunset date. Hard lessons were learned during COVID-19. Boards allowing temporary policies to address CDC recommendations were difficult to reverse once passed, for example, mask mandates and vaccination requirements.

Policy Revision and Review

The board should continuously review its written policies to keep them current. The superintendent is responsible for bringing to the board's attention all policies that are outdated or, for other reasons, appear to need revision. Policy revision should be accomplished in the same manner as policy adoption.

If hard copies are retained, the board should direct the superintendent to have policy and regulation manuals periodically reviewed for administrative updating and board approval. Additionally, from time to time, the board may undertake a process to review and revise all policies in its manual.

The board may hire an outside facilitator to conduct this review and revision process at its discretion. If applicable, the board and the outside facilitator will develop a schedule for the process, including opportunities for staff, parents, and community involvement.

Board Review of Regulations

The superintendent will issue district regulations that are not restricted to a board approval model. However, in particularly recent polarized instances, such as mandatory masks, vaccinations, and Title IX-related changes, superintendents issued regulations without prior discussion with their boards. This was problematic when it was brought to the board's attention that there was considerable parental outcry.

Superintendents must exercise sound judgment to maintain a 'no-surprise' understanding between boards and administration. Moreover, the board should not relinquish its right to review the regulations issued by the administration. The board should be provided with copies of all district-wide regulations. The board should officially approve regulations, especially when required by state or federal law or when significant community, staff, or student concerns arise.

Before issuance, regulations must be appropriately titled and coded.

Policy Communication

The board's policy manual is a public record, and it should be available for inspection at the district's administrative offices and on the district's website.

The superintendent should establish and maintain orderly procedures for preserving and disseminating district policies and regulations. Staff must be informed of policy changes regularly and promptly.

Monitoring Policy Implementation

It is paramount for the board to continuously monitor the implementation of its policies to ensure reasonable progress is being made toward achieving its goals and the school district's operation is consistent with its policies.

Title AGENDAS

Code po0165.1

0165.1 - **AGENDAS**

The Superintendent shall establish the agenda for School Board meetings in consultation with the Board Chairman. Individual members of the Board may place items for discussion on an agenda by advising the Superintendent of their desire to do so. A motion to rescind or to amend action previously taken shall be timely placed on the agenda since either motion may be considered a "proposition". The Superintendent shall establish reasonable procedures and deadlines for the receipt of requests to place items of business on the agenda and requests to make a presentation in the public discussion period. The agenda for regular Board business meetings, hearings, and workshops shall be prepared in time to ensure that a copy of the agenda may be received at least seven (7) days before the event by any person in the State who requests a copy and who pays the reasonable cost of the copy. The agenda shall contain the items to be considered in order of presentation.

A. Agendas

After the agenda has been made available public, changes to the agenda prior to the start of the meeting shall ~~be~~ only for good cause, as determined by the person designated to preside, and stated in the record. Notification of such change shall be at the earliest practicable time.

1. The agenda, along with any meeting materials and all backups must be made available by posting on BoardDocs in electronic form, excluding confidential or exempt information, shall be published on the Board's website at least seven (7) days before the event, and shall include any recommendations of the Superintendent. The only exception shall be items dependent on deadlines for submission or receipt.
2. The agenda for each ~~regular business~~ meeting shall be distributed to each Board member ~~so as~~ to provide proper time for the member to study the agenda. Generally, the agenda should be distributed no later than seven (7) days prior to the meeting or delivered so as to provide time for the study of the agenda by the member. However, every effort must be made in good faith to provide Board members with all backups fourteen (14) days prior to the meeting.
3. The Board shall transact business according to the agenda prepared by the Superintendent and Board Chairman. Individual Board members may add items to an agenda at least seven (7) days prior to a meeting. This request must be provided to the Superintendent. Board members are responsible for also providing backups when appropriate. ~~The order of business may be altered and items added at any meeting by a majority vote of the members present.~~
4. Any changes to policies or procedures regarding public participation, board meetings, or workshops, Speaker Forms, or the board agenda must be presented to the board as a proposition and pass with a majority vote.

B. Action or Proposition

An action agenda item is an item on the action agenda in which the Board will take official action by deliberation or vote. A proposition is an item before the Board for a vote, and includes, but is not necessarily limited to, all items on the agenda noted as unfinished business, consent, and action ~~nonconsent~~. A proposition may also include a vote on a motion to rescind or to amend action previously taken. A proposition does not include items wherever found on the agenda upon which the Board votes in its quasi-judicial capacity.

Quasi-Judicial - Quasi-Judicial is broadly defined as an action, or discretion of the board who are required to investigate facts, or ascertain the existence of facts, and draw conclusions from them as a basis for considering a proposition or take official action, and to exercise discretion of a judicial nature. I.e., workshops and discussion sessions might be considered quasi-judicial.

C. Discussion Items

The purpose workshops or discussion items is to allow Board members to raise issues of concern and/or interest for information and discussion amongst fellow Board members. Discussion items are not intended to be a propositional item or formal action. Discussion or workshop items are not intended to be an propositional item or formal action.

D. Consent Agenda

The Board shall use a consent agenda to keep routine or non-controversial matters within a reasonable time frame. Except for any item that a Board member pulls from the consent agenda and it is moved to the Action Agenda portion of the meeting, all items on the consent agenda may be approved in gross and without debate or amendment.

A member of the Board may request any item be removed from the consent agenda and defer it for individual discussion, public comment (if otherwise permitted), and action. No vote of the Board will be required to remove an item from the consent agenda. A single member's request shall cause it to be relocated as an action item eligible for discussion, public comment (if otherwise permitted), and action. Any item on the consent agenda may be removed and discussed as a nonaction item or be deferred for further study and discussion at a subsequent Board meeting if the Superintendent or any Board member thinks the item requires further discussion.

E. Special Meetings

The agenda for special meetings called by the Superintendent, or by the Superintendent on request of the Board Chairman, or on the request of a majority of the Board members, shall be prepared upon the calling of the meeting but not less than forty-eight (48) hours prior to such a meeting. The agenda for special meetings, along with any meeting materials available in electronic form, excluding confidential or exempt information, shall be published on the Board's website at least twenty-four (24) hours before the special meeting, and shall include any recommendations of the Superintendent. The order of business at special meetings of the Board shall be established by the Board.

Source: www.SDIRC.com

Chapter 20
Procedure

Why do you as a board member need to worry about procedures? Policy drives procedures. Board members are responsible for the policies, and superintendents are responsible for the procedures according to the guidelines. Procedures establish expectations and provide consistency for the school district's daily operations. For example, discipline is an issue in all school districts, whether dealing with staff or students. A procedure requires specific actions to gather relevant information, evaluate the situation, and support decision-making.

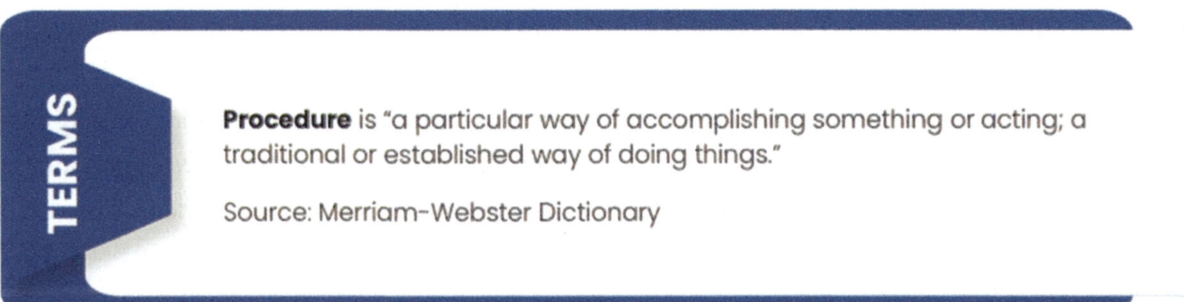

It's problematic if your school district does not have procedures because situations will tend to be handled differently. Certain administrators will deal with a problem in a manner they determine is best, leading to discriminatory practices and accusations. Procedures are a mitigation tool that should be established and utilized.

Who Controls Procedures?

Procedures, like processes, are generally administrative or operational functions. The superintendent and their administration would be responsible for this. However, it's perfectly acceptable for board members to inquire and understand. It's common for board members to receive communication from constituents about the treatment of their children. Referring the case to the superintendent is appropriate, but it's also an opportunity for board members to ensure consistency.

Policy Recommendations

Policy proposals are best accepted if presented comprehensively. As the board member recommending a policy change, cross reference the current policy with any statutes, rules, or recommendations. Then, cross out anything you want removed and add anything you want to add in green font color. This makes it easy for board members and district staff to recognize what is being recommended for removal and what is being recommended to be included.

Chapter 21
Crisis Management

Now that we've examined the differences between policies and procedures, it's up to the board members to unify these into a cohesive working plan for crisis management and emergency responses. The board and the superintendent must be aligned in their expectations during times of crisis. The midst of a crisis is not the right time to discover policies, procedures, and protocols are lacking.

In the unpredictable environment of public education, school boards must plan for a variety of crises that can impact the district's safety, well-being, and functionality. These crises can include natural disasters, school shootings, public health emergencies, and unexpected community crises or leadership changes.

Effective crisis management requires foresight, planning, and the ability to act quickly and decisively under pressure. This chapter examines the protocols school boards should expect to see in a written plan from the superintendent, based on the board's guidance on handling emergencies. It offers advice on communication, leadership, and decision-making during high-pressure situations.

The School Board's Role in Crisis Management

While the day-to-day management of school operations falls to the superintendent and staff, school boards have a critical role to play in crisis situations. The board must provide leadership, ensure effective communication, and make strategic decisions that protect students, staff, and the community. School boards are responsible for setting policies that guide the district's crisis response, monitoring the effectiveness of the response, and providing ongoing support as needed.

Key responsibilities of school boards during a crisis include:

- **Provide oversight and guidance**: The school board must ensure the district's crisis response is aligned with established protocols and resources are allocated appropriately.
- **Serve as decision-makers**: In some cases, the board may need to make decisions regarding closures, emergency funding, or policy changes.
- **Communicate with the community**: Boards serve as the link between the district and the public, and it is essential they ensure communication is clear, timely, and transparent during a crisis. Traditionally, the chair is designated as the board's primary spokesperson, in conjunction with the superintendent. During a crisis, having one board member as the designated point person is vital; however, all board members should attend press conferences to demonstrate unity and a collaborative effort.
- **Support recovery**: After the immediate crisis is over, the school board must support recovery efforts, ensuring students, staff, and the broader community receive the assistance they need.

Protocols for Handling Different Types of Crisis

1. **Natural Disasters**: Natural disasters, such as hurricanes, earthquakes, floods, or wildfires, require school boards to have clear, pre-established protocols for evacuations, facility closures, and coordination with emergency response agencies. Having a comprehensive disaster preparedness plan that includes guidelines for safe evacuations, communication strategies, and staff roles is essential for ensuring the safety of students and staff.

   Key Actions:
   » Ensure that all schools have disaster preparedness plans are regularly updated and practiced through drills.
   » Work with local emergency management agencies to coordinate efforts and align school district protocols with city, county, or state emergency procedures.
   » Develop plans for remote learning in the event schools must close for an extended period.
   » Establish a communication plan that includes notifying parents, local authorities, and other stakeholders about school closures, evacuations, or safety procedures.

2. **School Shootings and Active Threats**: School shootings are one of the most devastating crises a school district can face. School boards must have policies in place for preventing violence and responding quickly if an active shooter situation arises. These policies should include collaboration with local law enforcement, training for staff and students, and a clear chain of command for responding to threats.

   Key Actions:
   » Develop and implement comprehensive safety and security protocols that include measures to prevent school violence, such as school resource officers (SROs), surveillance systems, and emergency alert systems.
   » Ensure staff members are trained in emergency response procedures, including how to lock down classrooms, evacuate students safely, and administer first aid, if necessary.
   » Establish a crisis communication plan that includes notifying law enforcement, parents, and the media as quickly as possible with accurate information to prevent misinformation from spreading.
   » Work closely with local law enforcement and first responders to conduct regular drills and tabletop exercises to prepare for an active threat.

3. **Public Health Crisis**: Public health crises, such as a pandemic or an outbreak of infectious diseases, require school boards to be adaptable and responsive to rapidly changing situations. Board members must work with health authorities to make decisions regarding school closures, virtual learning, sanitation procedures, and vaccination policies, among others.

Key Actions:

- Work with local health departments and the Centers for Disease Control and Prevention (CDC) to stay informed on the latest health guidelines and to implement measures such as mask mandates, social distancing, and testing protocols.
- Develop plans for remote learning, including the provision of technology and internet access to ensure students can continue their education during school closures.
- Communicate transparently with parents, staff, and the community about the status of the crisis, the district's response, and any changes to school operations.
- Establish a process for monitoring the impact of the crisis on students' mental health and well-being and ensure access to counseling and support services.

4. **Leadership Crisis**: Crisis involving leadership, such as the sudden resignation or incapacity of a key administrator, can disrupt the functioning of a school district. The school board must be prepared to step in and make decisions about interim leadership, succession planning, and maintaining stability within the district.

Key Actions:

- Ensure the district has an up-to-date succession plan for key administrative positions, including the superintendent and principal roles.
- Communicate clearly with the community about the leadership transition and reassure stakeholders the district will continue to operate smoothly during the change.
- Provide support to interim leadership to ensure a smooth transition and continuity of operations.

Effective Communication During a Crisis

Communication is one of the most important aspects of crisis management. School boards must ensure information is shared quickly, clearly, and consistently with all stakeholders, including students, parents, staff, local authorities, and the broader community. Ineffective communication can lead to confusion, panic, and loss of trust in the district's leadership. The following are factors to be considered:

1. **Timeliness**: In a crisis, information must be communicated in real-time. School boards should establish protocols for quickly disseminating critical information through a variety of channels, including text alerts, emails, social media, and the district's website.
2. **Clarity**: Messages must be clear, concise, and free from jargon. Stakeholders need to understand what is happening, what actions they need to take, and how the situation will be managed.
3. **Transparency**: School boards must be transparent about what they know, what they are doing to address the crisis, and any uncertainties that exist. Providing regular updates helps to prevent rumors and misinformation from spreading.

4. **Consistency**: Communication should be consistent across all channels and from all spokespersons. This ensures the message is unified and that stakeholders receive the same information regardless of the platform they are using.

Decision-Making Under Pressure

During a crisis, school board members are often faced with high-pressure decisions that can have significant consequences. The ability to make quick, informed decisions is vital, but it is equally important that these decisions are made thoughtfully and with consideration for all stakeholders. The following help minimize poor outcomes:

1. **Stay Focused on Priorities**: In a crisis, it's easy to become overwhelmed by the sheer volume of issues that need to be addressed. School boards should stay focused on their top priorities: ensuring the safety and well-being of students and staff, maintaining clear communication, and ensuring continuity of education.
2. **Consult Experts**: School boards should rely on experts, including law enforcement, medical professionals, and emergency management personnel, when making decisions during a crisis. These experts can provide critical advice and guidance to ensure decisions are well-informed and effective.
3. **Maintain Flexibility**: Crisis situations are often fluid, with circumstances changing rapidly. School boards must be prepared to revise their decisions as new information becomes available and as the situation evolves.
4. **Support Staff and Families**: Decisions during a crisis should prioritize the mental and emotional well-being of students, staff, and families. School boards should ensure appropriate resources, such as counseling services, are available to support those affected by the crisis.

Post-Crisis Recovery and Reflection

Once the immediate crisis has been managed, the school board must shift its focus to recovery. This includes providing ongoing support to students and staff, addressing any long-term impacts, and conducting a thorough review of the crisis response to identify lessons learned. The following efforts lend to improving policy, procedures, and protocols:

1. **Recovery Support**: School boards should ensure students and staff have access to counseling and support services to help them cope with the aftermath of a crisis. This support should continue for as long as needed.
2. **Review and Improvement**: After a crisis, the school board should conduct a post-crisis review to assess their response's effectiveness, identify areas for improvement, and update crisis management protocols. This review should involve feedback from staff, students, parents, and other community stakeholders.

3. **Long-Term Planning**: Following a crisis, the school board should also engage in long-term planning to ensure the district is better prepared for future emergencies. This includes reviewing and updating safety protocols, improving communication systems, and providing additional training for staff.

Crisis management is an essential responsibility for school boards. Whether dealing with natural disasters, school shootings, public health crises, or leadership disruptions, school boards must be prepared to act quickly, communicate effectively, and make decisions that prioritize the safety and well-being of students and staff. By having clear protocols in place, maintaining strong relationships with community partners, and promoting a culture of readiness and transparency, school boards can get through even the most challenging crises with confidence and effectiveness.

Notes

Subsection 5.3: Hire, Fire, and Evaluate the Superintendent

Hiring, evaluating, and potentially terminating a superintendent is one of the school board's most profound responsibilities. This subsection highlights the significance of these decisions, emphasizing selection of a superintendent can shape the educational landscape of a district for years to come. The narrative begins with the critical first step—hiring a new superintendent. It underscores that this decision should not be viewed as a routine hiring process but demands a comprehensive and strategic approach. Casting a wide net and considering candidates beyond the immediate circle, boards will be able to find a leader who aligns with their vision and meets the district's unique needs.

Transitioning from one superintendent to another can be challenging, especially when the separation is contentious. Be cautious against rushing into a new hire without careful deliberation, as the situation's urgency may cloud judgment. During such transitions, it's advised to appoint an interim leader—someone trusted by the board—who can help maintain stability while searching for a permanent replacement. This approach ensures continuity in leadership and allows the board to take the necessary time to evaluate candidates and make a well-informed decision.

Subsequently, the chapter addresses the evaluation process that follows the hiring of a superintendent. This structured assessment is crucial for holding the superintendent accountable and ensuring alignment with the board's goals and expectations. The evaluation process is a formality and a governance tool designed to promote the superintendent's growth and improvement. By establishing clear criteria and objectives for evaluation, the board can foster an environment of transparency and accountability, ultimately leading to enhanced performance and better outcomes for students and the community.

Chapter 22
Hiring a New Superintendent

By far, this will be the most significant decision you make as a school board member. The best practice is not to treat this as another district hire that goes through the district HR department. To ensure you hire the best of the best, you will want to cast your net deep and wide. Even if you have someone in mind in-house for the position, don't limit yourself to what you know. Search firms beyond the state school board associations are sometimes helpful in guiding you through this transition. Don't be afraid of leaning on the advice of board members who have gone through the process.

When Separation Is Contentious

If your superintendent chooses an early separation of the contract, one mistake a board can make is rushing into the next hire. The process should be expedited urgently, but it is not a decision to be rushed into. The media is always quick to publicize the separation. Even though all eyes are on the board during this transition, superintendents do not often leave after a poor review or disciplinary action. Your focus should be on finding the right candidate, not the fastest one. During a search for a new superintendent, it's recommended the board appoint someone internally they can trust or tap a retired superintendent to act as the interim CEO while you carefully narrow down the candidates to interview. Ideally, this person will not apply for the permanent position because you want an unbiased ally you can lean on during the process.

Special Meeting to Discuss Separation

Navigating a problematic superintendent separation could be the most challenging and stressful time for the school board. A special meeting to discuss the next steps will be necessary.

Be prepared for possible communication breakdowns in cases where the separation is contentious. It's common for the superintendent to halt communication with selected board members during the final days of separation, which can present challenges for the board chair. This section aims to help you anticipate and prepare for the worst-case scenario should this occur. As the chair, be ready to plan and organize these special meetings, especially if the superintendent has adopted a hands-off approach.

During a contentious separation, the board, especially the chair, must heavily depend on the board attorney and clerk to organize and set the agenda for special meetings focused on the next steps. The board chair should ensure all relevant staff members are invited to these discussions—never assume their attendance. Keep in mind the superintendent employs staff members; if the departing leader intends to undermine the board, this can frequently happen. Holding a public special meeting to discuss the next steps without staff present to answer questions can negatively impact their confidence in the board. For these specially convened meetings concerning the superintendent's separation, adopt a proactive stance by ensuring the clerk, attorney, and board chair confirm the attendance of the chief financial officer, the lead procurement staff, and the head of HR for necessary insights. While your superintendent may or may not attend these meetings, there is a possibility they will remain silent and only be present to fulfill the terms of their contract.

Superintendent Search Firm

The board will need to decide whether to hire a search firm or not, and if not, who will be the point person to fulfill the board's wishes. The decision to engage a search firm depends on several factors. If your board is divided with strong opposing views, bringing in a firm can offer the needed neutral perspective. Furthermore, hiring a search firm is a sensible option if you aim to extend the search beyond your board's immediate connections. The board chair will need to call another special meeting to discuss the decision regarding hiring a search firm.

Hiring a superintendent search firm will likely go through your purchasing department posting a request for qualifications (RFP)/request for proposals (RFP) for the scope of work you are looking for. When amicable separations exist, the board can ask your superintendent to assist in the process; if not, you will need to lean on your school board chair, the board attorney, and an (interim) superintendent to guide the process. The team will collect professional proposals to present to the board for discussion and set interviews for the top two or three search firms, ultimately choosing one. Selecting the right search firm is the first step and will be as important as hiring the right superintendent.

Relying on a hiring firm to source candidates has pros and cons. While common, this approach may not always be ideal. Hiring firms can be costly, and their selection process may be influenced by internal preferences, particularly when utilizing your state school board association. However, search firms can offer access to a broader pool of candidates than a board might reach when selecting a national search firm.

The Job Listing

Engaging the right search firm will assist the board in outlining their priorities and the qualifications desired in the next superintendent. You can opt for either a national or an in-state search. Once the search firm has advertised the position, they will typically collaborate with the board clerk to distribute resumes to board members. After the application cut-off date, the board chair will coordinate with the search firm to schedule a meeting to discuss the top candidates. It is the search firm's responsibility to guide the board through this process in a structured and effective manner, working closely with the chair to ensure the discussions proceed smoothly. This can be considered as Round 1. You will want to lean on the search firm to lead you through an organized approach. At this point, no board member should communicate with any candidates.

To maintain the integrity of the process and ensure board members are aware of any potential candidates who remain unbiased during the search, the board can request specific information on the application. Candidates should be asked to explain how they learned about the position, whether they had prior communication with anyone from the search firm, the district, a vendor, or an organizational partner in the community, and if so, to identify who that was.

The Interview

The subsequent step involves preparing for the interviews. Ideally, conducting interviews during executive sessions with the board is preferred; however, not all states permit these discussions to be closed-door. If you're uncertain, confirm the requirements with your attorney. All board members are expected to attend each interview to ensure consistency and participate in the Q&A sessions. In a state like Florida, keeping candidate names confidential is not typically considered confidential information. While some candidates may seek anonymity, it's important to clearly state in your RFQ/RFP that they understand the implications of applying for a position in a state with open records. Ultimately, the board should determine whether transparency is beneficial. Publicly sharing candidate details could even yield valuable insights from their current district.

Some standard practices in superintendent interviews may be worth considering—or reconsidering. Many of these approaches stem from tradition or established board "norms." However, each school board should carefully evaluate its unique situation and customize the process to fit its needs. This role is the district's most significant and costliest hire, with far-reaching, long-term implications.

Round 1

Prepare the interview questions in advance. Having a few core or essential questions for each candidate is valuable, but this approach might not always be beneficial. Given candidates' diverse backgrounds and experiences, a uniform set of questions may not reveal the most relevant insights so including customized questions can provide a fuller picture. The questions will need to be fair and consistent across the board. Consider tailoring questions based on each candidate's portfolio to reflect the district's needs and unique experiences during the second or third round of interviews. Remember that candidates may communicate with one another after interviews. If all questions are identical, later interviewees may appear overly prepared, potentially gaining an unfair advantage. Each question asked of a candidate should have a follow-up question based on the answer given. This follow-up question may come from any board member. Here is another opportunity to vary the questions being asked of candidates.

Round 2

Once you've narrowed down the candidates to the top 5 or 6, the next step is to set the interview day. The firm should be the one that contacts each candidate and organizes the time. Since these are considered workshop settings, keeping the interviews fair and on the same footing is vital. In these situations, avoid live streaming the workshop. Your candidates should not be at a disadvantage if they are interviewed first. Keeping interviews on the same day consecutively is ideal. If not, avoid speaking with the media and broadcasting workshops until all candidates have been interviewed.

Round 3

Round three is the last step before the decision. Once the board has conducted the interviews in round 2, there will be 2-3 rising stars with whom you will want to go deeper into discussions as a board member. It is not uncommon to set a round of 15-minute interviews with each board member so they can understand the candidates' demeanor and compatibility. The board corporate and attorney will set the terms of questions and topics that might be off-limits.

Round 3 is a repeat of procedures in round 2. However, the best practice is to have a set of questions agreed upon ahead of time, with each board member having their own set of questions with a time limit for each board member's question and answer session.

Once all the interviews have been completed, the board will debate and deliberate. In a workshop or session, the board can only reach a consensus, and only during the official special meeting or business meeting can the board vote on hiring through a motion and a second.

Contract Negotiations

Once the board has cast its official vote, it will be important to review the terms of the superintendent's contract. Following this, the board will ask the consulting firm, the chair, and the attorney to negotiate a proposal on behalf of the board that will be submitted for a final vote. The board holds the superintendent accountable for the commitments made during the interview process. It is essential to document these commitments in writing, along with any "First Year Plan" the candidate may present, ensuring the candidate signs these documents. Furthermore, the contract should include clauses permitting termination if these commitments are not fulfilled. Additionally, any hiring commitments should be incorporated into the first-year evaluation of the newly appointed superintendent.

Takeaways

Approach the process with open eyes and confidence. As you go through the process of selecting a new superintendent, you must remain vigilant and informed. While the current superintendent may engage with candidates, these interactions can vary in tone and substance. Discussions about the district and individual board members may occur through various platforms, including phone calls and private meetings. Acknowledge that this is a regular part of the process.

Transparency is key; however, it's important to recognize that not all candidates may fully convey their intentions. Some may present a more polished version of themselves during the interview. Thus, you must carefully consider the authenticity of each candidate, as they are typically adept at navigating the interview process.

You might have a search firm, but do your due diligence and research the candidates. To further safeguard your decision, you must conduct a thorough background check. This includes scrutinizing media and social media presence. Investing in a reputable, independent investigator to provide a detailed report on the candidate and their family can yield invaluable insights. Additionally, never assume verbal agreements will suffice; document all critical points in writing. If a candidate needs to relocate their family to the district, ensure this is explicitly stated in the employment contract along with the potential consequences for non-compliance.

When drafting the superintendent's contract, choose your legal counsel carefully. Be aware that in some states, the superintendent may hire the school board attorney, which can lead to potential conflicts of interest.

Lastly, prepare yourself for criticism. Being a board member can be challenging, and it's essential to find your inner peace when making tough decisions that may be politically charged. Seek support through prayer and guidance beyond what you can see. If something feels off, trust your intuition when making this paramount decision that will have a lasting impact on the students in your community. Ultimately, you will be accountable for whether your choice leads to a negative or positive outcome.

Notes

Chapter 23

Superintendent's Evaluation

What Is It?

The superintendent's evaluation is a structured process that results in an official document developed by the board. Its primary aim is to assess the superintendent's performance, which is one of the school board's key responsibilities. At its core, this evaluation enables the board to make informed decisions regarding employment. Driven by the board, when executed correctly, this process serves as an effective governance tool that can enhance the superintendent's performance and result in success for the entire school district.

Who Should Lead the Evaluation Process?

The board chair leads this effort to ensure the integrity and fairness of the evaluation process. The chair's role is to guide the board and ensure all members are actively involved, thereby maintaining fairness and integrity.

The chair ensures the board is given an overview of the process and timeline and allows outside trainers to work with the board on the primary objectives and measurables.

When a new board comes together, the chair should set a board work session to review the objectives and measurables. The board, including new and existing school board members, will decide whether to add, delete, or alter the evaluation. The employment contract might require any changes to be acceptable to the superintendent, not the board will have to wait and renegotiate the terms on the anniversary of the superintendent's review or contract date. It is the job of every board member, not just the chairman, to know the terms in the superintendent's contract.

Evaluation Tools

Some school boards are composed of former administrators and teachers, which means the evaluation might mirror more of the rubric used for education professionals and employees. On the other hand, some boards have created their own to be more direct and simplistic. Either way, it is up to the board to ensure the evaluation is fair and encapsulates its priorities for the superintendent.

We return to the Strategic Plan, Annual Budget, Capital Plan, and School Board policy blueprints, which drive the superintendent's work. If rating the superintendent on Culture and Climate is not in the policies or strategic plan, evaluating them on these issues is unacceptable.

Every board will have objectives and a unique set of measurable goals. There may be an agreed-upon framework. However, a superintendent evaluation is not a one-size-fits-all document that can be replicated from another district. It must mirror the school district's mission and vision, along with identified priorities and challenges. The evaluation is based on the issues that matter to the district's unique DNA.

Superintendent's Evaluation

Please list the objectives under the appropriate categories in the space provided below.

1st: Board priorities, goals, and objectives

2nd: Current superintendent evaluation – evaluating priorities, goals, and objectives

3rd: Compare both lists acros all three categories

This exercise helps align the board's priorities with the superintendent's evaluation criteria, creating a clear path to success and growth by ensuring everyone is aligned.

Academic Bucket

The evaluation should assess whether the superintendent is driving academic success and outcomes for all students. As the lead educator and advisor for the school district, the superintendent ensures and maintains quality education. Does your evaluation align with the board's academic goals and objectives?

Common Priorities:

- Reading and Math Proficiency
- Graduation Rates
- Student Growth
- Student Assessment Tools
- ESE Student Needs

Board Academic Priorities

Academic Priorities In the Current Superintendent Evaluation

The two lists should match. If not, which board academic priorities are missing from the evaluation? The following areas show misalignment with the board and evaluation process:

Management Bucket

The evaluation should assess the superintendent's effectiveness as a leader and manager, including systems, staff performance, and financial integrity. It highlights the importance of their skills and capacity to handle multiple responsibilities.

For Example:

- Buildings
- Buses
- Budgets
- Bonds
- Teacher Evaluations
- State Compliance
- Culture and Climate Staff & Parent Communication

Board Management – Leadership Priorities

Leadership & Management Priorities in Superintendent Evaluation

The two lists should match. If not, which board academic priorities are missing from the evaluation? The following areas show misalignment with the board and evaluation process:

Accountability Bucket

The evaluation is a key tool for holding the superintendent accountable, solidifying the relationship between the superintendent and the board. Each board member's evaluation carries equal weight, regardless of the board's majority or minority status.

For Example:

- Communication with the board
- Follow through on commitments
- Transparency with information
- Accessibility to the board
- Working the strategic plan

Board Accountability Priorities

Accountability Priorities In the Current Superintendent Evaluation

The two lists should match. If not, which board academic priorities are missing from the evaluation? The following areas show misalignment with the board and evaluation process:

5. Evaluation Deadlines

Superintendent's Evaluation Deadlines to Know

Date to Submit ______________________________

Date to Meet with Superintendent to Review ______________________________

Date the Evaluations are Shared with Board ______________________________

Date to Review Evaluation as a Board ______________________________

Date that the Superintendent's Contract Is Up for Review ______________________________

Board Member's Exercises **Exercise 5**

Notes

Purpose of the Evaluation

The ultimate goal is to determine whether the board should continue with the superintendent's contract. If *yes*, the superintendent's evaluation may warrant a raise. A primary outcome is the superintendent will learn from and improve in the areas evaluated.

Components of Evaluation

The evaluation process may seem complex due to the intricacies and responsibilities of a superintendent's role. However, it essentially revolves around three interconnected priorities:

1. The superintendent's ability to act as an educational leader
2. The superintendent's responsibilities as the district manager
3. The superintendent's accountability to the board

All measurable aspects can be categorized into one of these three areas.

The "Exercise" section is designed to assist board members in identifying key priorities and aligning them with the evaluation process. By listing the areas the board considers most important and necessary and comparing them with the current superintendent evaluation, board members can ensure the review aligns with the board's goals and objectives.

State Guidelines

Some states have evaluation guidelines and critical objectives to measure and evaluate the superintendent. Before drafting a new superintendent evaluation, ask the board attorney if there is anything to be aware of. ***Here is an example from Virginia's code.***

Code of Virginia § 22.1-60.1. Evaluation of Superintendent

Each local school board shall evaluate the division Superintendent annually, consistent with the performance objectives outlined in the Guidelines for Uniform Performance Standards and Evaluation Criteria for Teachers, Administrators, and Superintendents, as required by § 22.1-253.13:5. 1999, cc. 1030, 1037; 2005, cc. 331, 450.

Evaluation Timeline

Once the board has a proper evaluation, the next step involves completing, reviewing, and submitting it. There should be a board calendar that has a timeline and a set of dates, which include:

1. Date to submit
2. Date to meet with superintendent to review
3. Date the evaluations are shared with the board
4. Date to review evaluations as a board
5. Date the superintendent's contract is up for review (determines next steps)

The chair leads the board on these matters; if not prescribed, responsibility should be identified in policy. Don't wait for it to just happen. The contract renewal should not be on the agenda before the board can evaluate the superintendent's performance. Questions must be asked in advance.

6. Other Details

Other Evaluation Details to Consider

- *Should evaluation be sent directly to the* ***board chair, board clerk,*** *or* ***superintendent?***
- Who do you submit the evaluation to?

  ____

- Reviewing this evaluation one-on-one with the superintendent is customary. Who will set these meetings?

  ____

Board Member's Exercises | **Exercise 6**

Evaluation Process

A good chairman will lead the process of keeping the board on track. The chair and the board clerk should work together to ensure an adequate timeline is put in place and the board is informed of important deadlines and next steps. The board clerk will have institutional knowledge based on experience, but it will be up to members to ensure processes are in place. It's important to be proactive especially if you have a laxed chairman and understanding the process will allow you to properly plan.

Subsection 5.4: Monitoring and Oversight

Effective monitoring and oversight are fundamental to school board governance, and this subsection emphasizes the role of information in this process. The chapter asserts that access to timely and relevant data is essential for informed decision-making, enabling board members to address challenges, evaluate options, and serve the interests of students and the broader community. When school boards prioritize transparency and accountability in disseminating information, they empower their members to engage in meaningful discussions, advocate for constituents, and make decisions to positively impact the educational environment.

However, it's important to highlight board member challenges with obtaining the necessary information. Often, superintendents may provide limited insights, which can lead to a power struggle between the administration and the board. This dynamic can complicate effective collaboration, as board members may be sidelined or unable to fulfill their responsibilities. The chapter encourages board members to recognize this struggle and seek to overcome challenges by establishing clear expectations for information flow and an organizational culture that values transparency. By doing so, boards can ensure all members are equally informed and equipped to make sound decisions.

Lastly, the chapter discusses the factors contributing to power struggles within school governance. These include a culture of control where superintendents may withhold information to maintain authority or a lack of confidence among board members to assert their roles effectively. This emphasizes that board members must take their oath seriously and fulfill their commitment to diligently monitor the district's operations. By engaging in proactive monitoring, conducting site visits, and maintaining open communication, board members can bridge the gap between themselves and the administration, ultimately enhancing the governance process and ensuring the school district's success.

Chapter 24
Information

In the continuously changing environment of school board governance, the importance of information goes beyond being a simple resource; it is the foundation upon which effective decision-making is built. The board's ability to oversee budgets, plans, and all necessary decisions hinges on access to relevant, timely information. It enables board members to navigate challenges, evaluate options, and ultimately make decisions that serve the best interests of students, educators, and the broader community. When board members are equipped with reliable and relevant data, they can engage in meaningful dialogue, participate in discussions, make informed votes, and advocate for the concerns and needs of their constituents.

Conversely, a deficiency of information can lead to decisions influenced by emotional responses or rooted in incomplete or misleading data, potentially resulting in unintended consequences that negatively affect the community. Therefore, it is imperative to cultivate an organizational culture emphasizing transparency and accountability in dissemination of information. By encouraging such an environment, school boards can ensure all members have equal access to comprehensive data necessary for making well-informed decisions. This reinforces the integrity and effectiveness of the governance process. Ultimately, recognizing and prioritizing the significance of information is essential for navigating the complexities of education leadership and making choices to yield positive and lasting impacts on the school district and its stakeholders.

The Importance of Being Informed

Being an informed and well-prepared member is central to your success. Information equates to knowledge, and knowledge is power. Everything hinges on what is known when making informed decisions and determining how to vote or participate in discussions.

Acquiring information may seem challenging. Typically, superintendents and staff provide board members with minimal details. This is because the more board members know, the more questions they ask. Fewer questions can lead the school board to accept whatever is presented without thorough scrutiny.

The Power Struggle

The power struggle within school governance is a genuine concern. While not all superintendents fit this mold, many struggle to keep their boards informed with meaningful and relevant information. This can create an ongoing power dynamic that complicates effective collaboration.

Boards often deal with a constant power struggle, whether among the board as a whole or between individual members. For decades, superintendents have taken on the board's authority through delegation. This has led to slowly handing over their authority to the point that it has become the norm due to a combination of reasons. Board members may have good intentions but have acquiesced due to trust in the superintendent, are volunteer members with full-time jobs who are too busy to invest the necessary time, or did not fully understand their role and authority according to state law. Also, a lack of confidence to make tough decisions merely exacerbated the situation.

The Root of the Struggle

Where does this resistance come from? Why are board members in Scottsdale, AZ, facing the same challenges as those in Drippings, TX? A longstanding culture of control characterizes the current influence of the leadership within a majority of these associations. We encourage you to balance your insights with experience and knowledge. By knowing the facts you will be able to challenge this "stinkin' thinkin'" or misguided mindset that permeates throughout the national and state associations.

An article from January 2024 titled "*13 Mistakes Board Members Make*" from the Connecticut Association of Boards of Education (CABE) and published by the National School Board Association provides valuable insight. Some of the mistakes illustrate common practices used to belittle or minimize members who do not conform or submit to the administration. Others can be used strategically at appropriate times for specific issues.

Two key points regarding information gathering are essential to understand and be prepared to hear repeatedly. These talking points have become repetitive and signal a power struggle. When hearing them, remember they often aim to undermine the value of requests for information. Common phrases include, "You're not supposed to get involved in day-to-day management!" "The board is trying to micromanage the administration," or "A board member is micromanaging."

Where does this mindset originate? Through common talking points and perspectives disseminated to board members through training and resources. For example, one association states: #5 "Can't see the forest for the trees." "Probably the greatest complaint by superintendents is that the board micromanages the administration. The more the board focuses on vision, the less it should be involved in day-to-day activities. Setting goals, monitoring their implementation through policy, and empowering the Superintendent to manage the district is critical and falls under the board's domain."

Here's what must be understood: If the goal is to be involved in daily operations to micromanage, don't! The board should establish the vision, set goals, monitor their implementation through policy, and enable the superintendent to manage the district.

However, problems arise when superintendents refuse to provide information while trying to fulfill monitoring responsibilities—a key term in the law that outlines the board's duties and authority. Members face a coalition of the superintendent and their supporters opposing requests for more information, claiming "micromanaging" or "day-to-day" information not relevant to the board's role. It is important to recognize this reaction is simply untrue.

Let's reiterate: members take a sworn oath to fulfill their duties, one of which is to "monitor" the school district's budget, vision, goals, and academic outcomes. The only way to effectively do this is through consistent and intentional monitoring, including research, site visits, town halls, and reviewing relevant information.

Additional Contributing Factors

Many factors contribute to power struggles. The following are provided as examples:

1. Many superintendents undergo educational leadership training at universities using similar textbooks and lectures from retired superintendents. Unfortunately, these programs can inadvertently teach superintendents how to navigate the system so they can pursue their objectives, often at the expense of transparency and collaboration with board members. This can lead to a situation where the superintendent's goals are met despite the board's will.
2. It is not uncommon for superintendents to hope board members overlook critical details and simply rubber-stamp proposals without asking challenging questions or seeking additional information. This tendency ultimately undermines the governance role boards are meant to fulfill.
3. Superintendent associations often lean toward a culture that inflates egos, perpetuated by former superintendents who lead these organizations. This environment minimizes the contributions of school board members, who frequently lack a Ph.D. and institutional knowledge as an educator. This leads superintendents to regard themselves as superior to board members, causing a struggle for authority and decision-making. Such perceptions complicate the relationship, making it increasingly difficult for board members to assert their responsibilities effectively.
4. Board members who ask questions and invest time researching and sharing their findings often face significant pushback when their ideas contradict the superintendent's views. If the superintendent hesitates to provide requested information, board members may need to vote "*no*." This hesitation can stem from concerns that if board members had sufficient information, they might reject the superintendent's proposal. Unfortunately, this creates a game-like atmosphere, forcing board members to decide to let go of specific issues or hold out for clarity.
5. Another source of resistance arises from the superintendent's knowledge or assumptions about how board members may vote on specific issues. If a superintendent senses a board member will oppose a proposal, they may withhold information from the member while providing more details to others who are more likely to support the item. This practice raises serious concerns and should be addressed, potentially through evaluations or discussions during meetings. Such behavior represents a betrayal of trust that needs to be called out.
6. On a positive note, board members are increasingly aware of their responsibilities, conducting due diligence, and expressing a desire to fulfill their duties. Many are also becoming better educated through professional learning resources. However, don't be surprised if the superintendent struggles with having less authority and resists sharing information to maintain control.

Common Struggles

Establishing Expectations

When accurate information is readily available, setting clear and realistic expectations for the board's activities and objectives becomes much more manageable. A consistent and transparent flow of information is an effective form of governance, ensuring that all members are on the same page and can engage in meaningful discussions.

Transparency with the Board

Transparency builds trust among parents, staff, and constituents and influences their trust in what is said and presented. When it is difficult to get a straight answer, or the superintendent resists giving backup information to the board, trust is minimized and roadblocks start forming.

Most Common Categories of Information Requests

1. **Research items:** Resources that help provide essential insights for issues brought up in a discussion but rely on the superintendent to provide.
2. **Constituent items:** Calls from constituents with an issue for members to look into "if" it is a common complaint or the superintendent wishes to ignore it before it's brought to the board.
3. **Agenda items:** Topics scheduled for discussion and approval during board meetings. Whether consent or action items, treating all agenda items with the same diligence and attention is important, each item deserves thorough consideration. Ultimately, it is vital to remember a board member is responsible for voting on each item presented, such as.
    a. **Contracts**
    b. **Budget amendments**
    c. **Annual budgets**
    d. **Policies**
    e. **Grants**
    f. **Requests for proposals**

When an agenda item is brought forward for approval, whether viewed as a routine matter or part of a broader consent agenda, each board member must comprehensively evaluate it. This means taking the time to thoroughly analyze the implications and details instead of casting a vote without sufficient consideration. While the superintendent plays a significant role in setting the agenda, it is ultimately the board's responsibility to assess and approve the items presented critically. This collaborative approach is essential for effective governance and decision-making.

Notes

Chapter 25
Fiduciary Responsibilities

UNDERSTANDING FIDUCIARY RESPONSIBILITY

Understand as a school board member, you have the authority and responsibility to make informed decisions where taxpayer dollars are involved. This is also your sworn duty. By law, the entire board could be held liable for not performing due diligence, which includes reviewing information and asking questions. Failing to do so would violate your fiduciary duties and could result in your being held responsible for malfeasance.

When encountering pushback from the superintendent or the board for asking too many questions or requesting relevant information, remind them it is the duty of the entire board, based on the oath and state law.

Fiduciary duty is a foundational principle that governs school board members' behavior and decision-making processes. It encompasses a commitment to act in the best interests of the school district, its students, and the community. This responsibility is not merely a legal obligation; it is also an ethical mandate that requires board members to prioritize the welfare of the educational environment above personal interests.

Breach of duty: This term encompasses actions involving personal gain from school contracts, misallocating school funds, or failing to exercise appropriate due diligence in decision-making.

Legal consequences: The repercussions of a breach can vary widely. Depending on the severity of the violation, a school board member may be subject to civil lawsuits, with specific penalties differing based on state regulations.

Key Components of Fiduciary Duty

These duties must not be taken lightly, as fiduciary responsibility has legal consequences. The following aspects are provided:

1. **Duty of care**: Board members must make informed decisions based on adequate information and sound judgment. This means actively participating in discussions, asking questions, and seeking expert advice when necessary to ensure well-founded decisions.

2. **Duty of loyalty:** This aspect focuses on the need for board members to act in the community's best interests. This includes students outside the district, including homeschool, private, and charter schools, because board members were elected to represent all residents and taxpayers. Additionally, they must avoid conflicts of interest and refrain from using their position for personal gain. This duty underscores the importance of transparency and honesty in all dealings related to the board's operations.

3. Duty of obedience: Board members must ensure their actions comply with the laws, regulations, and policies governing the school district and the board. This entails understanding their legal framework and ensuring board actions align with the district's mission and goals.

Malfeasance and Neglect of Duty

What Is It?

Malfeasance and neglect of duty refer to inappropriate conduct by elected officials or public employees. What does neglect or improper execution of official duties entail? Malfeasance occurs when a public official or individual takes on a responsibility but does not carry it out with the necessary care, skill, or diligence. While the action may be legal, negligence or improper execution can have adverse consequences.

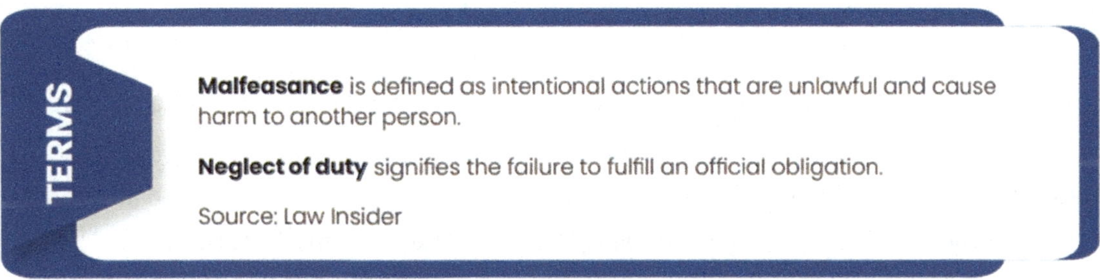

Understanding this is crucial because, in some states, like Florida, the governor can suspend an elected or appointed municipal official for malfeasance, neglect of duty, or other justifiable causes. Knowledge of these terms and their potential implications is required for upholding accountability and integrity as a public servant.

Consequences and Disciplinary Actions for Violating Fiduciary Duty

School board members who neglect their fiduciary responsibilities may face serious consequences, including removal from office, damaging their reputations, and disrupting governance. They could also encounter lawsuits for damages resulting from their actions or negligence, incur financial penalties in the form of fines, and, in severe cases, face criminal charges that include fines and jail time depending on the nature of the breach and applicable laws.

The failure to uphold fiduciary duty can also result in serious consequences for the district as a whole. Such violations can severely undermine community trust and credibility, causing parents, students, and faculty to lose confidence in the board's ability to govern effectively, which can take years to repair. Additionally, legal disputes arising from breaches can impose significant financial strains on the school district, diverting critical resources from educational programs and negatively impacting both students and teachers. Moreover, a breach can create a toxic board environment, leading to conflicts, low morale, and poor collaboration, hindering the board's ability to fulfill its mission and serve the community effectively.

Mitigating Risk and Exposure
To minimize risks associated with fiduciary responsibilities and potential misconduct, board members must have a solid understanding of relevant laws and the oath they have taken. One is less likely to be liable for actions if critical or inaccurate information is withheld and has gone on record to obtain it.

This due diligence entails understanding what is being approved before giving consent. If an item is presented for approval but lacks the necessary supporting information, and a vote is made, it may jeopardize fiduciary responsibilities.

In summary, consistently reviewing and expecting essential information is vital for sound decision-making and honoring the oath taken to fulfill duties effectively as a school board member.

Steps to Ensure Compliance with Duties

To promote adherence to responsibilities, school board members can take several proactive steps:

Ongoing education: Regular training and workshops help board members stay informed about their legal obligations and best practices in governance, enabling them to make informed decisions.

Establishing clear policies: Clear policies regarding conflicts of interest, financial oversight, and decision-making processes provide an ethical behavior and accountability framework.

Encouraging open communication: Creating an environment where board members are comfortable discussing concerns and asking questions lead to collaborative decision-making. Open dialogue helps prevent misunderstandings and ensure all perspectives are considered.

Information is paramount to school board governance and its success and effectiveness. Ultimately, a school board that prioritizes being well-informed is in a significantly stronger position to advocate for the needs of its students and educators. This contributes to the district's immediate welfare and the educational landscape's long-term success.

Notes

Notes

6

Section 6: **Budgeting and Budgets**

Objectives for Section 6: Budgeting and Budgets

1. **Clarify the Role of the School Board in Budgeting:** Understand the responsibilities of school board members in the budgeting process, emphasizing the necessity of informed participation and active engagement in setting financial priorities.

2. **Master the Five Steps of the Budget Process:** Learn the steps involved in budgeting, including guideline development, budget preparation, modification, approval, and management, to ensure a comprehensive understanding of effective budget governance.

3. **Enhance Accountability and Transparency:** Explore strategies to promote transparency in budget processes and ensure accountability among school administrators, ensuring budget decisions align with district priorities and stakeholder expectations.

4. **Comprehend the Purpose and Structure of School District Budgets:** Gain insights into the components of a school district budget, including its purpose in resource allocation and alignment with educational goals, to facilitate informed decision-making.

5. **Implement Effective Budget Monitoring Practices:** Develop skills to evaluate budget utilization and performance, enabling school board members to assess the superintendent's effectiveness and ensure resources are directed toward impactful educational initiatives.

In SECTION 6, we will explore the responsibilities of budgeting and monitoring the budget within school board leadership. This section is designed to equip you with the insights and strategies necessary for effectively governing the financial resources of your district.

In Chapter 26, we examine "Budgeting" as the board's role in the process. You'll learn how to actively engage in budget development, ensuring you are not just a passive approver but an informed and involved participant in setting priorities. This chapter outlines the five essential steps in the budgeting process, from establishing guidelines to ensuring accountability and transparency, highlighting the importance of these principles in effective governance.

Chapter 27 focuses on "Budgets" by providing a deeper understanding of what constitutes a school district budget. We will break down its purpose and components, emphasizing how a well-structured budget aligns with the district's educational goals and the board's priorities.

By breaking down these chapters into clearly defined sections, you will learn to transition your authority into actionable insights that enhance your district's financial health and educational outcomes. Your engagement in these processes will influence the quality of education provided to students.

Chapter 26
Budgeting

The Board's Role in the Budget Process

The board's role in creating the budget is the first step to overseeing and approving an annual budget. Members must be well-informed about the budget, which begins well before the final approval. One of your primary responsibilities is to oversee and approve the budget, and it is important not to vote unquestioningly on it. Your superintendent should ensure you're informed and involved in setting budget priorities throughout the year through workshops and regular updates leading up to the final budget presentation.

If your superintendent presents a budget to you without sufficient time for review or providing necessary backup information and then pressures you to approve it immediately due to a state deadline, it is important to take a stand. This tactic is often used when superintendents resist questioning or changing their priorities. Remember, the superintendent works for the board, and you have the right to fully understand and evaluate the budget before approving it. You may need to assert that you will not approve the budget if you are not adequately informed about its contents. Don't be surprised if you also get pushback from fellow board members because going along to get along is easy! However, when you're the only one trying to do the right thing and disrupt the status quo, that's when it becomes problematic. ***Scan the QR code to learn more with this Smart School Budgeting: Resources for Districts.***

5 Steps in the Budget Process

1. Development of the Guidelines Set By:

a. School Board Priorities
b. District Policy
c. Size of Budget
d. State Law
e. Schedule of Events and Dates

2. Budget Document Preparation

- The preparation will occur within each district department, facilities supervisor, and school administration. Once the initial budget drafts are created, they are typically reviewed by the school district's chief financial officer. After editing the budget, the CFO will send it to the superintendent for review. Again, there will be more edits before the budget is ready for the superintendent to present the draft budget to the board in a workshop setting. If this is not standard practice, you must set the expectations with your superintendent. Your superintendent is responsible for ensuring every board member can give feedback before it goes to the tentative draft.

3. Budget Modification

- The "tentative budget" is the budget that the board will approve with the understanding numbers will shift based on closing out of the books from the current school year. Cash on hand, revenues, reserves, or fund balance are the budget areas a board member needs to be aware of when the superintendent presents the final budget. Another shift in the "tentative budget" could be to over or estimate the student count for the budget year; state funding may shift during sessions, and it takes districts time to adjust to the latest calculations.

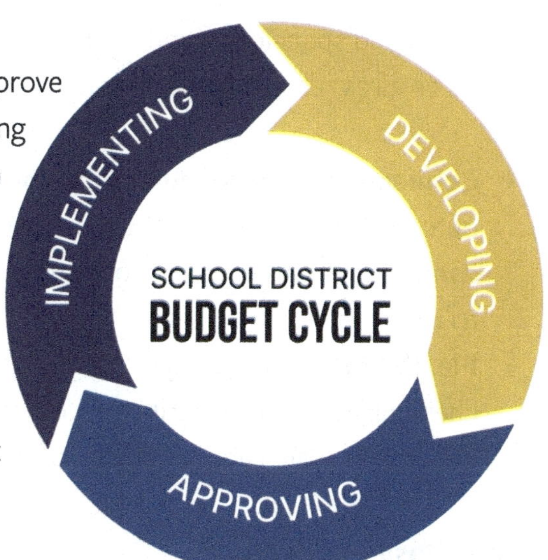

4. Budget Approval

- Each state has specific statutory requirements for approving the budget. Most states require public notice and hearings to approve the budget. The members must monitor the process to ensure the superintendent makes it transparent.
- Board members are responsible for understanding what they approve before giving their approval. Ultimately, the school board's primary role is to approve the budget by state statutes. However, many board members fail to conduct adequate research or succumb to pressure, approving a budget without sufficient clarification or supporting information. In extreme cases, entire boards have faced suspension or removal from office due to misconduct and neglect of their sworn duties.

5. Budget Management

- The superintendent will manage the district budget through their CFO. It is up to the superintendent to give board members routine reports on district finances. It is not uncommon for the superintendent to bring forward budget amendments for approval. Amendments could be a sign of poor department performance and management. Use the budget as a tool to monitor the performance of the superintendent's day-to-day management. The superintendent and CFO should be ready to give the board a clear explanation of why the amendment is needed. Amendments mean the budget for the department or school was either overspent for the specific line item, underestimated, or used for other purposes not budgeted or approved by the board.

Budget Models

There are many budgeting models and here we list the most common and efficient.

1. Priority-Based Budgeting

Priority-based budgeting (PBB) goes beyond departmental boundaries, funding specific initiatives that drive student success. For example, instead of simply allocating funds to the student services department, a PBB approach would specifically fund the truancy prevention program and all necessary personnel and resources. This ensures resources are directed to the areas of the most significant impact.

- **Connection Between Spending and Performance:** By linking budgeting decisions to performance outcomes, PBB enables school districts to allocate funds more effectively. This method encourages continuous assessment of how well programs achieve their goals, allowing districts to decide where to invest resources.
- **Flexibility in Budgeting:** Priority-based budgeting allows school districts to adapt their funding to changing needs and priorities. As new challenges arise or student demographics shift, PBB will enable districts to reallocate resources to the most relevant initiatives to current educational needs.

2. Zero-Based Budgeting

Zero-based budgeting (ZBB) requires every expense within the budget be justified from the ground up each year, starting with zero dollars. This approach forces decision-makers to critically evaluate and prioritize each expenditure based on value rather than relying on historical funding levels.

- **Strategic Prioritization:** By reviewing all expenses annually, districts can prioritize initiatives that align most closely with strategic goals and student needs. ZBB ensures only necessary expenses are included in the budget, which can be helpful for cost-cutting measures.
- **Resource Intensive:** Zero-based budgeting has significant advantages but is also resource-intensive. The process requires substantial time and effort from staff to thoroughly analyze and justify each expenditure, which can strain administrative resources.

3. Program Budgeting

This approach allocates funds based on specific programs and desired outcomes, focusing on each program's effectiveness in meeting educational goals.

4. Site-Based Budgeting

Site-based budgeting empowers individual schools to manage their budgets according to their unique needs, fostering local decision-making and accountability.

5. Student-Based Budgeting

This method allocates funds based on student enrollment numbers, providing more resources to schools with larger student populations and ensuring funding reflects the service demand.

Notes

Chapter 27
Budgets

According to William Hartman, the author of *School District Budgets*, the purpose of a school district budget is to *"establish the district's objectives and priorities; allocating resources; involving the public through budget hearings, school board decisions and other means of representative democracy; and, in some states, conducting budget elections."*

What Is a School District Budget?
A budget is a document that specifies a school district's planned expenditures and anticipated revenues in a given fiscal year. It also includes past and projected data and information relating fiscal elements to the district's education mission, organization, policies, programs, and outcomes.

This seems complicated, so let's break it down. The budget specifies a school district's planned expenditures and anticipated revenues based on historical data (including other past and projected data and information), program costs, contracts, and state/local education funding. These fiscal elements relate to the district's relevant education mission, organization, policies, programs, and outcomes.

Three Separate Elements Make Up a Budget

1. A description of the **educational program** to be provided by the school district
2. An estimate of the **expenditures** needed to carry out the desired programs
3. An estimate of the **revenues** that will be available to pay for the spending

The school district budget cycle diagram on page 149 illustrate a visual for the sequence of activities involved in planning the district's educational programs, estimating the needed expenditures and revenues to implement these programs, gaining the necessary approvals, and using the budget to assist in managing the district's operations.

Educational program is an organized set of learning activities designed, in the board's opinion, to enable learners to develop their potential and acquire the knowledge, skills, and attitudes needed to contribute to a healthy, democratic, prosperous, and sustainable economy.

Purpose of a School District Budget
The budgeting cycle immensely benefits the school district, constituents, and school board. A well-thought-out and comprehensive budget allows for accountability and transparency. As a management tool it empowers administrators to act within predetermined limits to execute their jobs and improve the district's educational

outcomes. For school board members, budgets are a way to control spending to align with their priorities and set expectations. A reasonable school district budget benefits every constituent, employee, and administrator, as it allows for clarity of purpose, the efficient allocation of resources, and transparency to the community on school district priorities (if adequately made available).

The Strategic Plan and the Budget serve as the main governance tools utilized by school boards.

5 Major Uses

1. Planning
2. Public Transparency
3. Legal
4. Control
5. Evaluations

1. Planning

The planning process begins with budgeting. The budget is the district's principal planning system, determining how much money will be spent on what and when. An important part of budgeting is aligning it with the stated goals of the school district and school board.

Does your budget support the board's strategic plan, priorities, and mission?
You want the answer to this question to be an unequivocal YES. Otherwise, your strategic plan, priorities, and mission will be nearly impossible to achieve – as they have been practically ignored.

During this stage, the district plans

1. Educational programs
2. Total cost of educational programs
3. Services offered to students
4. District office activities and supports
5. Resources needed and cost of resources

2. Public Transparency

Adequately ordered, the budget is a *transparent document for reviewing and approving the district's educational and fiscal plan*. This budgeting process allows the public and stakeholders to be involved in a process central to school district administration.

The review and approval of the budget can vary based on state laws:

1. From school board approval to submitting the local property tax levy required to support the budget to the voters.
2. In some states, proposed school district budgets require voters' approval and/or approval from cities or counties.
3. State law will determine the timelines and processes of the school board public hearings.

3. Legal

Once the budget has been approved, it becomes a functional legal document that serves as the legal basis for the school district administration to dispense public funds. With some exceptions, the approved budget authorizes the superintendent to expend revenues derived from local, state, and federal dollars as described in the budget.

As such, extra-budgetary expenditures must be approved by the school board, except in situations where the expenditure is less than a state-mandated or board-approved discretionary spending limit. Attempts to manipulate the budget, break up large extra-budgetary expenditures to adhere to discretionary limits, and misappropriate budgeted funds are significant problems. The school board must remain vigilant and informed as the body elected to represent the school district's constituent citizens.

Strategies you can use to maintain legal oversight of the budget and related expenditures include:

- Analyze budget amendments by asking for historical and relevant information before approving.
- Regularly ask for updates on the reserve balance.
- Question what funds, contracts, and vendors are being paid out of before approving the item.
- Know if funds are being siphoned from state or federal grants for other projects.
- Ensure relevant budget data is provided to compare past and present revenues and expenditures.
- Know the topline budget numbers and expenditures to date to analyze if spending is on pace, over budget, or under budget.
- Take this personal analysis as a reason to ask for specific expenditure reports from school and district administrators.
- Look for accounting inconsistencies, budgets not kept closely in check, and chronic overspending as evidence of incompetence or malpractice.
- Question budget amendments because these can sometimes signify mismanagement of funds.
- Look for accounts with under expenditures because this could indicate the administration is not following through on the board's funded priorities. For example, STEM programs, after-school tutoring, vocational education, etc.
- Be aware of account transfers and ensure funds are legally allocated.
- Keep the public as informed and updated as legally possible. This diffuses work and oversight to the party most impacted: constituent taxpayers.

4. Control

Over a budget's operating year, it serves as a management tool and control document. A well-outlined budget holds the superintendent, department heads, and principals accountable for their spending. This is important, as the natural mode of bureaucratic hierarchies, like a school administration, is to spend whatever they can and grow their respective departments' importance, resources, and power. The budget and the school board's unique position in approving it serve as the basis for the taxpayers' control over school district expenditures.

BUDGETARY CONTROL

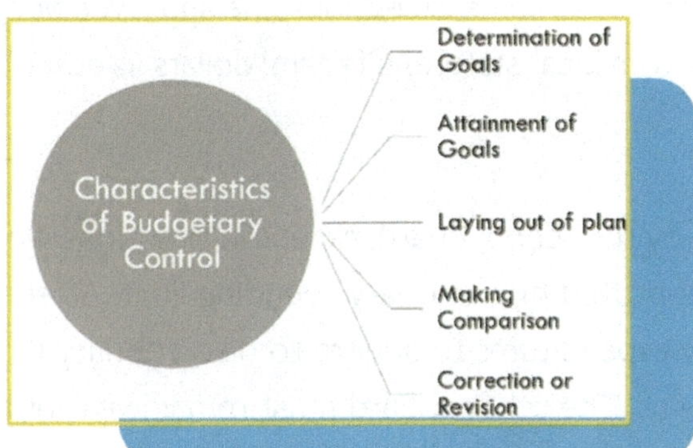

Throughout the fiscal year, the budget functions as a critical management control document. The budget holds the superintendent, department heads, and principals accountable for their financial decisions and strategic plans. It serves as the foundation for overseeing expenditures within the school district. The budget should be utilized to monitor under-expenditures in school-based programs, district departments, and priority initiatives. Tying the budget to the strategic plan ensures that short- and long-term goals are met.

BEFORE APPROVING AN EXPENDITURE CULTIVATE THE PRACTICE OF:
#1 Ask the superintendent how the items up for approval (e.g., all contracts) relate to the strategic plan.
#2 Ask the superintendent if this was originally approved in the annual budget and, if so, where specifically?

In light of this, the budget monitors *underspending* in school-based programs and departments. Some examples of this include STEM programs and literacy resources. The budget document serves as the measurement against which *over-expenditures* are compared.

5. Evaluations

The budget is a yardstick against which you can measure progress toward district goals, especially since you considered these on the front end when formulating and voting on the budget. Some factors which you can evaluate the superintendent on success are:

- Budgeting process
  - Budget accuracy (over/under)
  - Transparency
  - Include the board
- Adhering to state and federal laws?
  - Reserve or fund balance minimums set by state/board
- Expenditure control?

- Does the budget promote accountability?
- Does the budget link resource allocation to student outcomes compared to performance indicators?
- Is it implementing the district's strategic plan?

Case Scenario: Ensuring Effective Budget Utilization in School Districts

As school boards set their priorities for the academic year, it is essential to ensure budget allocations align with approved initiatives and are effectively utilized. A recurring challenge arises when funds are allocated to underused programs, leading to unnecessary budget requests for subsequent years.

STEM Initiative Utilization

At the end of the school year, a board member discovered approximately 90% of the funds allocated for the STEM initiative, which had been approved for each school, had gone unused. Despite this significant underutilization, schools submitted requests for continued funding for the STEM program for the following academic year. This raised concerns about the efficiency of budget planning and resource allocation.

Key Issues Identified

Underutilization of Approved Programs – Most of the allocated funds for the STEM initiative had gone unspent, indicating a disconnect between the board's priorities and the schools' implementation of these programs.

Lack of Accountability –The schools did not adequately justify the underutilization, leading to questions about accountability and the effectiveness of monitoring processes.

Continuation of Unused Programs –The schools' requests for additional funding for a program that saw little use suggest a lack of strategic planning and evaluation.

Analysis

Need for Regular Reviews –The situation highlights the necessity of assessing funded programs on an ongoing basis. Regular reviews can help identify underutilized initiatives and facilitate adjustments to future budgets based on actual usage and effectiveness.

Accountability Mechanisms – Establishing clear accountability measures for schools to report on the utilization of funds can encourage responsible spending and ensure resources are directed toward initiatives that yield results.

Strategic Planning – Schools should be encouraged to develop strategic plans that align with board priorities and demonstrate how they will effectively utilize allocated funds before requesting additional resources.

Recommendations

1. Implement a Utilization Review Process. Require schools to provide periodic reports on the usage of allocated funds and the outcomes of funded initiatives. This should be integrated into the budget approval process for the following year.

2. Establish Clear Performance Metrics. Develop specific metrics to evaluate the success and utilization of programs like the STEM initiative. This will help the board make informed decisions about funding based on actual performance.

3. Create a Contingency Funding Model. Consider allocating a portion of the budget for new initiatives based on the previous year's utilization rates. If a program is underutilized, funds can be redirected to more effective initiatives, promoting a culture of accountability and efficiency.

4. Prepare for the Next Budget Cycle. The board will ask the superintendent to implement Zero-Based Budgeting (ZBB) for the next budget cycle to ensure programs request only what they truly need.

Takeaways

This case underscores the importance of ensuring budget requests are grounded in actual program utilization and effectiveness. By implementing regular reviews, establishing accountability mechanisms, and involving stakeholders in the evaluation process, school boards can make more informed decisions that prioritize the effective use of resources. Ultimately, this approach will lead to more strategic budgeting, ensuring funds are allocated to initiatives that enhance students' educational experience.

Notes

Notes

7

Section 7: **School Board Finance**

Objectives for Section 7: School Board Finance, Procurement, Contracts, and Fraud

1. **Understand School District Finance Basics:** Gain a foundational understanding of school district finance, including the various funding sources, types of funds, and their purposes, to make informed decisions during budget approvals.

2. **Navigate the Procurement Process:** Learn the procurement procedures for acquiring goods and services effectively, including recognizing the differences between RFPs, RFQs, and RFOs, to ensure transparency and fairness in contract approvals.

3. **Evaluate Contracts Thoroughly:** Develop skills to assess contracts presented to the board, ensuring they align with district goals, adhere to budgetary constraints, and comply with procurement policies for responsible financial governance.

4. **Recognize and Combat Fraud:** Identify common forms of fraud within school districts, understand the factors contributing to fraud, and implement strategies to promote a culture of accountability and transparency.

5. **Implement Financial Safeguards:** Explore best practices for safeguarding district finances, including setting spending limits, rotating contractors, and establishing clear procurement policies to mitigate risks associated with financial mismanagement and fraud.

School board finance is an intricate and multifaceted subject, but with dedicated effort to understand its complexities, you can equip yourself to make informed and impactful decisions. Section 7 is designed to demystify the components of school district finances, procurement processes, contract approvals, and awareness of fraud. Each chapter within this section offers valuable insights and frameworks that will help you take on these responsibilities with confidence.

As you read through this section, keep in mind it is not intended for a single read-through. The information presented here serves as a comprehensive resource you can revisit repeatedly, allowing you to deepen your understanding and refine your approach to the various financial aspects of school governance. By breaking down each topic into clearly defined chapters, you will gain clarity on your duties and the authority vested in you as a school board member.

Chapter 28, "School District Finance Basics," introduces you to the basics of school district finance, shedding light on the often convoluted state and federal funding mechanisms. It emphasizes the importance of familiarizing yourself with different types of funds and their purposes, ensuring you can interpret budget documents.

In Chapter 29, "Understanding Procurement," you will explore the procurement process, detailing the steps necessary to ensure fair and transparent acquisition of goods and services. Understanding the distinctions between Requests for Proposal (RFP), Requests for Quotation (RFQ), Requests for Qualification (RFQ), and Requests for Offer (RFO) will enhance your ability to make thoughtful and strategic decisions when approving contracts.

Chapter 30, "Contract Approvals," focuses on key contractual responsibilities of the school board. It outlines the steps you must take to ensure contracts align with district goals, are financially sound, and adhere to legal requirements. This chapter reinforces the need for vigilance and thorough review to protect the district's interests.

Finally, Chapter 31, "School District Fraud," addresses the overlooked issue of fraud within school districts. By examining common fraud schemes and identifying the factors that facilitate fraud, you will be better positioned to implement safeguards and promote a culture of accountability within your district.

As you engage with Sections 6 and 7, remember informed decision-making is grounded in knowledge and vigilance. Your proactive involvement in understanding budgetary items, finance, procurement, contracts, and fraud will ultimately contribute to a stronger, more transparent educational environment for the students and community you serve.

Chapter 28
School District Finance Basics

School district finance is riddled with complicated state and federal formulas. However, don't let the complexity of the funding mechanisms overwhelm you. Your first budget cycle may feel like drinking from a firehose with an insurmountable amount of information coming at you in the form of numbers and pages.

In this chapter, we have broken down the fundamental elements of school district finance so you can understand the budget better before you approve it. Depending on state statutes and Department of Education policies, every state's budget documents will vary regarding required information. For our purposes, we want to give you as a school board member the fundamental elements so you can make informed decisions based on the information most commonly presented during the budget (and contract) approvals

The school district budget comprises many separate funds due to the funding sources and the accounting and accountability associated with each. It is important to understand the names and purposes of each fund, the funding sources that go into it, and, finally, the expenses associated with each.

Get Familiar With Your School District's Funding Types

There are four main categories, each containing several subcategories:

1. **General Operating Fund**
2. **Special Revenues Funds**
    - Federal Fund
    - Food Service Fund
    - Debt Service Fund
    - Capital Projects Fund
    - Community Fund
3. **Proprietary or Enterprise Fund**
4. **Fiduciary Funds**
    - Medical Insurance Trust Fund

Understand Each Fund's Purpose

- **General Operating Fund** – This fund is the school district's chief operating fund. It accounts for all financial resources except those accounted for and reported in another fund. A district may have only one general fund.

Saint Paul Public Schools
Proposed Revenue and Expenditures Summary
Fiscal Year 2023-24

	Estimated Beginning Fund Balance	Revenue	Expense	Net Change in Fund Balance	Estimated Ending Fund Balance
General Fund	$165,721,421	$766,654,615	$801,094,756	($34,440,141)	$131,281,280
General Fund Fully Financed	$0	$0	$0	$0	$0
Food Service	$7,580,115	$28,782,398	$33,615,466	($4,833,068)	$2,747,047
Community Service	$12,071,056	$33,635,302	$35,149,600	($1,514,298)	$10,556,758
Community Service Fully Financed	$0	$0	$0	$0	$0
Building Construction	$125,279,340	$135,000,000	$114,685,153	$20,314,847	$145,594,187
Debt Service	$48,424,260	$56,763,413	$51,333,088	$5,430,325	$53,854,585
Total All Funds	**$359,076,192**	**$1,020,835,728**	**$1,035,878,063**	**($15,042,335)**	**$344,033,857**

Percent of Total Revenue

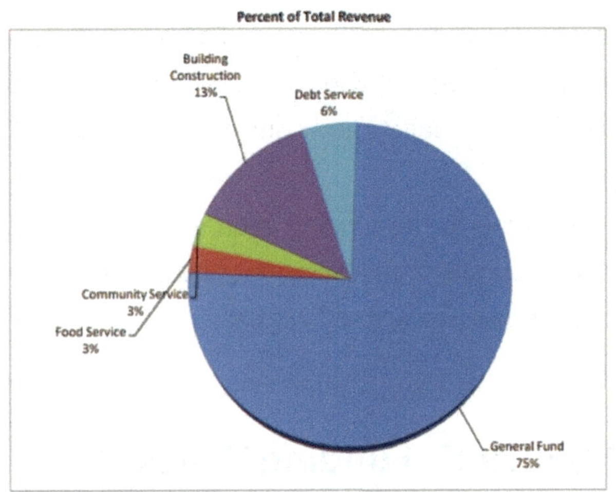

Percent of Total Expenditures

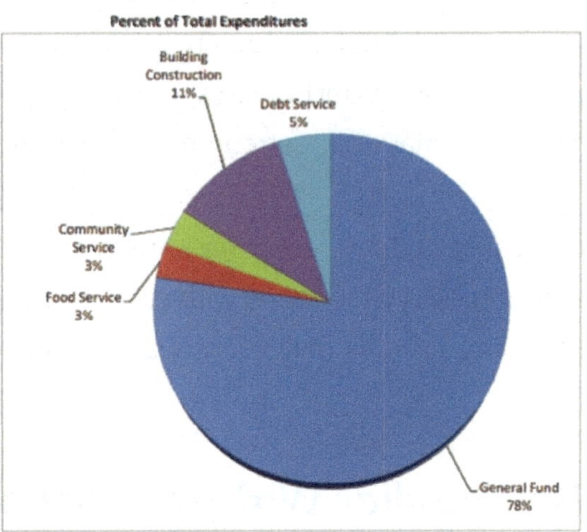

Estimated beginning Fund Balance is based on the March 20, 2023 Revised Budget

Source: St. Paul Public Schools FY 2023-2024

- **Federal Fund** – These are primarily targeted funds for specific programs like IDEA and Title programs such as Title IX under federal law.

- **Food Service Fund** – These funds primarily come from federal and state resources and are provided specifically for breakfast and lunch programs.

- **Debt Service Fund** – These funds account for financial resources that are restricted, committed, or assigned to expenditure for principal and interest. Debt service funds should be used if legally mandated, as well as to accumulate resources for the payment of general long-term debt principal and interest maturing in future years.

- **Capital Projects Funds** – These funds account for financial resources that are restricted, committed, or assigned to expenditure for capital outlays, including the acquisition or construction of capital facilities and other capital assets (other than those of proprietary funds and trust funds). The most common source of capital project funding is the sale of bonds or other capital financing instruments.

A separate fund may be used for each capital project, or one fund may be used, supplemented by the classification project/reporting code. For example, Building Construction.

- **Community Fund** – A fund serves as a dedicated financial resource to support various community education programs, including early childhood education, adult basic education, school readiness, recreational activities, and civic engagement. This fund is sourced from multiple avenues: local community service fees paid by patrons participating in programs, property tax levies collected from the community, and financial assistance from state and federal governments, alongside grants from organizations such as the Department of Education. The funds are allocated to numerous initiatives, including programs and nonpublic student activities, and are managed in a reserve account within the community service fund.

- **Proprietary or Enterprise Funds** – These funds account for any activity for which a fee is charged to external users for goods or services. Enterprise funds are required to be used to account for any activity whose principal revenue sources meet any of the following criteria:
  - Debt backed solely by revenues from fees (thus, not debt supported by the full faith and credit of the school district)
  - Legal requirement to recover costs through fees and charges
  - Policy decision of the governing board of management to recover the costs of providing services through fees or charges

  Enterprise funds can be used for activities such as food service programs, bookstore operations, athletic stadiums, community swimming pools, and the rental of the high school's performing arts center.

- **Health Fund or Trust Fund** – A fund that accounts for assets held by a school district in a trustee capacity for others—e.g., members and beneficiaries of pension plans and other post-employment benefit (OPEB) plans, external investment pools, or private-purpose trust arrangements—and that therefore cannot be used to support the school district's programs. For example, in this illustration, the district maintains a "self-insured" health care common in larger school districts.

School District Expenditures

After understanding the various funds, the next step in reading a budget is to grasp the expenses or expenditures your district is responsible for paying. These costs are routine; therefore, you should become familiar with the cost categories to the extent an expenditure or a new price is out of the ordinary. By becoming familiar with your budget, you will identify areas of opportunity to reduce costs and perhaps stop politically charged additions such as a DEI position, new books that could be age-appropriate, etc. ***See St. Paul Public Schools FY 2025 chart as a sample breakdown of expenditures by fund for a school district.***

FY25 Expenditures by Fund

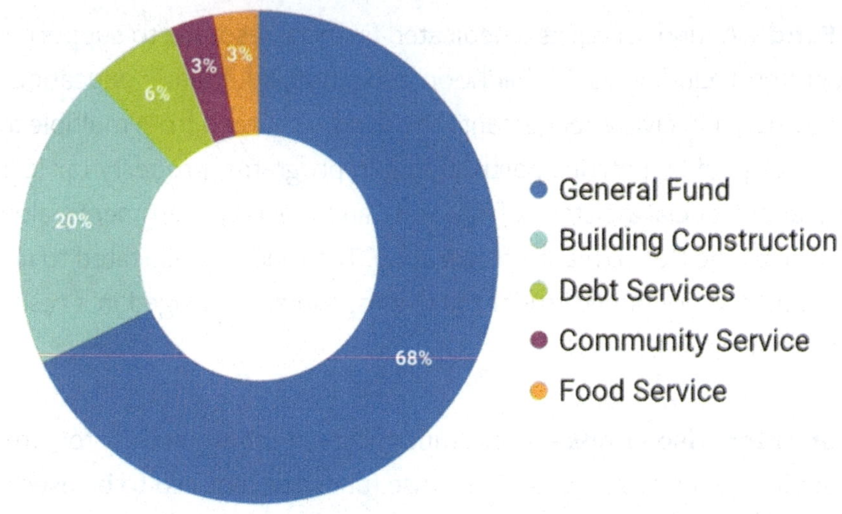

Inspire students to think critically, pursue their dreams and change the world.

13

Expenditure categories commonly within a specific fund(s):

- Salaries – General fund
- Employee Benefits – General fund
- Health and Safety – General fund
- Curriculum – General & Federal fund
- Food Services – Federal & General fund
- Student Support Services – General & Federal fund
- Transportation – Capital fund
- Facilities – Capital fund
- Utilities – Capital fund

School District Revenues

Understanding school district finances begins with recognizing the primary revenue sources. Across the country, school districts receive funding from three primary sources: federal, state, and local.

Federal funding is primarily program-specific and often aims to support educational initiatives for disadvantaged students or specific programs. State funding has a broader application, covering various expenses such as salaries and capital projects, depending on state-imposed regulations. Local funding is the most flexible and forms the foundation of a school district's overall budget.

FY25 General Fund Revenue Sources

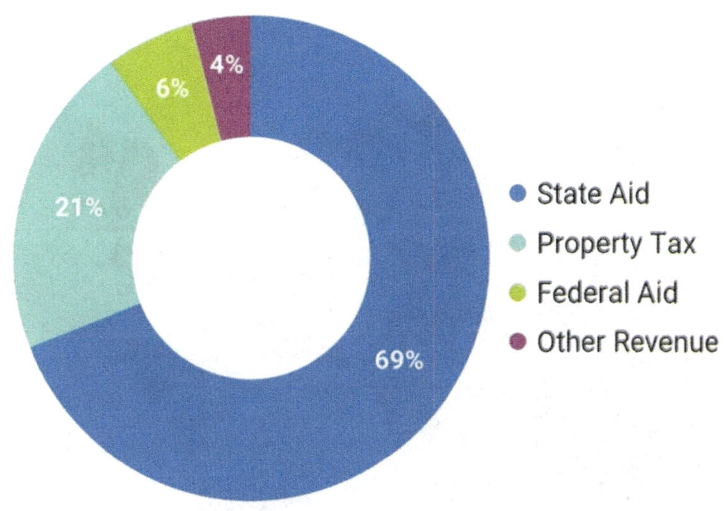

Inspire students to think critically, pursue their dreams and change the world.

11

Federal funds come from federal taxes, state funds are generated through state taxes, and local funds are primarily sourced from property taxes. Other funding sources, such as grants and donations, contribute only a small portion to a district's overall funding. ***See St. Paul Public Schools FY 2025 chart to get a rough breakdown of these sources of funds typical for a school district.***

Understand School District Funding Structure

As the following graphics shows, most states utilize a student-based funding model, followed by resource-based and program-based models. Some states employ a combination of these approaches.

Student-Based Funding
School districts receive funding based on the number of students enrolled or attending. Additionally, districts may receive extra funding based on specific characteristics of enrolled students, such as low income, disabilities, or being English Language Learners.

Resource-Based Funding
In this model, school districts receive funding based on the anticipated costs of resources and inputs, such as staff salaries and instructional materials, adjusted for the number of students, teachers, and administrators within the district. Most funding is linked to staffing ratios for various roles at different grade levels, including teachers, counselors, and administrators. This type of aid is distributed without regard to a district's property wealth or per-pupil spending.

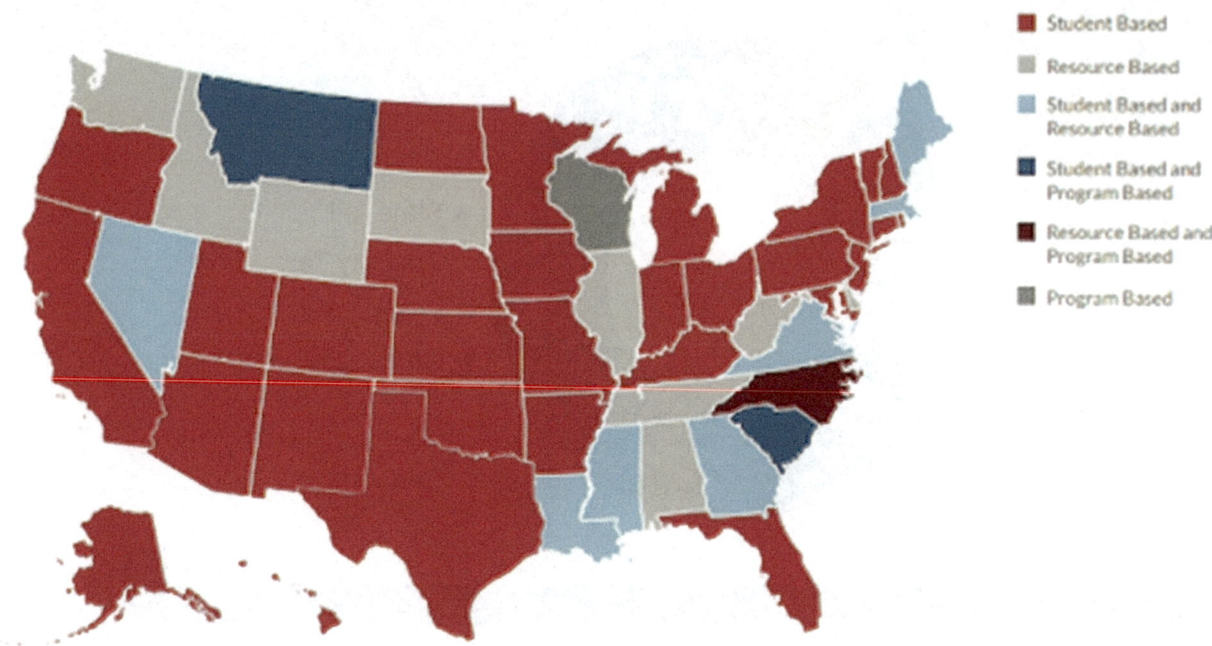

Source: "FundEd: National Policy Maps—A National Overview of State Education Funding Policies," EdBuild, 2021, http://funded.edbuild.org/national#formula-type.

Federal Funding & Programs

Federal Educational Funding, the smallest part of a school district's revenue (when compared to local or state), is allocated for specific purposes or uses and has mandatory reporting requirements. This has developed into the government's well-known practice of dictating mandates, typically with attached money strings, as so-called ***funded mandates***. However, funding is only provided for a limited period, but the mandates usually remain. Federal funding comes from two kinds of grants and different rules govern how the funds may be spent.

Federal Grants

1. **Formula grants**: Determined by Congress and allocated to states, funds are granted to school communities without an application process.
2. **Discretionary grants**: Awarded using a competitive grant application process for states and school communities.

Annual Federal Programs

Federal funding and its processes can be complex, as there are 30+ federal educational grant programs. Primarily provides funding to all states and districts on an annual basis through formula grants.

Title I: Economically Disadvantaged

$16B per year (approximate). The largest federal funding program focuses on improving the academic achievement of disadvantaged students.

- **Title I (Part A):** Provides funding to schools with a high percentage of students from low-income families to ensure all students meet challenging state academic standards.
- **Title I (Part A, Section 1003 G):** Provides funding to the lowest-performing schools to raise students' achievement.

Title II: Professional Development for Educators

$2B per year (approximate) grant funding supports effective instruction and improves the quality of educators and administrators. It aims to increase student achievement consistent with challenging state academic standards.

Title III: English Language Learners

$737M per year (approximate)

- **Title III (Part A)** funds schools to advance the education of English Learners (ELs), ensuring these students can achieve English language proficiency while meeting academic standards.

Title IV: Student Support and Academic Achievement

- **Title IV** (Part A—$1.17B per year, approximate) provides funding opportunities for students to access a well-rounded education, improve their use of technology to achieve academic success and increase their engagement in STEM activities.
- **Title IV** (Part B—$1.2B per year, approximate) provides funding for various activities that advance student achievement, such as after-school programs, summer school programs, digital learning, family involvement, and other forms of education and remediation beyond the traditional school day.

IDEA: Special Education & Students with Disabilities

$13.45B per year (approximate) second largest federal funding program *Provides funding opportunities for the education of students with special needs and disabilities, supports early intervention, and improves the use of technology in the classroom for special education.

Perkins V: Career and Technical Education

$1.26B per year (approximate) provides funding opportunities for career and technical education to prepare students for careers in current or emerging professions, industry sectors, or occupations, technical skill proficiency, prerequisite courses or postsecondary credentials, career exploration at high school or middle school levels, work-based or other applied learning opportunities, dual or concurrent enrollment program opportunities, and postsecondary credits.

Other Federal Programs

Title IX

Congress enacted Title IX in 1972 to ensure girls and women have access to the same educational opportunities and programs as boys and men. Title IX authorizes any federal agency that provides such assistance to issue regulations to enforce the prohibition of sex discrimination. It also allows the termination of financial aid when an institution does not voluntarily comply. ***Scan the QR code to read more about Title IX.***

Title IX states:

"No person in the United States shall, based on sex, be excluded from the participation in, be denied the benefits of, or be subjected to discrimination under any education program or activity receiving Federal financial assistance."

Who does Title IX apply to?

All schools, local and state educational agencies, and other institutions receiving federal financial assistance from the Department of Education.

These recipients include:

- 17,600 local school districts
- Over 5,000 post-secondary institutions
- Charter schools
- For-profit schools
- Libraries
- Museums

A recipient of funds from the Federal Department of Education must operate its educational programs or activities without discrimination based on sex.

Examples of Title IX obligations include:

- Recruitment, admissions, and counseling
- Financial assistance
- Athletics
- Sex-based harassment
- Discipline
- Employment

Trump (47) Administration Returns Title IX to 2020 Rule

Summary

On January 31, the U.S. Department of Education (DOE) announced that, effective immediately, it will enforce the original Trump-era Title IX regulations from 2020, rather than the regulations established during the Biden administration (the 2024 Rule). The reinstated 2020 Title IX regulations limit claims of sexual harassment to those based on the sex assigned at birth, following President Trump's January 20, 2025, executive order mandating all federal executive agencies to recognize only "two sexes: male and female."

Overview

On January 9, 2025, a federal district court invalidated the 2024 Rule. However, the court did not clarify how long institutions would have to adjust to the new legal framework or whether the DOE intended to return to previous regulations. The DOE has confirmed that the court's decision reinstates the enforcement of the 2020 Rule for Title IX.

The DOE no longer interprets Title IX's prohibition against discrimination "on the basis of sex" as including discrimination based on sex stereotypes, sexual orientation, gender identity (including transgender status), or sex characteristics.

President Trump's January 20, 2025, Executive Order titled "Defending Women from Gender Ideology Extremism and Restoring Biological Truth to the Federal Government" instructs federal agencies to promptly retract any guidance inconsistent with the Executive Order, which asserts that the federal government should recognize only sex assigned at birth, thereby excluding nonbinary identities.

In accordance with the Executive Order and the federal court's invalidation of the 2024 Rule, the Department of Education (DOE) has issued a Dear Colleague Letter (DCL). This letter confirms that educational institutions must ensure their policies and investigations align with the 2020 Rule. This guidance is effective immediately and applies to all ongoing Title IX investigations.

The DCL emphasizes that all schools receiving federal financial assistance must implement or maintain policies that comply with the 2020 Rule. This change takes effect immediately and applies to all open investigations, regardless of the regulations in place when the conduct occurred. ***Scan the QR Code to read the Dear Colleagu Letter dated February 4th, 2025***

One Time Federal Funding

Approving one-time funding grants can be challenging for districts without a clear plan for when the funding ends. To avoid complications, it's important to set specific expectations regarding the duration of the program and the funding. Many districts find themselves in difficult situations when they postpone adjustments until the funding period concludes, often resulting in last-minute financing efforts.

As a board member you can promote sound fiscal planning by asking key questions, such as, "Is this a non-recurring grant?" and "Does the item we approve have clear timelines and expectations that align with the end of the funding?" For example, if the approval involves hiring new staff, to ensure transparency, the new hire must fully understand the contract terms and how they relate to the duration of the funding. By taking these proactive steps, the board can ensure your district's financial strategies are sustainable and well-planned.

Understanding Elementary and Secondary School Emergency Relief (ESSER)

The Coronavirus Response and Relief Supplemental Appropriations (CRRSA) Act, 2021, was signed into law on December 27, 2020, and provided an additional $54.3 billion for the Elementary and Secondary School Emergency Relief (ESSER II) Fund. ESSER II Fund awards to State Education Agencies (SEAs) are the same proportion as each state receiving funds under Part A of Title I of the Elementary and Secondary Education Act of 1965, as amended, in fiscal year 2020.

American Rescue Plan (ARP) Act

The American Rescue Plan (ARP) Act was signed into law on Thursday, March 11, 2021. This comprehensive $1.9 trillion package, which included a massive allocation of $122 billion designated explicitly for the ARP Elementary and Secondary School Emergency Relief (ARP ESSER) Fund, represents a substantial response to the challenges posed by the COVID-19 pandemic.

These funds were allocated to State Education Agencies (SEAs) and Local Education Agencies (LEAs), known as the State Department of Education and School Districts, to facilitate the safe reopening of schools and ensure the continuation of in-person learning amidst ongoing public health concerns.

The primary goal of the ARP ESSER Fund was to address the significant impacts of the coronavirus pandemic on students, families, and school communities across the United States. However, this financial support has led some districts into financial difficulties because they utilized the funds beyond their original intent. The funds were intended to help schools implement necessary safety measures, provide resources for academic recovery, and promote overall student well-being. In a later section, we will review how school districts utilized these funds for ongoing expenses. Now that the funding has run out, school districts face deficits if they do not revert to spending levels minus ARP funds. The times are never easy when districts have to cut back so staying transparent with department heads, staff, and parents is vital if it is a one-time grant. ***Scan the QR code for additional federal grant information.***

Case Scenario: Addressing Financial Challenges in a School District

Background: As we enter 2025, the local school district finds itself in a precarious financial situation. The expiration of American Rescue Plan (ARP) funds, rising inflation, and a notable decline in student enrollment due to prolonged COVID-19 lockdowns and controversial mandates have led to a significant budget shortfall. Using ESSER (Elementary and Secondary School Emergency Relief) funds for recurring expenses rather than one-time costs has exacerbated the financial strain. As a result, the school board must take immediate and strategic actions to align expenditures with the current economic reality while ensuring the continued delivery of quality education.

The Board Meets for the Financial Overview

The chief financial officer presents a comprehensive financial report revealing a projected budget deficit of $4 million for the upcoming fiscal year. The board learns enrollment has decreased by 25%, significantly impacting the district's funding. With ESSER funds already allocated to ongoing expenses, the board recognizes the urgent need for a sustainable financial strategy.

Board Members Discuss Options

Establishing a Financial Recovery Task Force: A Financial Recovery Task Force would be formed to identify cost-saving measures and ensure fiscal responsibility. It would consist of board members, district administrators, and community stakeholders, providing diverse perspectives in decision-making.

Implementing a Budget Realignment Policy: A suggested policy mandates a thorough review of all departmental budgets with a zero-base budget process. Each department must justify its expenditures so funds can be reallocated to prioritize essential services and programs directly impacting student learning.

Evaluating Personnel Costs: The board discusses assessing staffing levels. It recommends a temporary hiring freeze on non-essential positions and a review of current staffing structures to identify potential redundancies and inefficiencies.

Streamlining Operational Expenses: It is vital to conduct a comprehensive audit of operational expenses, including utilities, maintenance, and transportation. Identifying areas for cost reduction, such as renegotiating contracts or consolidating services, could yield significant savings.

Pursuing Alternative Funding: The board emphasizes seeking alternative funding opportunities.

Long-Term Strategic Planning

Developing a Sustainable Financial Plan: The board acknowledges the necessity of creating a long-term financial sustainability plan. This plan should address immediate budgetary concerns while outlining future growth and resilience strategies, including diversifying funding sources.

Reevaluating Educational Programs: A comprehensive evaluation of all educational programs is proposed to assess their effectiveness and alignment with community needs. This evaluation can guide program consolidation or enhancement decisions and ensure resources are allocated efficiently.

Takeaways

In conclusion, the board is taking proactive measures to address the impending financial challenges actively. By implementing strategic policies, effectively managing costs, enhancing revenue generation, and engaging the community, the school board aims to stabilize its finances while continuing to provide a quality education.

Notes

Chapter 29
Understanding Procurement

Procurement Process

Understanding the procurement process and confidently approving contracts is paramount for school board members. With a firm grasp of procurement procedures, you can effectively fulfill your responsibilities and ensure the district's best interests are served. A thorough understanding of the procurement process allows for informed decision-making, promotes transparency, and ensures accountability. It will empower you to advocate for the efficient and effective allocation of resources, ultimately benefiting the students and the entire school community.

In this summary, we'll provide an overview of school district procurement processes and procedures, highlighting the significance of differentiating between an RFP, RFQ/RFQ, and RFO, the involvement of school board members, the role of the purchasing department, district policies on rotating contractors or bids, and the overall importance of comprehending this essential process.

RFP, RFQ/RFQ, and RFO

These are standard procurement methods used by school districts. RFP stands for Request for Proposal, typically used when the district requires a detailed solution or service. RFQ stands for Request for Quotation and is used when the district seeks pricing for a specific product or service. RFQ can also be Request for Qualifications, which is used when the district requires particular professional qualifications. RFO stands for Request for Offer and is used when the district explores and seeks general information or offers from potential vendors.

School Board Member Involvement

As a school board member, you will encounter procurement processes when acquiring goods or services for the district. You'll review and approve the procurement policies, procedures, and contracts to ensure they align with the district's goals, objectives, and strategic plan. The board's and superintendent's responsibility is to ensure transparency, fairness, and adherence to legal requirements in the procurement process.

Purchasing Department Role

The purchasing department within a school district is responsible for managing the procurement process. The board's role is on the front end, setting goals, budget, policy and approving vendors; it is also in the final stage of approving the contract during a business meeting. Everything else in the middle will be handled through the purchasing department. They review and evaluate bids or proposals received, ensure compliance with district policies and legal requirements, negotiate contracts, and monitor vendor performance. The purchasing department ensures the district obtains the best value while maintaining high-quality standards. It is always best practice and sometimes required by board policy or state law for the purchasing department to create a purchasing manual.

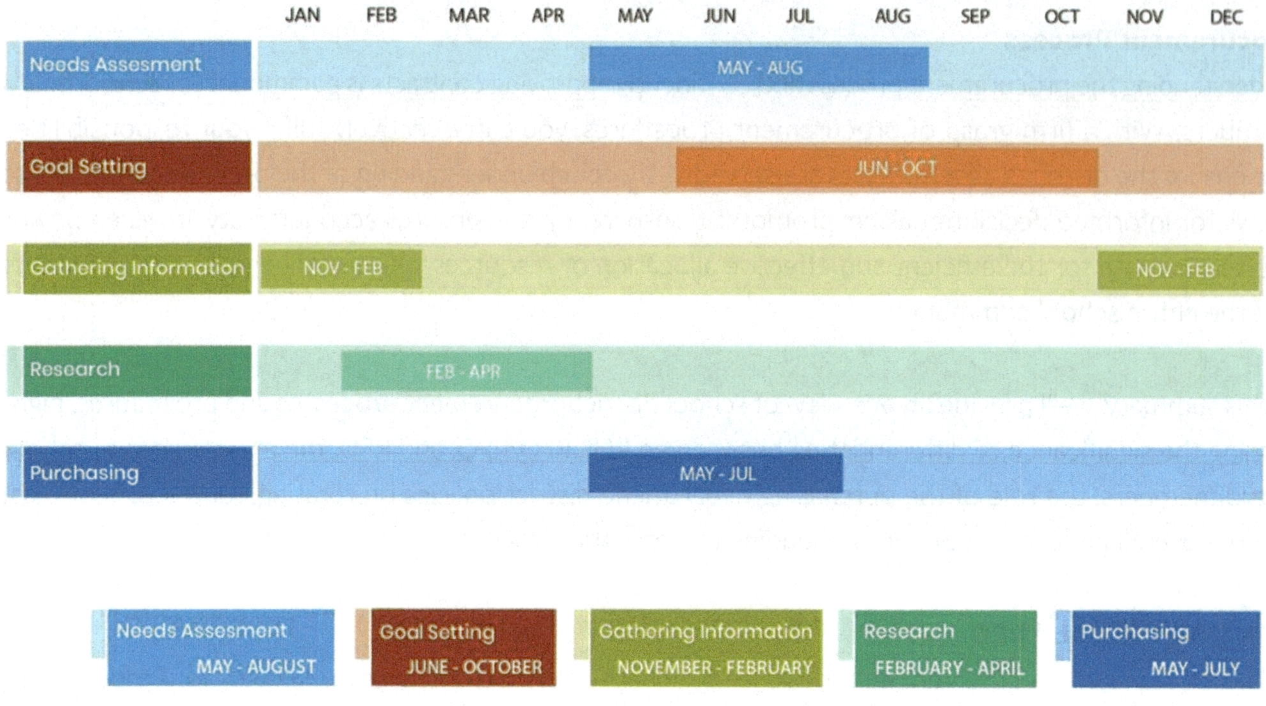

Source: www.K!2Prospects.com

Board and State Policy on Rotating Pre-Approved Contractors or Bids

Some school boards and states have policies in place that require the rotation of pre-approved contractors or bids. This policy aims to promote competition, prevent nepotism/corruption, and provide opportunities for a diverse range of vendors. The district can ensure fairness and equal opportunities for all qualified vendors by rotating pre-approved contractors or bids.

School district procurement processes and procedures are essential for acquiring goods and services and working efficiently and transparently. School board members oversee and approve these processes to ensure accountability and the district's best interests. Adhering to district policies and processes enhances fair and equal opportunity vendors should expect.

Spending Limits Within Policy

It's necessary to establish safeguards when securing bids and approving vendors, particularly when setting policies on spending limits. While not every purchase may require prior board approval, ensuring it aligns with the district's strategic goals, capital plan, and annual budget is essential. Moreover, many boards grant the superintendent spending authority up to a specific amount. This authority is often further delegated to others with associated spending limits. It is imperative to thoroughly review the spending authorities within the district and implement safeguards accordingly.

Procurement Methods Used by School Districts

- **Request for Proposal (RFP):** This method is typically used when the school district requires a detailed solution or service. Potential vendors are issued an RFP outlining the district's requirements and requesting detailed proposals that address specific needs. Vendors are evaluated based on their qualifications, experience, pricing, and proposed approach. The district then selects the vendor that best meets its requirements.

- **Request for Quotation (RFQ):** This method is a document that outlines the requirements and asks vendors to provide pricing and payment terms. The main focus of this RFQ is the pricing aspect, and often, the lowest-priced bidder is awarded the contract.

  The RFQ method is used when the school district seeks pricing for a specific product or service. Potential vendors are issued an RFQ requesting pricing information. Vendors submit quotations, the district evaluates the quote, and selects the vendor offering the most favorable terms.

- **Request for Qualification (RFQ):** This "RFQ" (not to be confused with "Request for Quotation" refers to a document used to ask potential suppliers or vendors for information about their background and experience in providing a specific good or service. The school board and purchasing agent are primarily interested in the vendor's skills and knowledge rather than pricing.

  The response is typically called a **statement of qualifications (SOQ**) rather than a bid.

  It is important to differentiate between these two RFQs to avoid confusion. While an RFQ for qualifications is focused on the vendor's capabilities and experience, an RFQ for quotes is primarily concerned with pricing and payment terms.

- **Request for Offer (RFO):** This method is used when the school district seeks general information or offers from potential vendors. Unlike the RFP and RFQ methods, the RFO does not require vendors to provide detailed proposals or pricing. Instead, vendors are asked to submit general information about their capabilities, experience, and offerings. The district may use this information to create a shortlist of potential vendors for further evaluation or negotiation.

  These procurement methods allow school districts to solicit and evaluate vendor proposals, quotations, or general offers. This enables them to make informed decisions when acquiring goods or services that meet their needs.

These examples demonstrate how RFP, RFQ/RFQ, and RFO methods can be used in various procurement scenarios. The school board must review and evaluate the proposals, quotations, or offers received, ensure compliance with procurement policies, and make informed decisions that benefit the district and its students.

Four Examples of When a School Board May See the Methods of RFP, RFQ, and RFO in the Procurement Process

1. Request for Proposal (RFP):

- **Technology Upgrade**: The school district wants to upgrade its computer systems and software. An RFP is issued to solicit proposals from technology vendors, outlining their solutions, pricing, implementation plans, and ongoing support.
- **Construction Project**: The district plans to build a new school facility. An RFP is issued to seek proposals from construction companies detailing their construction plans, cost estimates, project timelines, and previous experience with similar projects.

2. Request for Quotation (RFQ):

- **School Supplies**: The district needs to purchase school supplies for the upcoming academic year. An RFQ is issued to multiple vendors, requesting quotations for specific items, quantities, and delivery timelines. The quotations are reviewed, and the vendor that offers the best value is selected.
- **Maintenance Services**: The district requires maintenance services, such as HVAC repairs or landscaping. An RFQ is issued to obtain vendor quotations, specifying the scope of work, estimated hours or materials required, and pricing. The quotations are reviewed and the vendor that provides the most competitive and comprehensive quote is selected.

3. Request for Qualifications (RFQ):

- **Architectural Services:** If a school board plans to construct a new school building or renovate an existing facility, they may issue an RFQ to solicit qualifications from architectural firms. The RFQ would ask the firms to provide information about their experience in designing educational facilities, their team's expertise, and examples of previous projects.
- **Legal Services:** When a school board needs legal representation or advice, they may issue an RFQ to gather qualifications from law firms. The RFQ would request information about the firm's experience in education law, the qualifications of their attorneys, and references from other school districts they have worked with.
- **Consulting Services**: If a school board requires specialized expertise or guidance in a particular area, such as curriculum development or strategic planning, they may issue an RFQ to seek qualifications from consulting firms. The RFQ would ask for details about the firm's experience in the education sector, their consultants' qualifications, and examples of successful projects they have completed.
- **Educational Services:** If a school board is looking for external providers to offer supplementary educational services, such as tutoring programs or after-school enrichment activities, it may issue an

RFQ to gather qualifications from interested organizations. The RFQ would ask for information about the organization's experience in providing educational services, its program offerings, and testimonials from other schools it has worked with.

4. **Request for Offer (RFO):**
   - **Transportation Services**: The district is exploring transportation options for students. An RFO is issued to gather information and offers from transportation companies, outlining their services, fleet size, driver qualifications, and pricing structure. The offers are reviewed, and the most suitable provider is selected based on the district's requirements and budget.
   - **Food Services**: The district is considering outsourcing its food services. An RFO is issued to obtain offers from food service providers, detailing their menu options, nutritional standards, pricing models, and experience in serving school districts. The offers are reviewed, and the provider that best aligns with the district's goals and requirements is selected.

Evaluate Your Procurement Policies

School board members need to review and analyze board policies and understand procurement practices to explore opportunities for efficiency. The policy areas listed below outline best practices in purchasing and serve as a framework for board members. Note: Every state has specific laws and regulations that govern your board policies and procedures.

- **Procurement Policy:** Establishes guidelines for the procurement process, including the principles of fairness, transparency, and accountability. It outlines the procedures for soliciting bids, evaluating proposals, awarding contracts, and managing vendor relationships.
- **Competitive Bidding Policy:** The district must seek competitive bids for significant purchases or contracts. It sets thresholds for when competitive bidding is required and outlines the process for soliciting bids, evaluating responses, and awarding contracts based on the best value.
- **Vendor Selection Policy:** Outlines the selection criteria and process. It emphasizes the importance of evaluating vendors based on price, quality, reliability, and past performance. The policy also encourages the board to consider diverse suppliers and promotes fair competition.
- **Conflict of Interest Policy:** Addresses conflicts of interest in procurement. It requires board members and employees to disclose potential conflicts and prohibits them from participating in decisions or transactions where a conflict exists. The policy ensures purchasing decisions are made objectively and in the district's best interest.
- **Ethical Standards Policy:** Establishes ethical guidelines for board members and employees involved in purchasing. It prohibits bribery, kickbacks, and any unethical practices related to procurement and emphasizes the importance of integrity, honesty, and adherence to legal and regulatory requirements.
- **Cost Savings Policy:** Encourages board members and employees to seek cost-saving opportunities in the purchasing process. It promotes volume discounts, cooperative purchasing, negotiation with

vendors, and exploring alternative suppliers. It aims to maximize the district's purchasing power and achieve cost-effective procurement.

- **Vendor Performance Evaluation Policy:** Outlines the process for evaluating and assessing vendor performance. It establishes criteria for evaluating vendors' adherence to contractual terms, quality of goods or services, timeliness, and customer service. It ensures vendors consistently meet the district's expectations and provides a basis for vendor selection and contract renewal decisions.
- **Contract Management Policy:** Governs the management of contracts throughout their lifecycle. It outlines procedures for contract administration, monitoring performance, and enforcing contract terms. It emphasizes the importance of maintaining accurate records, addressing contract disputes, and ensuring compliance with contractual obligations.
- **Sustainability and Social Responsibility Policy:** Encourages the consideration of sustainability and social responsibility factors in the purchasing process. It promotes using environmentally friendly products, supporting local businesses, and adhering to fair labor practices. Thus, the district's purchasing practices align with its social and environmental stewardship commitment.
- **Training and Professional Development Policy:** Emphasizes the importance of training and professional development for board members and employees involved in purchasing. It encourages ongoing education to stay updated on best practices, procurement regulations, and industry trends. Thus, the district's purchasing decisions are informed and based on the latest knowledge and skills.

School Districts Purchasing Cycles

The K-12 education purchasing cycle differs from other sectors due to its specific timelines and considerations. Most education purchases occur during the spring and summer to prepare for the new school year. This unique cycle is driven by various factors, including legislative session requirements, the need to operate within set timelines, and budget constraints based on state and local funding estimates that require decisions to be made well before the new school year.

Phase 1 - Needs assessment: May – August

Beginning in May and continuing over the summer, administrators start looking at the year and assessing how it went. Each school district is an entity unto itself with its own unique needs, so assessments of what works and what doesn't work are particular to each district as well as each school within that district. One program may be working wonderfully for the high school but the same program in the middle school may need to be reevaluated. In this step, data is gathered and analyzed, and it is this analysis that provides the platform for setting goals for the following school year. The needs assessment covers staff, programs, materials, technology, etc.

Phase 2 - Goal setting: June – October

Goal setting starts at the beginning of the summer and continues through early fall. It is the result of the needs assessment. Usually, the board or a committee made up of administrators, staff, parents, and community members meets over the summer to analyze the data gathered and decide what will drive the school district to success during the next school year.

Phase 3 - Gathering information: Nov – Feb

Once the needs assessment and goal-setting phases are complete, information has to be gathered. Just getting the information on vendors who are credible can take weeks. The process typically begins in late October or early November.

Phase 4 - Research: Feb – Apr

Once the information is gathered, then purchasings research begins on each company, its strengths and weaknesses, its options, materials, etc. During this time, school districts will take an in-depth look at the vendors and why one is better than another. This process continues through March or April.

Phase 5 - Purchasing: May – July

After all the steps of the purchasing cycle are completed, it is time to decide which materials, programs, technology, etc. to buy. Before purchasing can occur the contracts must come to the board for approval, usually takes place in the summer, so it is ready for use at the beginning of the school year.

Stop the "Use It or Lose It" Culture

Stop wasteful spending by understanding the "use It or lose It" principle. So what is it? In all levels of government, including school districts, towards the end of the budgeting cycle, there is a period of "use it or lose it" versus, in a business world, it could be referred to as a "use it or save it." However, this is the government, and most department heads and principals will be in a mad dash to use their budget allocations to justify their department budgets and waste monies that could be saved.

Be mindful of frivolous contracts in the last few months of the budget year. The end of the school year brings about a rush for administrators and schools to use up remaining funds. Whether it's imperative to use up millions of dollars in larger districts or a few hundred dollars, no one wants to let that money go unused. This "use it or lose it" practice drives the urgency to make unnecessary purchases to ensure every dollar is utilized. Vendors feed off knowing this and train their salespeople to take advantage of this mentality common with government bureaucracies, which is even a part of most school district vendors' sales and marketing plans.

Knowing this is a real issue, board members should talk to their superintendent if they see unnecessary last-minute spending. Some boards have been known to direct the superintendent to put into place the end-of-the-year purchase deadlines three months before the end of the budget year - without notice to department heads to curb this practice.

Chapter 30
Contract Approvals

Approval of contracts is a primary task for a school board, carried out during business meetings to keep the district's operations running smoothly and on schedule. Most spending within a school district will come to the board as a contract. However, several essential steps must be taken before a contract reaches the board for approval. As a board member, it is valuable to understand your role and stay vigilant in certain areas to safeguard the district's best interests.

Step 1
The board must consider several factors before approving a contract. Does the contract align with the overall strategic plan? Have the goods and services been pre-approved within the annual budget? Have all the necessary procurement procedures been followed? These questions help ensure the contract is in line with the district's goals, financially feasible, and compliant with procurement regulations.

Step 2
Once you have determined the contract meets these criteria, the next step before approval is to review a copy of the document. This copy should be attached to the agenda and included in the backup materials provided by the superintendent. This best practice ensures you have all the necessary information to make an informed decision.

If the superintendent presents an item for approval without attaching the contract, especially when it involves financial implications, you must address this with them. Make it clear you will not vote for any request that does not have proper supporting documentation. This approach ensures transparency and accountability in the approval process.

Having the board's eyes on the contract is vital to catch any omissions or discrepancies before approving it. For instance, you may discover the contractor does not have the required insurance or proof of insurance. Additionally, the contract may not cover the project expectations discussed during the board review. By actively reviewing contracts, you fulfill your fiduciary responsibility for every dollar the district spends and ensure compliance with policies, budgetary constraints, procedures, transparency, and accountability.

Step 3
Moving an item from consent to action is okay, especially when money is involved. It is worth noting contracts often appear on the agenda as consent items and are approved without any board discussion. When placed on the agenda as an action item, the superintendent must provide a brief explanation, and the board can ask questions or explore concerns with the staff and/or the superintendent.

Many contracts are often considered routine or recurring. However, it is essential not to overlook them, as hidden within these seemingly routine contracts may lie instances of nepotism or unnecessary spending. For example, the fuel cost provided by a specific vendor, trash services, lawn services, cleaning services, or even the contract with the health insurance broker may not have been reviewed in years, potentially resulting in missed pharmaceutical rebates. Pay attention to these recurring contracts, as they can lead to cost savings for the district.

Board members should know the procedures for contract approval, and staying vigilant in reviewing them is crucial for school board members. By doing so, you can ensure contracts align with the district's strategic plan, adhere to budgetary constraints, follow proper procurement procedures, and promote transparency and accountability. Your active involvement in the approval process helps safeguard the district's resources and ultimately benefit the students and the school community.

Use Caution When Approving Recurring Contracts

Transparency and Accountability: Board members ensure transparency and accountability in the procurement process by thoroughly reviewing routine contracts. This allows them to verify that contracts are awarded through fair and competitive processes without favoritism or nepotism. This scrutiny helps maintain public trust and confidence in the district's operations.

Compliance and Risk Management: Even routine contracts must comply with legal and regulatory requirements. By reviewing these contracts, board members can ensure all necessary documentation, such as insurance coverage or proof of insurance, is in place. This helps mitigate potential risks and protects the district from liability.

Long-Term Impact: Seemingly routine contracts can have long-term implications for the district. Board members can assess their effectiveness and relevance by regularly reviewing and revisiting these contracts. If they no longer serve the district's best interests, you can identify opportunities for improvement, renegotiation, or termination. A proactive approach to these contracts ensures district's resources are allocated wisely and efficiently.

Learn to Identify Potential Cost-Saving Opportunities

Remember that all contracts matter. One area of potential fraud and one of the number one regrets of most organizations and businesses is allowing routine to creep into their policies, practices, and procedures. Pay attention to unusual spikes in cost and budget amendments. There are several reasons why board members need to adopt the mindset of "Trust but Verify." By actively reviewing contracts and exploring cost-saving opportunities, board members can help maximize the district's financial resources and ensure taxpayer dollars are used efficiently. These efforts contribute to the overall economic health of the district and support the delivery of quality education to students.

Competitive Bidding: By encouraging competitive bidding, board members can ensure the district obtains goods or services at the best possible price. This process allows multiple vendors to submit proposals, allowing the district to compare prices and choose the most cost-effective option.

Vendor Evaluation: Regularly evaluating vendors can reveal cost-saving opportunities. Board members can assess whether the current vendor still provides the best value for the district or whether there are alternative vendors offering similar goods or services at a lower cost.

Reviewing Service Levels: Assessing the level of service vendors provide can reveal areas where cost savings can be achieved without compromising quality. Board members can evaluate whether certain services can be scaled back or modified to reduce costs while meeting the district's needs.

Energy Efficiency: Reviewing contracts related to energy consumption, such as utilities or HVAC services, can lead to cost savings through energy efficiency initiatives. Board members can explore options for energy-saving equipment, innovative building technologies, or renewable energy sources to reduce long-term operational costs.

Contract Renegotiation: Periodically renegotiating contracts with existing vendors can result in cost savings. As market conditions change, board members can leverage these changes to negotiate better terms, lower prices, or improved service levels.

Routine Contracts: Fuel, trash services, lawn services, cleaning services, bus parts, food services, insurance brokers, tires, or chicken may appear insignificant on the surface. However, by closely reviewing all contracts, board members can identify potential cost-saving opportunities, waste, and fraud. It may be as simple as the district negotiating better terms, exploring alternative vendors, or uncovering missed opportunities for discounts or rebates. These cost savings can increase over time and positively impact the district's budget.

Notes

Chapter 31

School District Fraud

First and foremost, waste and fraud can be avoided with the right policies, procedures, safeguards, and oversight. One of the last things you want to happen on your watch is fraudulent activity. It's not good for you, and it gives the district a black eye when asking voters for referendums. It does happen, and most of the time, it occurs by those with longer tenure and who trust is bestowed upon. It is an uncomfortable situation for managers and board members to be in. "How dare you question a beloved loyal employee?" and most will not. However, there needs to be a "Trust but Verify" culture in your district, no matter who or how long an employee with the district or a board member has been in office.

In a unique research report in 2021, Weaver and Tidwell examined the various forms of school district fraud, ranging from small-scale incidents where an employee misuses funds for personal expenses to elaborate schemes that involve diverting significant amounts of district funds into fake bank accounts.

To identify the most common fraud traps in today's school districts, the researchers examined 57 fraud cases reported publicly nationwide. By understanding these emerging fraud trends, school board members can monitor the district's procurement process and adapt their policies to ensure there are internal controls and protect the district from falling into similar traps.

SCHOOL DISTRICT FRAUD SCHEMES

Fraud Category	# of Cases	$ Loss
Misuse of Funds / Theft (Case/Check/CreditCard	27	$
Vendor Fraud (Kickbacks / Conflicts of Interest)	17	$$$
Phishing Scams	7	$$$$
Payroll Fraud	6	$$
Total	57	

Source: Weaver & Tidwell

The following is an outline of the most common fraud found. In addition, since the report in 2021, we have pulled case analyses to illustrate more current examples of fraud. These analyses reveal that fraud can affect districts of all sizes. Smaller schools often lack robust internal controls and proper segregation of duties, making them more vulnerable to fraudulent activities. On the other hand, larger districts with a high volume of transactions and disbursements may face challenges in detecting fraud due to the sheer scale of their operations.

Three Factors That Open the Door to Fraud

Before we begin analyzing the cases, it's important to identify a few factors that can be monitored to prevent fraud: motivation, opportunity, and lack of surveillance or supervision.

1. **Motivation**: This is the most challenging factor to detect. Financial pressures individuals face are often hidden. These pressures may stem from a lavish lifestyle, relationship breakdowns, family members needing financial assistance (such as for college tuition), competition, or medical expenses. Another motivating factor could be a disgruntled employee who feels undervalued due to a culture of nepotism or who feels overworked and underappreciated.

2. **Opportunity**: This is where you, as a member of the organization, play a vital part . Fraud is more complex to commit when there are limited opportunities to do so. For example, fraud becomes much more likely if an employee is given a purchasing card (P-card) with minimal oversight—without having to provide receipts, spending limits without approvals, or if a school employee can easily steal cash from the register due to a lack of safeguards. By removing these opportunities, fraud and waste can be significantly reduced.

3. **Lack of Surveillance**: Insufficient internal controls increase the chance of fraud. Opportunities for fraudulent activities expand when checks and balances, safeguards, and regular internal and external audits are absent.

Understanding Fraud

Understanding fraud and its various forms is the first step to preventing financial loss. However, greedy and arrogant individuals often try to outsmart the system despite one's best efforts. Early detection is key to minimizing financial damage, as some fraud cases can go undetected for years.

Boards must remember these three critical factors that contribute to exposing their districts to fraud and waste. Strong policies and training can guide employees on expected behaviors and ethical standards. Waste occurs when employees evade accountability due to lax oversight, which is entirely avoidable. In contrast, fraud involves secrecy and deception. Detecting fraud requires the involvement of the board, other employees, the community, and a superintendent who takes fraud and waste seriously by setting up a system of oversight and accountability through surprise audits, anonymous tip lines, continuous monitoring, and ensuring the right individuals are placed in positions that follow established procedures and protocols. These measures can help mitigate losses to the district, which ultimately detracts from students' learning experiences and erodes trust in the district and the board.

To analyze different fraud cases, researchers categorized them into five distinct types. They assessed the financial impact of each category, providing valuable insights into the potential losses school districts may face due to these fraudulent activities.

Common Forms of Fraud in School Districts

P-Cards

One of the most common forms of fraud in the misuse of funds category involves employees using district credit cards, or P-cards, for personal expenses. These expenses may include fuel for personal vehicles, home improvements, utility bills, gift cards, individual travel, and more. This type of fraud is often committed by superintendents, department heads, coaches, and principals.

Fraudulent activities are typically concealed because cardholders have complete control over their purchases without adequate oversight, such as proper authorization and reconciliation. Some cardholders falsely claim to have submitted expense reports, taking advantage of the confusion during the transition to remote work. Another tactic to mask fraud is allocating charges across multiple budget codes, making detection more difficult. Additionally, fraudulent purchases may be concealed by using third-party payment processors like PayPal and Square.

Implementing established controls can prevent P-card fraud. While P-cards facilitate daily operational purchases, board members must know who possesses a card and impose limits on their spending.

Anyone with a P-card, including board members, the superintendent, and other administrators, must understand the policies, procedures, and consequences of card misuse or fraud. Clarifying these guidelines is essential because individuals will always claim, "I didn't know I couldn't use it for..." and you can fill in the blank.

To strengthen controls further, the district can work with card issuers to set up merchant category codes and approve spending limits. Additionally, approval procedures should require receipts and a second person to verify the information and ensure it matches.

Phishing Scams

External parties perpetrate these scams, redirecting payments for legitimate vendors, contractors, or bond payments. Fraudsters send emails to employees under the guise of legitimate vendors, requesting changes to payment instructions, such as ACH information. Over the last several years, phishing scams have become more prevalent and sophisticated, with fraudsters quickly moving stolen funds overseas, making recovery difficult. Some fraudsters use software to mask their location and identity, thereby avoiding detection. Prevention measures include dual-factor verification for change requests, restricting access to vendor information, employee training on identifying phishing scams, investing in technological controls like spam filtering and anti-phishing software, and implementing policies for reporting threats.

Payroll Fraud

While payroll fraud is less common, it still occurs. Some examples include ghost employee schemes, where an unemployed employee colludes with a school clerk to clock in. Other instances involve payroll supervisors changing names on checks before they are printed or payroll clerks forging supervisor signatures to authorize overtime payments without approval. Additionally, fraud can occur when employees leave the district but are not removed from the payroll; someone with access may change the bank account information to divert payments into their account.

PAYROLL FRAUD SCHEMES

Description of Scheme	$ Loss
Ghost Employee	$122,000
Forged Payroll Checks	$320,000
Unauthorized Overtime	$23,500
Reduction of Income Taxes	$8,400
Unauthorized Salary from Federal Funds	$125,000
Unauthorized Bonuses	$30,000
Average Loss	**$105,000**

Source: Weaver & Tidwell

Petty Cash and Fundraisers

Cash and checks are also susceptible to fraud in school districts, particularly in funds managed by individuals handling student activity funds, booster funds, or campus funds. Although their financial impact is smaller than that of credit card fraud, such schemes occur more frequently and are more challenging to detect.

Case Scenario: Booster Fraud

SCENARIO

A longtime Hawaii public schools administrator, Nitta, stole over $400,000 from Mililani High School's booster club and retired from the athletic director position in 2021. He was ordered to pay back the full $406,000 he stole from the school, which he did. Over five years he stole from the school, didn't pay taxes on the ill-gotten income, and used the money to fund personal trips. The former athletic director (76) was ordered to serve probation and pay back the full amount.

This section emphasizes the importance of oversight and having proper systems in place. Regardless of an individual's age or reputation, ensuring transparency and established procedures for anyone responsible for public funds is essential.

Vendor Fraud

Vendor fraud is another category that includes fake accounts, invoice kickback schemes, and conflicts of interest. Fake accounts occur when a vendor is set up in the system that does not exist or has existed in the past but was never removed from the system. They are easier to detect in smaller districts.

Kickback schemes involve superintendents, department heads, and board members awarding contracts to vendors in exchange for kickbacks, such as cash payments, equipment, discounts, or job opportunities. These schemes can be challenging to detect, but red flags may include higher costs for services or equipment compared to other school districts, evidence of payments made to vendors without services rendered, or connections between vendors and district personnel involved in the selection process.

Having policies that require conflicts of interest statements, ethics training, and rotation of contracts can curb abuse of power that can sometimes occur when an employee influences the selection of a vendor or contractor for personal benefit, and even by doing this, there will still be those who will lie and scam the system for personal gain.

Case Scenario: Fake Vendor Invoices

In late 2023, a former Chief Learning and Talent Officer for Tulsa Public Schools (TPS) pleaded guilty to conspiracy to commit fraud.

Devin Fletcher, who pleaded guilty to the charge, admitted in court to working with another person to create, alter, and fabricate fraudulent invoices, purchase orders, and supporting documents to defraud TPS and the Foundation for Tulsa Schools, according to a report from KTUL Channel 8 in Tulsa, Oklahoma.

The foundation is a public charity organization that aims to build a better community through supporting TPS by providing education resources via donated funds.

Fletcher's scheme cost the school district and the foundation more than $603,000. He faces a maximum sentence of 20 years in prison plus a period of supervised release, restitution, and monetary penalties.

Fletcher was hired as TPS's Chief Academic Officer in August 2016 and later promoted to Chief Learning and Talent Officer. According to court records, from August 2018 through March 2022, Fletcher and another person stole from the district and the foundation. In his signed plea agreement, Fletcher admitted he and another individual had created fake invoices and purchase orders to commit fraud. "I utilized my position at Tulsa Public Schools to make these documents appear legitimate and vouched for services that were never provided," his plea agreement stated. According to court records, the money was shared among Fletcher, his accomplice, and at least two vendors or consultants. Before being terminated, Fletcher resigned in June 2022, a common practice that helps avoid public scrutiny of superintendents and school boards. This practice can sometimes lead to agreements being made behind closed doors, which may go undetected by the public.

Case Scenario: Bribery and Vendor Kickbacks

Former Houston Independent School District (HISD) Chief Operating Officer Brian Busby is facing over 35 years in prison for an alleged bribery scheme that cost the district millions of dollars.

Busby and HISD contract vendor Anthony Hutchison, both from Houston, were charged on December 14, 2021, and are awaiting trial. According to the United States Attorney's Office in the Southern District of Texas, a federal grand jury issued a 33-count superseding indictment in April 2022, which included additional tax charges against both men.

Hutchison, operating under Southwest Wholesale, allegedly entered into long-term contracts with HISD to provide grounds maintenance services for schools. The indictment claims from 2011 to 2020, Hutchison systematically overbilled HISD and inflated service invoices, resulting in millions of dollars lost for the school district. He is accused of paying Busby some of his inflated profits in cash and through home remodeling services.

The indictment further states Hutchison secured purchase orders for construction, repair, landscaping, and maintenance jobs at specific HISD schools by paying cash bribes—primarily kickbacks—to HISD personnel and the board president, who facilitated his business dealings with the district.

Five individuals have already pleaded guilty in connection with the scheme: Rhonda Skillern-Jones (former HISD board of education president), Derrick Sanders (officer of construction services), Alfred Hoskins (general manager of facilities, maintenance, and operations), Gerron Hall (area manager for maintenance - south), and Luis Tovar (area manager for maintenance - north). As part of their pleas, they admitted to conspiring with Busby and Hutchison by accepting bribes in exchange for helping to award contracts to Hutchison or not obstructing their approval.

Busby and Hutchison are charged with conspiracy, bribery concerning programs receiving federal funds, witness tampering, and wire fraud. If convicted, both could face significant prison time.

According to the state attorney's office, Busby allegedly assisted in awarding HISD construction and grounds maintenance contracts to Hutchison in exchange for cash bribes and substantial home remodeling services. Hutchison is said to have funneled cash for these bribes by writing company checks to vendors, who then cashed the checks and provided Hutchison with the money. Court records indicate Hutchison falsely stated on the memo line of the checks the funds were payments for work performed on HISD properties. Furthermore, Busby allegedly attempted to conceal his involvement in the bribery scheme by depositing the proceeds into multiple bank accounts.

In response to these allegations, HISD stated, "HISD has also implemented additional internal procedures to safeguard against the type of conduct alleged in the charges."

Lack of Oversight

Lastly, let's talk about the final type of fraud not listed in the 2021 report that has resonated to the top based on trust. From tires to chicken wings, if there is a will, there is a way for employees to scam the system. The larger the fraud, the more likely it is that various factors are all at play, such as motivation, opportunity, and a lack of internal controls or surveillance.

Another common factor in these cases is too much trust. However, in all these situations, the individuals involved eventually get caught due to greed and arrogance.

Case Scenario: Tire Gate

Burkeen, the former city mayor and Assistant Chief of Indian River County's Emergency Department, was convicted in 2020 and sentenced to 12 years for stealing more than 1,000 tires before retiring in 2018.

Burkeen was accused of ordering about $300,000 in tires from Vero Beach Goodyear stores between June 2014 and February 2018, billing them to the county, and then selling them by word of mouth and online advertising, using the alias Percipher Pucklebrush. In his last year on the job, he purchased 984 tires for $215,000.

After Burkeen's retirement, the former Emergency Services Director contacted the sheriff's office after noticing several *tire purchases did not match any fleet vehicles*. Investigators determined Burkeen, who had worked for Indian River Fire Rescue for 30 years, was *the lone person authorizing tire purchases.*

Investigators discovered Burkeen had been buying tires with county money, not for emergency vehicles but to sell and keep the proceeds for himself. That led to a grand theft charge against Burkeem.

Fire officials told the sheriff's office that most of the tires Burkeen had bought did not fit any of the fleet's vehicles. They also noted that tire changes for the fire engines were not handled at the fire stations.

Investigators said Burkeen had convinced his subordinates and Goodyear staff the tire purchases were legitimate. He'd told Goodyear managers the county kept a stockpile of tires for motorists who would sue the county for damages from potholes.

Case Scenario: The Chicken Wing Heist

A former food service director at a school district in the Chicago area was sentenced to nine years in prison after admitting she'd stolen $1.5 million worth of chicken wings. Vera Liddell, 68, who served in the director role for Harvey School District 152 near Chicago, pleaded guilty on Aug. 9, 2024, to theft and operating a criminal enterprise, according to WGN, ABC News, and CBS News, citing prosecutors. Liddell stole the mounds of meat intended to be for take-home meals for students learning remotely during the COVID-19 pandemic.

Liddell's job involved placing orders with Gordon Food Services, the school district's leading supplier. Between July 2020 and February 2022, she placed the orders and billed but kept the chicken wings. Between August and November 2021, Liddell ordered more than 11,000 cases of chicken wings from the food supplier and then picked *up the orders herself in a district cargo van.*

The chicken theft operation was uncovered during a 2023 audit, which revealed the district's food service department had exceeded its annual budget by $300,000 halfway through the school year. Authorities were notified after the school district's business manager found unusual invoices for chicken wings. *This item was deemed odd. It is not served to students because it contains bones.*

Takeaways

In both of these cases, there are similarities. Who would have suspected tires or chicken wings? Look for the obvious. These ordinary items were purchased and approved by the same individuals and were picked up in a government vehicle by the "managers." In the case of the wings, what began as a friends and family discount that flew under the radar became a lucrative scheme until someone reviewed the invoices. Just like in the Burkeen case, where the chief immediately recognized the tires did not match the vehicles, in the Liddell case, the business manager noted bones could not be served to students.

Motivation, trust, opportunity, and a lack of oversight all contributed to situations that nearly went unnoticed, resulting in both individuals being sent straight to jail. These are real cases and genuine breaches in controls. Ultimately, the responsibility falls back on the board. Oversight is the board's job; you must ask questions, pay attention to details, and invest the time to understand the systems to remain alert to abnormalities – especially before a vote.

As a key decision-maker, you have the fiduciary responsibility to review and approve all district spending and contracts. This duty extends to serving as the vigilant representative of taxpayers' interests. It is important to understand and respect the separation of duties while following the specific protocols set forth by your superintendent.

Even though you might not need to immerse yourself in the minutiae of daily operations, it is beneficial to familiarize yourself with the overarching protocols. Reviewing the district's procurement manual can uncover practices that might deviate from established guidelines or regulations.

Moreover, a reliable tip line for reporting suspicious purchasing activities, fraudulent behavior, or instances of waste must be established. This tip line should be easily accessible to all employees and vendors, promoting an environment where everyone can contribute to identifying and preventing wasteful spending and potential fraud. You can enhance accountability within the district by encouraging transparency and open communication.

Notes

8

Section 8: **Internal and External Influences**

Objectives for Section 8: Internal and External Influences

1. **Differentiate Recommendations from Mandates:** Understand the importance of distinguishing between recommendations and mandates from external agencies and committees, enabling informed decision-making to prioritize the needs of students and the community.

2. **Leverage Committees for Effective Governance:** Explore the role and types of committees within school governance, recognizing how they can enhance the board's effectiveness through research and informed recommendations.

3. **Navigate Labor Union Dynamics:** Gain insights into the implications of labor union contracts and relationships, understanding how they affect fiscal responsibility and transparency in decision-making processes.

4. **Build Strong External Relationships:** Recognize the significance of building relationships with key community stakeholders, including local law enforcement, health departments, and other organizations, to support the district's goals and enhance educational opportunities.

5. **Engage with Associations and Political Influences:** Understand the impact of various educational associations and political influences on school governance, equipping board members to navigate these dynamics effectively while prioritizing the best interests of students.

As we enter this section, we will explore the internal and external influences shaping school board leadership and decision-making. This section intends to understand how various pressures and relationships impact your responsibilities as board members, ultimately guiding you toward achieving success in your roles.

In Chapter 32, "Recommendations vs. Mandates," we will explore the challenges of distinguishing between advice and authoritative directives. Board members frequently encounter recommendations from committees, consultants, and external agencies. Understanding how to evaluate these suggestions while maintaining decision-making authority is essential. This chapter emphasizes the importance of informed choices that prioritize the needs of students and the community over mere compliance with external pressures.

Chapter 33 will examine the role of "Committees," within the school governance framework. Committees are instrumental in conducting research, providing insights, and formulating recommendations that help boards make informed decisions. We will explore the various types of committees, their purposes, and how they can enhance members' effectiveness as leaders.

In Chapter 34, we will address the dynamics of "Labor unions". While school boards may not be directly involved in negotiations, understanding the implications of union contracts and the relationships with these organizations is vital for ensuring fiscal responsibility and transparency in your decision-making processes.

Chapter 35 will broaden members' scope to include the "External Relationships," that impact school governance, particularly the importance of building strong community relations. As board members, they must be able to connect with local stakeholders, including parents, community organizations, law enforcement, and state legislators, to garner support for a positive educational environment.

Finally, Chapter 36 will explore the "Associations," surrounding school boards and their potential impact on governance. We will discuss the various challenges that arise from political influences within these organizations and how to navigate them effectively.

Chapter 32
Recommendations vs. Mandates

Handling recommendations can be particularly challenging for board members. This section will help you understand your role and authority to manage any pressures that may arise effectively. Sometimes, you might not follow the suggestions from committees, partners, external government agencies, or consultants. That's okay! With the complexities of a school board's responsibilities, it's wise to gather as much information as possible before making decisions that could impact student learning, the wider community, or financial commitments.

You need to understand the differences between recommendations and mandates, so we will discuss these in more depth. We want board members to clearly understand the separation between these concepts, especially when working with other government agencies.

TERMS

Recommendations: The **recommendations** of a person or a committee are their suggestions or advice on the best thing to do.

Mandate: If a government or other elected body has a **mandate** to carry out a particular policy or task, they have the authority to carry it out as a result of winning an election.

Source: Collins Dictionary

Remember, recommendations made to the board, whether by a consultant, superintendent, committee, or agency, are meant to guide the decision-making process. However, recommenders are advice with no authority and should not be viewed as a must or, in other words, a mandate.

While these recommendations may stem from a specific perspective or goal focusing on particular issues, they often lack the comprehensive understanding of the diverse dynamics you have acquired as a board member through your observations and experiences. Trust your research and insights, using these recommendations to support or challenge your ideas.

Board members may start with specific viewpoints, so be comfortable with adjusting your opinions based on the recommendations you receive, whether you choose to accept all, some, or none. This adaptability is entirely acceptable; you engage with these individuals because they contribute value to the conversation. One of the worst mistakes any elected official can make is sticking to their vote out of stubbornness to admit they were wrong. A successful representative will always be willing to change their opinion based on new information or evidence.

When you feel uneasy about rejecting recommendations, you are not alone; this is understandable, primarily when volunteers have dedicated time to serve on committees or the board has invested funds in consultants.

If you know this going into it, communicate to these individuals that while the board welcomes input, the ultimate decision rests with you. Set clear expectations from the beginning, ensuring everyone understands the committee's role in reviewing, researching, discussing, and potentially making formal recommendations to the superintendent for the board's consideration.

Below is a case scenario that can illustrate practical applications you may face. It cannot be stressed enough. Ultimately, you were elected to represent the voice of the people, parents, and constituents in your community, and the board holds the final authority over the tough decisions being made. Do not hand over your authority because of pressure or fear of retribution. You must vote according to your conscience and the evidence you have gathered. The responsibility lies with the board, so fully embrace your decisions and be willing to accept any criticism.

Case Scenarios: Evaluation Recommendations

Evaluating School Start Times: In a school district focused on enhancing student well-being, a committee was established to assess the potential benefits and drawbacks of changing school start times. This committee, which included parents, teachers, administrators, and healthcare professionals, met over several months to conduct extensive research, review existing studies, gather data from other districts, and discuss how start times affect student health and academic performance. After thorough deliberation, the committee reached a consensus and submitted a formal recommendation to the superintendent, proposing school start times be shifted later to improve student sleep patterns and overall well-being.

The superintendent then presented the committee's recommendation to the school board for consideration. Anticipating a constructive dialogue, the board arranged a meeting to hear public comments from the community. However, during this meeting, many parents strongly opposed the proposed change. They expressed various concerns, including logistical challenges such as difficulties with after-school activities, childcare arrangements, and the potential disruption to family schedules. The dominant sentiment among the parents was that altering the start times would create more complications than it would resolve.

In light of this strong opposition, the school board deliberated on the committee's recommendation. Ultimately, most board members voted against the proposal, citing the significant concerns raised by parents, the potential disruptions it could cause to families, and worries about how to fund the recommended changes. Only two board members supported the recommendation, with one arguing the committee's research had been thorough and should be taken seriously.

Question

In this scenario, a question arises: Which board member would you say is not voting with the best intentions based on rational consideration?

A) Two board members opposed the recommendation, swayed by the testimonies of community members, teachers, coaches, students, and parents, which they felt outweighed the committee's research.

B) One member opposed the proposal because, despite the research, she believed the safety of K-5 students waiting at bus stops in the morning darkness was a significant concern. She was particularly troubled by young children getting off the bus to find an empty house, as older siblings would arrive home later. She felt the recommendation did not adequately address this issue.

C) One member favored the recommendation, believing the potential benefits outweighed the challenges. This member expressed a willingness to invest time in addressing as many constituents' concerns as possible.

D) One board member, moved by the public comments, recognized the community's concerns and was aware of the likely funding issues associated with the change. Nevertheless, he ultimately voted to favor the recommendation because he wanted to honor the committee's efforts. He was concerned about upsetting the community members participating in the research process.

Takeaways

Evaluating the votes, it becomes clear all sides are justified in their decisions, as each member acts according to their beliefs and values. The majority voted against the proposal in response to the strong concerns expressed by parents, prioritizing community feedback and the potential impact on families. Conversely, option D—the board member who supported the recommendation—sought to honor the committee's hard work and research despite acknowledging the community's significant concerns.

Ultimately, the key takeaway is board members should always vote according to their conscience, regardless of whether their views align with recommendations. You must avoid making votes solely out of fear of criticism or emotional responses. All decisions should be grounded in what is best for the students. Striking a balance between the insights of committees and experts and the voices of the community is essential. A thoughtful approach considering both perspectives can lead to more informed and effective decision-making, building trust and collaboration within the school district.

Chapter 33
Committees

Committees assist a school district in researching, recommending, and implementing policies and procedures. They allow for a division of labor and participation by internal and external individuals in this process. The board or the superintendent can create committees. Typically, the board will have committees focusing on policy and financial issues, while superintendents create committees focusing more on operational matters. A committee can be Standing, Special, Select, or Advisory, depending on the purpose, length of time necessary for the effort, and the issue it is probing. These public meetings must comply with Sunshine/open meetings laws, such as public comments, announcements, minutes, etc. Check your statutes and policy for committee information.

Purpose of Committees

Committees are groups of individuals who gather to research an issue or seek solutions to a particular problem affecting the district.

Therefore, a committee's purpose relates to how and why it was created. Committees often conduct research to provide recommendations. They can also function as advisory committees to ensure the board and superintendent are current on a specific topic. If a standing committee is in place, it will typically provide some annual review or assessment.

Who Runs Committees?

The purpose of the committee will determine who will run it. However, each committee will select or vote on a chair who will lead in setting the time and place and creating the agenda.

Types of Committees

As mentioned previously, committees are formed for various reasons. They can be a Standing Committee, Special Committee, Select Committee, or Advisory Committee. All of these committees are organized differently and utilized to meet specific needs. For example:

Standing Committee – A committee that is permanent or semi-permanent in nature. For example, a capital needs review is done annually to support budget requests.
Special Committee – A committee set up to conduct research and make one-time recommendations to the board. For instance, a committee was set up to research teacher salaries and benefit increases in other districts.
Select Committee – Created to investigate or research a specific incident or topic, e.g., addressing student behavior in the classroom and the impact of increasing or reducing SRO involvement.
Advisory Committee – A group with specific knowledge and expertise to advise on a particular topic, issue, or concern; typically has citizen participants.

Sample Committees and Descriptions

BOARD OF EDUCATION
2024-2025 Committees
For Internal Use Only

Committee Descriptions	Members
Executive Committee The Executive Committee is composed of the board elected officers, including the President, 1st Vice President, 2nd Vice President and Secretary.	Roxanne Martinez Tobi Jackson Dr. Michael Ryan Anael Luebanos
After School Coordinating Board The After School Coordinating Board advises and provides support for the District's before and after school programming.	Dr. Michael Ryan Wallace Bridges * Kevin Lynch Dr. Camille Rodriguez
Board Audit The Board Audit Committee assists the Board in fulfilling its oversight responsibilities regarding internal and external audits, the system of internal controls, and the District's process for monitoring compliance with law and regulations. The Board Audit Committee must be voted on by the Board and select its chair from within the Committee.	Tobi Jackson* Dr. Michael Ryan Anael Luebanos Quinton Phillips
Facilities The Facilities Committee serves in an advisory role to the Superintendent and the Board in all areas of District facilities and infrastructure needs. The committee addresses issues related to growth, development, and the facilities needed to provide an optimal learning environment for students.	Tobi Jackson Dr. Michael Ryan * Wallace Bridges Kevin Lynch
Finance The Finance Committee collaborates with the Superintendent and Chief Financial Officer by reviewing and providing feedback on financial issues. This committee addresses matters pertaining to the school District's budget development and related recommendations to the Board.	Roxanne Martinez Tobi Jackson Anael Luebanos Kevin Lynch *
Legislative The Legislative Committee assists in developing the District's federal and state legislative priorities and provides feedback throughout the federal and state legislative sessions.	Roxanne Martinez Tobi Jackson Anne Darr * Quinton Phillips
Policy The Policy Committee works closely with the appropriate staff to draft new or refine current policies, processes and protocols, that are then brought to the board for formal action.	Anael Luebanos Anne Darr Quinton Phillips Dr. Camille Rodriguez *
Racial Equity The Racial Equity Committee studies District practices and policies and offers suggestions to ensure equitable practices at all organizational levels.	Roxanne Martinez Anael Luebanos Wallace Bridges Quinton Phillips *
Safety and Security The Safety and Security Committee addresses the safety and well-being of the students and staff within the district. The committee provides safety recommendations and central coordination of safety efforts such as school safety and security audits, policy development, and training.	Roxanne Martinez* Wallace Bridges Anne Darr Quinton Phillips

*Committee Chair

Source: www.fwisd.org

Chapter 34
Labor Unions

Many school districts have to contend with unions and union contracts. Though school boards are not directly involved in negotiating the contracts, they are responsible for being aware of the terms and conditions. The result does have a direct impact on the budget. However, any contract is not binding until the board approves it and the authorized parties sign it.

What's the Difference

In the simplest terms, the difference is whether private and public employees can be forced to participate in a union based on voting for *agency shops*. When a shop is authorized, dues or special fees will apply to all employees, whether an individual is a member or nonmember.

The National Right to Work Legal Defense Foundation currently identifies 26 states and the territory of Guam as having right-to-work laws, which means 24 states have forced union laws. The Michigan Legislature approved legislation to repeal the state's Right-to-Work Law, which took effect in February 2024.

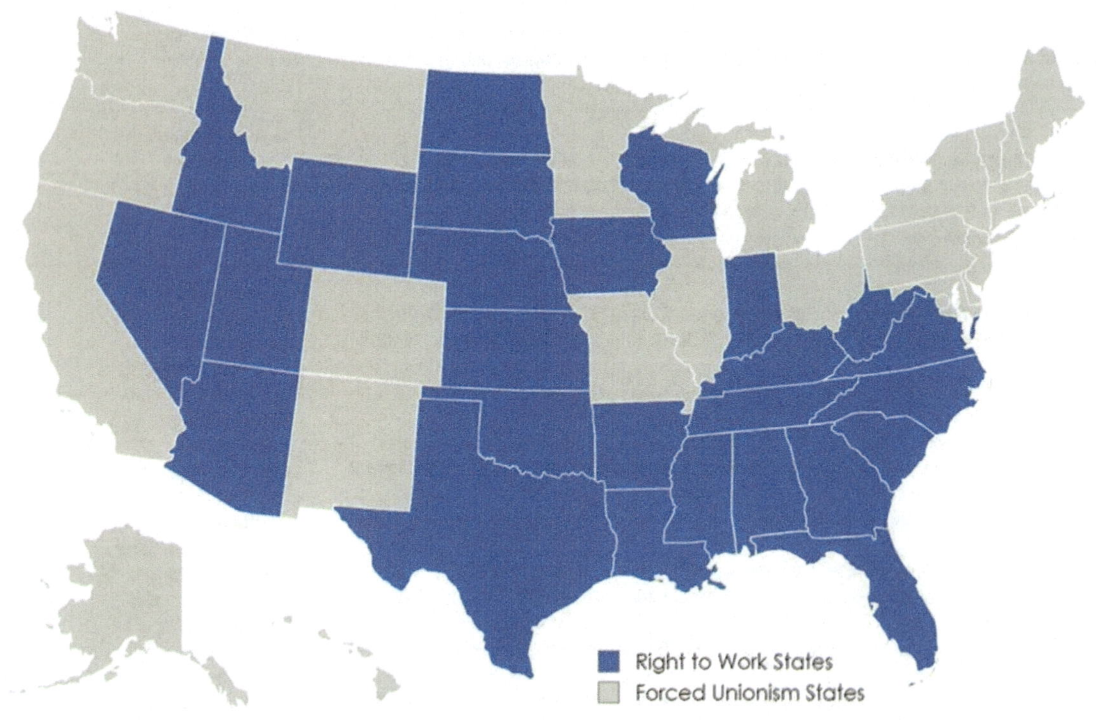

Source: National Right to Work Legal Defense Foundation (NRWLDF)

Each state has its own set of laws governing how unions can operate. Whether a state has laws regarding unions or the right to work, all states have some form of organized labor.

Why it Matters

Whether a school board is required to vote on a union contract or not, there are affiliations with national unions such as the National Education Association (NEA) and the American Federation of Teachers (AFT). States typically have associations such as the Virginia Education Association (VEA), Arizona Education Association (AEA), or Florida Education Association (FEA). These associations operate in the Right to Work states, identify as labor organizations or labor unions, function like unions, and are affiliated with national unions.

School Board Responsibility

Regardless of the state, school board members must know the type of labor laws they must follow. Though not all states are forced unions, it's important to understand the role of unions and associations.

The superintendent is responsible for ensuring union contracts are negotiated and the budget is sufficient for staff, salaries, and benefits increases. The negotiations typically determine the outcomes of these three aspects.

Board members should read the contract and ask questions about anything they are concerned about or unsure of before voting to approve it.

A Letter of Historical Significance

There were many periods throughout the late 1800s and early 1900s when unions fought to protect workers and their workplaces. There have been many benefits over the years in the private sector. However, a different perspective was taken regarding unions and their place in the public sector.

As this letter reveals, President Franklin D. Roosevelt was not favorable to public employees unionizing. To paraphrase, the letter states public servants are to serve the public, the taxpayer. If they had the right to strike, they would have done a disservice by not fulfilling the government's operations and obligations.

Letter on the Resolution of Federation of Federal Employees Against Strikes in Federal Service

August 16, 1937

My dear Mr. Steward:

As I cannot accept your invitation to attend the Twentieth Jubilee Convention of the National Federation of Federal Employees, I am sending greetings and a message using this method.

Reading your letter of July 14, 1937, I was especially interested in the timeliness of your remark that how the activities of your organization have been carried on during the past two decades "has been in complete consonance with the best traditions of public employee relationships." Organizations of Government employees have a logical place in Government affairs.

The desire of Government employees for fair and adequate pay, reasonable hours of work, safe and suitable working conditions, development of opportunities for advancement, facilities for fair and impartial consideration and review of grievances, and other objectives of a proper employee relations policy, is basically no different from that of employees in private industry. Organization on their part to present their views on such matters is both natural and logical, but meticulous attention should be paid to the special relationships and obligations of public servants to the public itself and to the Government.

All Government employees should realize that the process of collective bargaining, as usually understood, cannot be transplanted into the public service. It has its distinct and insurmountable limitations when applied to public personnel management. The very nature and purposes of Government make it impossible for administrative officials to represent fully or to bind the employer in mutual discussions with Government employee organizations. The employer is the whole people who speak by means of laws enacted by their representatives in Congress. Accordingly, administrative officials and employees alike are governed and guided, and in many instances restricted, by laws that establish policies, procedures, or rules in personnel matters.

Particularly, I want to emphasize my conviction that militant tactics have no place in the functions of any government employee organization. Upon employees in the Federal service rests the obligation to serve the whole people, whose interests and welfare require orderliness and continuity in the conduct of Government activities. This obligation is paramount. Since their own services have to do with the functioning of the Government, a strike of public employees manifests nothing less than an intent on their part to prevent or obstruct the operations of the Government until their demands are satisfied. Such action, looking toward the paralysis of Government by those who have sworn to support it, is unthinkable and intolerable. It is, therefore, with a feeling of gratification that I have noted in the constitution of the National Federation of Federal Employees the provision that "under no circumstances shall this Federation engage in or support strikes against the United States Government."

I congratulate the National Federation of Federal Employees on its twentieth anniversary of founding and trust that the convention will be successful in every way.

Very sincerely yours,

Mr. Luther C. Steward,
President,
National Federation of Federal Employees,
10 Independence Avenue, S.W., Washington, D.C.

Case Scenario: Janus v. American Federation of State, County, and Municipal Employees, Council 31, et al. (2018)

This precedent-setting case for public service employees overturned previous cases and restored individuals' 1st amendment rights. Liberty Justice Center reported the following:

*In a major victory for First Amendment rights, the U.S. Supreme Court ruled on June 27, 2018, in **Janus v. AFSCME**, that non-union government workers cannot be required to pay union fees as a condition of working in public service. This landmark case restores the First Amendment rights of free speech and freedom of association to more than five million public school teachers, first responders, and other government workers across the country.*

The U.S. Supreme Court ruled in favor of the plaintiff. The following are a few relevant excerpts from the ruling,

"Petitioner Mark Janus is a state employee whose unit is represented by a public-sector union (Union), one of the respondents. He refused to join the union because he opposed many of its positions, including those in collective bargaining."

The official filing document has a syllabus (summary) that includes the following:

1. The District Court had jurisdiction over the petitioner's suit. The petitioner was undisputedly injured, in fact, by Illinois' agency fee scheme, and a favorable court decision can redress his injuries.

2. The State's extraction of agency fees from nonconsenting public-sector employees violates the First Amendment.

3. For these reasons, states and public-sector unions may no longer extract agency fees from nonconsenting employees. The First Amendment is violated when money is taken from nonconsenting employees for a public-sector union; employees must choose to support the union before anything is taken from them. Accordingly, neither an agency fee nor any other form of payment to a public-sector union may be deducted from an employee, nor may any other attempt be made to collect such a payment unless the employee affirmatively consents to pay. ***Scan the QR code to view the Supreme Court decision.***

Case Scenario: Friedrichs v. California Teachers Assn., 578 U.S. (2016)

Petitioners were public school employees who sued the California Teachers Association and others. They argued that dues for non-members, which were extracted based on the agency shop arrangement and the opt-out requirement, violated the First Amendment.

Ballotpedia reported the following related to this case:

In a case that labor unions and those in the right-to-work movement watched closely, the court addressed the constitutionality of requiring public employees to pay agency shop fees to public-sector unions in ***Friedrichs v. California Teachers Association****. Agency shop fees are dues paid to compensate a labor union for any collective bargaining, contract administration, or grievance adjustment purposes conducted on behalf of the employees; the fees are equal to the amount of union dues. A group of California teachers argued that these fees were a violation of their First Amendment rights.*

The U.S. Supreme Court's unsigned *per curiam* opinion was based on an equally divided eight-member court, which affirmed the judgment of the lower court to stand. **Scan the QR code to view the Supreme Court Per Curiam judgement.**

Case Scenario: Knox v. Service Employees Int'l Union Local 1000, 567 U.S. 298 (2012)

This is another California case that concerns public employees and the rights of non-members. The filing concerns agency shops that force non-members to pay special fees and any subsequent increases to further the union's political and ideological activities.

The Legal Information Institute (LII) at Cornell Law School houses many cases. The following comes from LII's resources as stated in the syllabus (summary),

California law permits public-sector employees in a bargaining unit to decide by majority vote to create an "agency shop" arrangement under which a union represents all the employees. Even employees who do not join the union must pay an annual fee for "chargeable expenses," i.e., the cost of nonpolitical union services related to collective bargaining.

The opinion, authored by Justice Alito, states, "The judgment of the Ninth Circuit is reversed, and the case is remanded for further proceedings consistent with this opinion." This equates to a return to the lower court via an *order of certiorari*. This technical term means "to be more fully informed," which means the U.S. Supreme Court is asking for additional information. **Scan the QR code to view the Supreme Court opinion.**

Notes

Chapter 35

External Relationships

Building Impactful Community Relations

Candidates running for the school board often cite improving community relations as a campaign goal. But what are community relations, and what relationships should school board members foster? Is it merely parents and groups involved with education? Or is it more broad?

School board members need to understand the arena they have entered. Knowing what to accomplish during a term is equally important. It isn't easy to accomplish much without the support of others, so it's necessary to identify the various entities that can help reach identified goals. Building positive relationships is key to the board's and district's success.

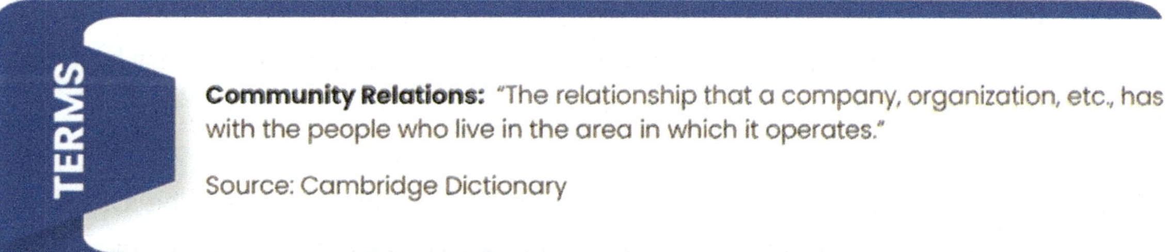

As the definition implies, community relations involve more than parents. They involve any public or private group that supports students' education from various perspectives. The following are examples of public and private entities and agreements to consider.

Types of Agreements

Various organizations and departments participate in some capacity with school districts. Three types of agreements facilitate transactions: Memorandum of Agreement (MOA), Memorandum of Understanding (MOU), and Interagency Agreement (IA). Though the agreements have different names, they serve the same purpose. The parties decide which agreement to use. Not all agreements have funding, but all agreements are binding. This requires board members to review and approve them before the authorized parties sign them.

Local Law Enforcement

Districts rely on law enforcement for school resource officer (SRO) support, whether from the county sheriff or local police department. Many districts enter into a Memorandum of Agreement (MOA) or contract arrangement to provide school security.

Keeping students and schools safe is foremost on the minds of parents and community members. Over the past several decades, school shootings have occurred and are on the rise around the country. SROs are the first line of defense when any type of incident occurs. Whether it's a fight in the hallway, a weapon in a student or employee locker or vehicle, dealing with illegal substances, inappropriate behavior, or a bullying incident, SROs are on sight to take immediate action.

Law enforcement officers are trained to recognize behavior and actions the average person doesn't notice. They identify patterns and can help mitigate human behavior issues and make recommendations for discipline protocols. They can sometimes prevent an incident before it has time to develop. They also provide written reports regarding incidents. When a suspension is presented to the board, members rely on the written record to support the action. SRO relationships can be invaluable.

State Department of Health

School districts typically have a local state health department within proximity. However, the majority of districts seek to hire health professionals. It's common to hire a nurse or other type of health professional. Many districts will hire a nurse who rotates among two or three schools, or each school may have one on staff, depending on the number of students in the school.

Nurses are hired to assist with various medical needs throughout the day. These could be as minor as a bloody nose or a cut finger from a playground accident. Other assistance can include administering prescription drugs students may need during the day, taking a student's temperature to determine whether they should be sent home, or calling an ambulance because a student broke a bone.

An increase in student behavior concerns has facilitated the hiring of other medical professionals. Determining and evaluating the cause of behavior changes requires the assistance of trained professionals. These interactions can be invasive and may require parental permission before pursuing any discussions.

Due to rising medical considerations, school districts compete with the local health department for limited resources. To help minimize or eliminate competition, districts might consider utilizing an MOA or contracting support with the local health department.

State Department of Social Services

Another local state department is social services. All school districts need these services in some capacity. Many districts hire social workers to assist with foster care or socio-economic issues.

This is another service where the state and district compete for professional services. Rather than increase employee roles, districts should consider an MOA or contract to meet student needs. This can minimize or eliminate competition for limited resources between the state department and school district to meet student needs. This can often be a win for all parties involved.

Local County Officials

Some state school districts have funding authority, whereas others have a system where the local county authority funds the school. This would be the district's board of supervisors, county commissioners, or city council.

The funding authority organization is vital to school districts. School boards must communicate the district's demands regardless of the entity with funding authority. Transparency raises public awareness and ensures appropriate funding.

Positive working relationships with those who allocate funding provide a range of benefits. First, it builds trust. Second, productive conversations tend to foster support for a buy-in of the school district's vision and needs. Both are important to help ensure sufficient revenue is generated to meet budgetary requirements.

Local and Regional Community Colleges

Many students seek to further their education, but attending a four-year institution may not be affordable or of interest. Community colleges are a good alternative. The value of working with these institutions goes beyond academics.

School board members can obtain data regarding regional economic opportunities. This is beneficial for high school career counselors. Community colleges align their programs with the region, particularly for career and technical education (CTE). These courses provide students with job skills and allow them to remain close to family and live in their hometown.

The cost of higher education deters many, so community college is an affordable alternative. Not only are the courses less expensive, but room and board are often eliminated, which is a savings. Students can also apply for grants for various academic and CTE programs, internships, or apprenticeships with local businesses to meet employment needs.

Understanding the full scope of academic programs and opportunities within the district and region can enhance a community's education and economic viability.

Non-Profits

All communities have a plethora of nonprofits that seek to provide some type of service to school districts. Board members must ensure these organizations meet a need rather than merely following a trend or agenda.

School boards should be judicious in deciding how to spend district funding. Though the board is not involved in the day-to-day operations, it has a fiduciary responsibility. If a non-profit doesn't align with the strategic outcomes of the district's efforts, then it should not be funded.

School board members should request periodic reviews of programs provided by outside organizations and determine if there is any return on investment. There should be measurable objectives for all programs to determine value to the district.

State Legislators

The House and Senate generate state education laws. School board members should work with their representatives in these bodies. Meeting with them before the legislative session and discussing issues that impact student learning, safety, and funding can be beneficial.

State legislators sponsor and present bills every legislative cycle. It's prudent as a school board member to follow what bills are being presented, who is sponsoring them, understand what they are attempting to accomplish, and what groups are involved. There will be many education bills in some years, and in others, there will be only a few. Either way, having a positive working relationship with your state legislators is essential.

The Local Community

Those closest to the district who have children in the schools, who work and live in the community, and who vote are the people to communicate with frequently. They will likely attend meetings, send emails, request information, and participate in district committees, events, and programs. Encountering them in the grocery store, restaurants, games, or just walking down the street is likely.

However, trying to please everyone is not a good strategy. Members will sometimes gain support from some but not from all. You'll need to develop a thick skin because there will be some pushback regardless of what is said or voted on. The best remedy is to have a foundation, stand on it, and be consistent. This will, in time, build a level of trust and respect.

Cultivate Enduring Professional Relations

There are many considerations when it comes to developing relationships. As a school board member, you need to understand the position's legal authority and role. It's equally important to surround yourself with those who can assist, in some capacity, to ensure valuable data and information are presented and necessary support is provided.

Ensuring sufficient funding is one of the primary responsibilities of a school board member. The position requires regular and open communication with the funding authorities in the district, county, and state. Making decisions about resource allocation will be a continual task.

Whether the district hires employees or contracts for services from various public or private sources, members must be vigilant in determining what is best for the district. Decision-making has many aspects and should not be done in a vacuum. Being a school board member is a team sport if the objective is to have a thriving and efficient district.

The following examples showcase various agreements, each designed to illustrate the distinct terms and conditions that may be present in different contractual arrangements.

Scan the QR code to view the MOU for School Resource Officer (SRO), Brevard Public Schools, FL.

Scan the QR code to view the MOU for Behavioral Health and Prevention Services, Kimberly School District, ID.

Scan the QR code to view the MOA for Drug Testing Services, Kentucky Center for School Safety, KY.

Notes

Chapter 36
Associations

Wall of Resistance

As a board member, you may sometimes feel like you're against a wall of resistance in a system designed to protect itself rather than promote meaningful change for students. While the challenges may feel overwhelming, every small effort you make can contribute to positive change. Your concerns are valid; there is indeed a protective framework surrounding public education that can make it challenging to implement necessary reforms. Public education operates with layers of influence that often overshadow the needs of students.

Politically Driven

The majority of these associations have lost their way and become loyal to political platforms. This shift continues even as the quality of education declines year after year. The mandates imposed by the Federal Department of Education, state boards, and governors often feel suffocating, draining the vitality of classrooms. The educational agenda is tossed around chaotically, like a wiffle ball bouncing in all directions.

Avoid Distractions

That is why you must not lose sight of your purpose. Without this constant reminder, you may become drained and worn out. You will need to learn to pick your battles, especially if you are in the minority on the board. You cannot fight every battle; instead, you must choose wisely and be strategic about where to invest your energy. Many distractions and issues will ultimately not matter in the long run. For example, spending two hours in a board workshop debating the color of a new school building is insignificant compared to the long-term changes involving policy, budgets, and strategic plans.

Focusing on what truly impacts students and the educational system is essential. The superintendent can distract the board to be preoccupied with busy work, diverting attention from meaningful discussions. Their mindset often suggests they are "the experts" who should not be questioned. This can lead to a board of rubber-stampers and cheerleaders for the district rather than active participants in shaping effective educational policies.

Maintain Your Authority

While these administrators may feel empowered within the protective cocoon built around them through these associations and fellow lifelong bureaucrats, you must maintain your empowerment by reminding yourself of your authority as outlined in your state statutes. Familiarize yourself with the organizational chart that places the community, board, superintendent, and staff in their proper order. Remember that for decades, these education experts have often gone unaccountable, leading to wasteful spending they are reluctant to relinquish, as well as a decline in academics due to the time wasted on political agendas and unnecessary focus on non-core essential content.

In previous discussions, we explored the roles of the National School Board Association and various state associations. New board members must enter this role with a clear understanding of these complexities. Be prepared for pushback when you attempt to enforce or create policies that challenge the prevailing political agenda.

Since 2020, the focus of these associations has drastically shifted from merely safeguarding funding to actively pushing politically charged issues that are counterintuitive and being funded by taxpayers who are not politically aligned with their agendas. Ultimately, initially intended to foster collaboration and professional development, these associations have transformed into breeding grounds for political activism and lobbying. When they push their agenda at the state or national capitol, the first thing they will tout is their membership numbers to advance an agenda you may or may not agree with.

Stop Funding

Moreover, these national and state K-12 associations and lifelong bureaucrats rely on membership from public school leaders and the tax dollars received from each public school student. Without public schools, these organizations would lose their purpose. Their existence often hinges on crises that necessitate membership, which can lead to complacency and an unwillingness to embrace meaningful change. Across the 50 states, these associations frequently act as cogs in the wheel of public education. They are more concerned with maintaining their memberships and protecting their positions than focusing on the needs of the students they are meant to serve. This is why public education is frequently referred to as a "machine"— it is surrounded by associations, unions, and bureaucracies prioritizing their interests over student welfare. Focusing on what truly impacts students and the educational system is essential.

As a board member, you must recognize that you approve budgets and control spending. You can refuse to allocate funds for memberships that do not serve your district's best interests. Beyond the annual membership dues, significant costs associated with conference fees, travel expenses, and accommodations can be scrutinized. While it may be challenging to make these changes, you have the power to adjust the budget to prevent unnecessary expenses from burdening taxpayers. Suppose district staff wish to participate in these associations. In that case, they should do so at their own expense rather than using public funds to support agendas that may not reflect the community's values.

In 2021, school boards across the country set an example. They declared, "enough is enough," by withdrawing from state associations when they felt the National School Board Association undermined parental rights. This collective action emphasizes the importance of prioritizing student needs over political agendas.

You will quickly notice the outrageous membership dues the board approves yearly without proper oversight. The dues can be eliminated. While it may be easier said than done, it is entirely within your authority to adjust the budget to prevent these costs from impacting your district's finances. Expect pushback, as many staff members enjoy attending conferences and appreciate the opportunity for a paid trip away from the office. These associations typically do not host their conferences at budget-friendly venues; instead, they are often held in luxury hotels, with taxpayers footing the bill for these overpriced accommodations, meals, and parking fees.

Keep in mind, if you start eliminating these costs and ties for staff, you are expected to set an example of being a good steward of taxpayer money by cutting connections with associations yourself that do not align with your community's values or goals.

8. External Influence Costs

To understand the gravity of the costs associated with outside influence, ask your superintendent for the following information:

Please provide a detailed list of all associations funded by the board, along with the associated costs and the purpose of the funding. This will help evaluate how these expenditures align with the district's priorities and goals.

Request a breakdown of the annual staff travel budget, including travel costs and registration fees, to prioritize students' educational needs over external interests.

Request a routine staff summary report that explains why staff members want to join the associations and their key takeaways from the meetings and conferences.

Require the superintendent to provide the board with an annual report on the legislative platform of each association the board is funding through membership and other associated costs.

Board Member's Exercises | **Exercise 8**

Familiarize Yourself Before You Fund

Finally, you must research and conduct your due diligence before agreeing to fund these expenses. Click through the associations' websites, review their resources, pay close attention to their legislative platforms, and determine whether you can support these views and costs.

Notes

Common K-12 public education associations, organized alphabetically by acronym. It aims to enhance your research and understanding of the various organizations involved in K-12 education.

1. AASA - American Association of School Administrators (*www.aasa.org*)
2. AAHPERD - American Alliance for Health, Physical Education, Recreation and Dance (*www.aahperd.org*)
3. AASL - American Association of School Librarians (*www.ala.org/aasl*)
4. ACTFL - American Council on the Teaching of Foreign Languages (*www.actfl.org*)
5. AECT - Association for Educational Communications and Technology (*www.aect.org*)
6. AERA - American Educational Research Association (*www.aera.net*)
7. AESA - Association of Educational Service Agencies (*www.aesa.us*)
8. AFT - American Federation of Teachers (*www.aft.org*)
9. ALAS - Association of Latino Administrators and Superintendents (*www.alasedu.net*)
10. AMLE - Association for Middle Level Education (*www.amle.org*)
11. ASBO - Association of School Business Officers International (*www.asbointl.org*)
12. ASCD - Association for Supervision and Curriculum Development (*www.ascd.org*)
13. ASCA - American School Counselor Association (*www.school counselor.org*)
14. ASIS - ASIS International, Advancing Security Worldwide (*www.asisonline.org*)
15. CEC - Council for Exceptional Children (*www.cec.sped.org*)
16. CEFPI - Council of Educational Facilities Planners International (*www.cefpi.org*)
17. Childhood Education International (*www.ceinternational1892.org*)
18. COSA - Council of School Attorneys (*www.NSBA.org*)
19. CoSN - Council for School Networking (*www.cosn.org*)
20. IRA - International Reading Association (*www.reading.org*)
21. ISTE - International Society for Technology in Education (*www.iste.org*)
22. NAEA - National Art Education Association (*www.arteducators.org*)
23. NAESP - National Association of Elementary School Principals (*www.naesp.org*)
24. NAEYC - National Association for the Education of Young Children (*www.naeyc.org*)
25. NAfME - National Association for Music Education (*www.nafme.org*)
26. NAGC - National Association for Gifted Children (*www.nagc.org*)
27. NASSP - National Association of Secondary School Principals (*www.nassp.org*)
28. NBEA - National Business Education Association (*www.nbea.org*)
29. NCSS - National Council for the Social Studies (*www.ncss.org*)
30. NCTE - National Council of Teachers of English (*www.ncte.org*)
31. NCTM - National Council of Teachers of Mathematics (*www.nctm.org*)
32. NEA - National Education Association (*www.nea.org*)
33. NSBA - National School Boards Association (*www.nsba.org*)
34. NSSA - National School Attorneys Association (*/www.nationalschoolattorneysassociation.org*)
35. NSTA - National Science Teachers Association (*www.nsta.org*)
36. PTA - National Parent Teachers Association (*www.pta.org*)
37. SETDA - State Educational Technology Directors Association (*www.setda.org*)
38. USDLA - United States Distance Learning Association (*www.usdla.org*)

9

Section 9: **Shaping the Culture and Climate in Your School District**

Objectives for Section 9: Shaping the Culture and Climate in Your School District

1. **Address Nepotism and Fairness:** Recognize the detrimental effects of nepotism on morale and productivity, and learn how to implement clear policies to promote fairness and integrity within the school district.

2. **Develop Effective Student Discipline Policies:** Understand the importance of establishing and monitoring student discipline policies to create a safe and conducive learning environment, addressing contemporary challenges in classroom management.

3. **Prioritize School Safety and Security:** Explore the board's responsibilities in developing robust safety plans and collaborating with law enforcement to ensure the safety and security of students and staff within the school district.

4. **Navigate Political and Cultural Issues:** Examine the challenges presented by politically charged topics, such as Critical Race Theory, and learn how to maintain a focus on educational priorities while addressing community concerns.

5. **Promote Transparency and Trust in Curriculum:** Understand the significance of curriculum transparency in building trust with parents and the community, and learn how to implement policies to ensure stakeholders are informed about educational materials and programs.

As a school board member, you are instrumental in shaping and nurturing the culture and climate within your districts. This section addresses the fundamental aspects contributing to a positive educational environment for students, staff, and the broader community. The following chapters will explore key themes, ranging from nepotism and discipline to safety, political and cultural issues, and the ongoing debates surrounding equality and equity in education.

Chapter 37, "Nepotism," begins our exploration by defining nepotism and highlighting its negative impact on morale and productivity within school districts. We will discuss the importance of implementing clear policies to prevent favoritism and ensure fairness in the workplace for all staff members. As a board member, your commitment to addressing nepotism builds a culture of integrity and accountability.

Chapter 38, "Student Discipline," can be a nonissue when met with effective discipline policies to maintain order and promote a conducive learning environment. We will examine the evolution of student discipline practices and the board's role in ensuring policies are implemented fairly and consistently.

Chapter 39, "School Safety and Security," outlines the board's responsibility for establishing robust safety plans, collaborating with law enforcement, and monitoring and enforcing safety measures. The board's proactive approach to safety is vital for creating a secure educational environment.

Chapter 40, "Examining Political Cultural Issues in Schools," examines the challenges posed by politically charged topics such as Critical Race Theory (CRT). We will explore the importance of focusing on educational priorities while addressing the concerns of parents and the community regarding curriculum content.

In Chapter 41, "Equality vs. Equity," we will clarify the distinctions between equality and equity and their implications for policy-making and resource allocation. The chapter will also address the challenges and controversies arising from equity initiatives and how these can impact all students' education quality.

Chapter 42, "Curriculum Transparency Builds Trust," highlights the necessity for open communication among school boards, educators, and parents regarding educational materials. We will discuss how transparency can rebuild community trust and ensure parents are informed about their children's education.

Finally, Chapter 43, "Adapting to Change," encourages school board members to embrace the rise of school choice and recognize the diverse needs of families in the community. We will explore strategies for collaboration with alternative education providers and ensure the district remains relevant and responsive to the needs of all students.

As you read through this section, remember that your leadership is instrumental in cultivating a positive culture and climate in your schools. Each chapter provides valuable insights and actionable steps to enhance the educational environment for everyone involved.

Chapter 37

Nepotism

What Is Nepotism?

Nepotism is the unfair practice of granting advantages, privileges, or positions to relatives or friends through the authority of a person in power. It can occur in various environments, especially educational settings, where fairness should prevail.

Why it is Detrimental to Morale

Nepotism can lead to several problems within a school district, resulting in a hostile environment, decreased productivity, and lost talent. As a board member, you are likely part of the largest employer in the district, making it essential to identify and address nepotism. Its effects can include:

1. **Unfairness**: Nepotism creates an environment where individuals feel undervalued, leading to resentment and low morale.
2. **Reduced Performance**: Favoring unqualified individuals can harm overall workplace performance.
3. **Loss of Talent**: High-performing individuals, including employees and students, may leave for opportunities that recognize merit.
4. **Conflict**: Favoritism can lead to disputes among team members and staff.
5. **Legal Risks**: If not addressed, nepotism can result in legal challenges for the district.
6. **Damaged Culture**: Favoritism undermines the overall integrity of the school district.

Policies and Procedures

School boards must implement clear policies and procedures to prevent nepotism. As a board member, you are responsible for abstaining from voting on contracts or positions involving family members or close friends. Even if a formal policy is not yet in place, abstaining is important because it sets a precedent.

Once policies are established, the superintendent must ensure all department heads, principals, and HR staff are trained on them. Those making recommendations for contracts or hires must also be aware of these policies and face consequences for violations.

Impact on Student Morale

Nepotism and favoritism can disadvantage students in clubs, teams, and competitions. When coaches favor relatives or friends over more qualified players, it creates a hostile atmosphere that can alienate students and parents. This behavior is easily noticed and can lead to dissatisfaction within the school community.

West Allegheny School District

Nepotism Policy Acknowledgment

Nepotism: The West Allegheny Board of School Directors understands that school directors and district administrators are not to use their positions to benefit either themselves or any other individual or agency apart from the total interest of the school district. Furthermore, the Administration shall not recommend and the Board of School Directors shall not hire any person who is a relative or spouse of an administrator or school board member. Questions regarding this policy may be clarified during the interview. Please read the Nepotism Policy and sign the Nepotism Acknowledgement below.

Acknowledgement Regarding Nepotism

I, ___________________________ do hereby acknowledge that I have reviewed the West Allegheny School District's Nepotism Policy and I understand the policy. I further acknowledge that any questions I may have had regarding the nepotism policy have been answered to my satisfaction. Listed below are any and all affiliations I have with any District employees or members of the Board of School Directors as defined in the West Allegheny School District's nepotism policy. I understand that West Allegheny School District will rely on the statements made below. In the event an employment offer is made by West Allegheny School District and it is subsequently determined during my employment with West Allegheny that the affiliations* listed below do not completely disclose all affiliations as required by the nepotism policy, West Allegheny School District may discharge me and I understand that my conduct shall constitute just cause for discharge.

*Are you related to any administrator or board member of the West Allegheny School District? **Affiliation shall also mean** any relative defined as a parent, spouse, brother, sister, son, daughter, grandchild, grandparent, aunt, uncle, nephew, niece, first cousin, father-in-law, mother-in-law, sister-in-law, brother-in-law, son-in-law, daughter-in-law, stepfather, stepmother, stepdaughter, stepson, or anyone under the legal guardianship of an administrator or school director, or the spouse of an administrator or school director.

Affiliations: (Please list below.) If none - check ☐ **NONE-NOT APPLICABLE**

Signature ____ Date_____________

West Allegheny School District

Nepotism Policy

The West Allegheny Board of School Directors recognizes that it represents all the citizens of the school district and has been entrusted by the public with the educational development of its children. The Board, as a body and as individuals, understands that school directors and district administrators are not to use their positions to benefit either themselves or any other individual or agency apart from the total interest of the school district. To promote the best interest of the entire district, it is necessary to avoid partiality and preferential hiring, promotion or compensation. The Board also recognizes that employees of the District coming under the supervision of, reporting to, or engaging in duties under the authority of a relative, may give rise to a perception of a conflict of public and personal interest. Because of this concern, the Board deems it appropriate to adopt a policy governing the employment duties of such persons.

To this end, the Board adopts the following policy regarding hiring of relatives:

A relative shall be defined as parent, spouse, brother, sister, son, daughter, grandchild, grandparent, aunt, uncle, nephew, niece, first cousin, father-in-law, mother-in-law, sister-in-law, brother-in-law, son-in-law, daughter-in-law, stepfather, stepmother, stepdaughter, stepson, or anyone under the legal guardianship of an administrator or school director, or the spouse of an administrator or school director.

The administration shall not recommend and the Board of Directors shall not hire any person who is a relative of an administrator, a school director or the spouse of an administrator or school director of the West Allegheny School District.

An inquiry of relationship will be included with each application of employment. If a person is hired contrary to this policy, and the relationship becomes known, the person shall be dismissed from his/her position immediately.

Excluded from these provisions are those who hold a yearly renewable position and acquired that position before the appointment or election of the related administrator or board member.

A relative may serve as an unpaid volunteer for the school district.

No two (2) employees from any one (1) family may be employed at the same school. For the purposes of this policy, **from one (1) family** is interpreted to mean employees living in the same household and/or siblings, children, spouse, parents, or in-laws of the employee.

No portion of this policy shall be construed to violate and laws of the Commonwealth or Federal government or the collective bargaining agreements, between the West Allegheny School Board and the district employees.

This policy shall take effect immediately and shall not be applied retroactively to any present employee.

Source:www.westasd.org

Case Scenario: Nepotism Among Coaches

A parent stops you in the mall to share their frustration about a situation regarding the boys' lacrosse team. Coach Smith has been giving significant playing time to his nephew, Tyler, despite Tyler's inconsistent attendance at practices and lack of skills compared to other players. This favoritism frustrates other team members, who feel their hard work is overlooked.

Steps to manage the situation

1. Acknowledge the Concern: Ask for the parent's number and suggest they allow you to set up a meeting for them to share this information with the superintendent or their representative.
2. Set a Meeting: Ask the superintendent to schedule a meeting with the parent.
3. Follow Up with the Parent: Call the parent if the superintendent did not follow through.
4. Listen to Concerns: As a board member, you should be open to hearing complaints from parents about Coach Smith's decisions.
5. Support Policy Development: Work with the superintendent to develop or enhance policies regarding playing time and team selection. Ensure these policies are communicated clearly to the coaching staff and the players.
6. Follow-up: After addressing the issue, check in with parents to see if there have been improvements in the situation. Continued feedback is vital to ensure favoritism does not persist.

It is easy for these matters to become overly complicated, potentially diverting your focus from essential responsibilities. Refusing to delve into the school district's daily operations is vital. Your primary duty as a board member is to formulate and implement policies that proactively eliminate any culture of nepotism and favoritism. By attentively addressing the concerns of students, parents, and staff members and taking decisive action when necessary, school boards and superintendents can cultivate an atmosphere where every student and employee enjoys equal opportunities for success and growth.

Takeaways

Keep the Golden Rule for board members in mind: If you witness favoritism or nepotism, you must speak up. Ignoring such issues can set a troubling precedent, enabling justifications for similar behaviors in the future.

Notes

Chapter 38
Student Discipline

In today's educational landscape, the significance of discipline within schools cannot be overstated. In an age of cell phones, social media, hyperactivity, and a culture of lawlessness, order and discipline within schools have reached challenging levels. The board's role in this is guided by its ability to identify and address the challenges through policy and budgetary action. As an integral component of effective learning environments, discipline shapes not only the academic outcomes of students but also their overall well-being. The evolution of student discipline policies from 2014 to 2024 highlights the role of board oversight, policy formulation, and funding for ensuring a safe and conducive learning environment. By examining past practices and current challenges, proactive measures in addressing discipline-related issues that affect students and educators must be considered.

Student Discipline Policies from 2014 - 2024

The ongoing discussion about student discipline dates back to 2014 when federal agencies issued nonbinding civil rights guidelines to educate local school districts about enforcing civil rights laws.

During President Obama's administration, this guidance highlighted the potential for schools to violate federal civil rights laws if they disciplined students of color at significantly higher rates than white students.

In January 2014, the US Department of Education (USDOE) and the US Department of Justice (DOJ) released a *"Dear Colleague Letter"* (DCL) addressing school discipline. During this announcement, then Secretary of Education Arne Duncan stated, "Racial discrimination in school discipline is a real problem today, and not just an issue from 40 to 50 years ago." The US Department of Education emphasized the need to reconsider the effects of disciplinary practices on students, especially those from marginalized backgrounds.

The DCL warned school districts that how they handled student discipline could lead to unlawful discrimination based on race if not administered equitably. It stressed that even seemingly neutral disciplinary policies could disproportionately affect students of a specific race, which would violate Title VI of the Civil Rights Act of 1964. Therefore, if the Office for Civil Rights (OCR) found a school district's policies led to such disparities, the district might risk losing federal funding unless it entered into a resolution agreement with the OCR.

This assertion—suggesting schools could breach the Civil Rights Act due to disparate impact—sparked significant debate. Critics argued this marked a stark shift from traditional enforcement methods since the guidance was labeled as "non-binding" and did not mandate specific policies. Nevertheless, the threat of investigations led many districts to alter their disciplinary practices, often prioritizing compliance over maintaining a safe learning environment.

Policy-Based Reactions

Some reforms involve changing policies that dictate how districts, schools, and educators respond to student misbehavior rather than solely relying on programs.

Targeted strategies, such as early-warning indicator systems, utilize extensive administrative databases to predict which students might struggle academically or exhibit behavioral issues. The goal is to identify these students early before problems become more pronounced. While research on the effectiveness of early-warning systems in reducing exclusionary discipline is still limited, studies suggest systems are unlikely to be effective without accompanying behavioral support strategies.

Trump (45) Administration Cancels 2014 Practices

Teachers reported experiencing chaotic classrooms and felt unsafe due to their inability to manage students with behavioral issues effectively. The narrative presented to the Federal Commission on School Safety mirrored these concerns, ultimately influencing the Trump administration in 2018 to revoke Obama-era guidance. The investigation was sparked following the Parkland shooting on February 14, 2018. A deep look into school-based discipline practices, known as restorative justice practices, were touted as best practices through the Obama administration's guidance, highlighted as an example of success from schools that had implemented them to the greatest extent, namely in Chicago and Broward County, Florida. This district includes Marjory Stoneman Douglas High School, where a former student tragically took the lives of 17 individuals. Critics contend school discipline guidance contributed to such incidents, leading to a decline in school climate and safety.

Though the Trump administration successfully redirected many of the harmful policies and directives, the effects of the 2014 policies continue to linger, manifesting through passive discipline policies and the fear of being investigated for disproportionate discipline numbers. This has caused Post Traumatic Stress Disorder (PTSD) among school administrators who lived under the threat of DOE investigations during the Obama era.

Student Code of Conduct

The school district's code of conduct is a tool for establishing and enforcing uniform expectations. It should not be a document that simply collects dust once finalized. Issues evolve; for example, a code of conduct from five years ago might not address current concerns like AI plagiarism, vaping, cell phones, and smartwatches. These are just a few instances of how the educational environment changes. It's important to adjust to stay on top of important issues in the current code of conduct. By ensuring students understand the rules and the associated consequences, we can improve order, allowing for a greater focus on teaching and learning, which is the board's primary goal. Your responsibility is not to manage the intricate details; that falls under the superintendent's duties. Instead, your role is to ensure the code of conduct supports a safe and productive learning environment for all students.

U.S. Department of Justice
Civil Rights Division

U.S. Department of Education
Office for Civil Rights

December 21, 2018

Dear Colleague:

The purpose of this letter is to inform you that the Department of Justice and the Department of Education are withdrawing the statements of policy and guidance reflected in the following documents:

- Dear Colleague Letter on Nondiscriminatory Administration of School Discipline dated January 8, 2014; and

- Overview of the Supportive School Discipline Initiative dated January 8, 2014.

Additionally, the Department of Education is withdrawing the following related documents:

- *Guiding Principles: A Resource Guide for Improving School Climate and Discipline,* dated January 8, 2014;

- Appendix 1: *U.S. Department of Education* Directory of Federal School Climate and Discipline Resources, dated January 8, 2014;

- Appendix 2: Compendium of School Discipline Laws and Regulations for the 50 States, Washington D.C., and Puerto Rico, dated January 8, 2014; and

- School Discipline Guidance Package FAQs, dated January 8, 2014.

The Dear Colleague Letter on Nondiscriminatory Administration of Discipline ("Guidance") discussed the legal framework that the Departments employ to analyze complaints of discrimination under Title IV of the Civil Rights Act of 1964 (Title IV), 42 U.S.C. §§ 2000c *et seq.*, and Title VI of the Civil Rights Act of 1964 (Title VI), 42 U.S.C. §§ 2000d *et seq.*, and its implementing regulations, 34 C.F.R. Part 100. Title IV authorizes the Attorney General in certain circumstances to institute a lawsuit against public school boards, colleges, and universities upon receiving a complaint

Page 1 — Dear Colleage Letter

[OCR-000113]

of discrimination. Title VI prohibits discrimination based on race, color, or national origin by recipients of Federal financial assistance. The Guidance presented and analyzed, under Titles IV and VI, a number of factual scenarios involving the application of school discipline, and indicated what conclusions the Departments might reach in each scenario.

On March 12, 2018, President Trump announced the formation of a Federal Commission on School Safety. President Trump directed the Commission to study and make recommendations regarding several issues, including whether the Guidance and associated documents should be rescinded. On December 18, 2018, the Commission recommended that the Departments rescind the Guidance and associated documents.

States and local school districts play the primary role in establishing educational policy, including how to handle specific instances of student misconduct and discipline, and in ensuring that classroom teachers have the support they need to implement appropriate discipline policies. States and local school districts must also comply with the antidiscrimination protections contained in federal law, including Title VI. The Departments have concluded that the Guidance and associated documents advance policy preferences and positions not required or contemplated by Title IV or Title VI.

Accordingly, the Department of Education and the Department of Justice have decided to withdraw and rescind the Guidance and associated documents. The Departments are firmly committed to vigorously enforcing civil rights protections on behalf of all students. The robust protections against race, color, and national origin discrimination guaranteed by the Constitution, Title IV, and Title VI remain unchanged, and continue to be vital for educational institutions in the United States.

This letter does not add requirements to applicable law and is not intended to, and does not, create any rights, substantive or procedural, enforceable at law by any party in any matter civil or criminal. If you have questions or are interested in commenting on this letter, please contact the Department of Education at ocr@ed.gov or 800-421-3481 (TDD: 800-877-8339); or the Department of Justice at education@usdoj.gov or 877-292-3804 (TTY: 800-514-0383).

Sincerely,

/s/	/s/
Kenneth L. Marcus	Eric S. Dreiband
Assistant Secretary for Civil Rights	Assistant Attorney General
U.S. Department of Education	U.S. Department of Justice

Page 2 — Dear Colleage Letter

Source: www.govinfo.gov

Top Issues of Teacher Turnover

Though there are multiple reasons why teachers choose to leave the profession, the following are significant contributors. Of these six reasons, five are associated with chronic discipline issues.

1. **Lack of Support:** Many are overwhelmed by insufficient administration support, including a lack of resources, mentoring, and opportunities for professional development.
2. **Burnout:** Heavy workloads, large class sizes, extensive paperwork, and responsibilities that extend beyond the classroom lead to burnout.
3. **Classroom Management:** Struggles with managing student behavior and discipline create a stressful work environment, prompting many to leave the profession.
4. **Limited Professional Growth:** A lack of opportunities for advancement and professional development leads to dissatisfaction.
5. **Negative School Culture:** A toxic culture is created by limited or nonexistent collaboration among staff and strained relationships with colleagues and administrators.
6. **Low Salaries:** Competitive pay is essential, and when salaries are not aligned with the position's demands, other opportunities are considered.

High Absentee Rates

The level of absences is tied to various factors, with discipline and safety being the primary ones. The District of Columbia has one of the highest rates of chronic absenteeism in the country, with Alaska having the highest average at 48.6%. Across K-12, 43% of district students were chronically absent in the 2022-2023 school year, and 37% were truant. Absenteeism is especially prevalent among high school students, with 60% chronically absent.

Chronic absenteeism rates are significantly higher in certain schools, especially those in disadvantaged neighborhoods. For example, in the District of Columbia Public Schools, high schools on the east side have rates ranging from just under 80% to nearly 90%. Ballou High School is particularly concerning, with 89.3% of its students classified as chronically absent. Districts in these situations must pay urgent attention to addressing issues related to discipline, safety, security, and ineffective policies.

According to data compiled by Stanford University education professor Thomas Dee in partnership with The Associated Press, an estimated 6.5 million additional students became chronically absent. The data covers 40 states and Washington, D.C., and provides the most comprehensive absenteeism accounting nationwide. According to Dee's analysis, absences were more prevalent among Latino, Black, and low-income students.

Stay Proactive

School board members are responsible for ensuring students receive a quality education. Frequent teacher absences or calls out disrupt the learning process. Furthermore, a district that lacks substantial consequences and discipline leads to higher rates of bullying and fighting, creating an unsafe environment for students and driving up absenteeism.

WARNING SIGNS

OF DISCIPLINE AND MANAGEMENT ISSUES IN DISTRICTS

School boards need to remain vigilant and attentive to various signs that could indicate more profound issues. When warning signs are overlooked or dismissed, serious consequences impact the entire school community. Student performance declines, school morale takes a significant hit, and the overall atmosphere within the district begins to become hostile and unwelcoming. Some of the impacts include the following:

High Absenteeism Rates: This reflects disengagement or dissatisfaction with the school environment for both students and teachers.

Student Enrollment Drops: A drop in student enrollment indicates that families are unhappy with the school or the overall culture.

Underperforming Schools: Declines in academic performance signal underlying issues with teaching methods or a lack of adequate support for struggling students. Many teachers are overwhelmed by disruptive behavior and unable to give all students

Parent Engagement: Parents' continual interaction with the school board for assistance with urgent matters highlights a genuine concern for their children's education and overall well-being.

Substitute Teachers: Difficulty retaining substitute teachers can be significantly affected if discipline is an issue.

Bus Drivers: The inability to keep school bus drivers is attributed to low pay and unruly students, which leads to anxiety and turnover.

Teacher Turnover: A noticeable rise in teacher turnover is a red flag that teachers are not receiving support or that working conditions are challenging. If it's a management issue, turnover is typically higher at specific locations.

Taking decisive action can improve discipline is through implementing the following:

1. Analyze exit surveys of employees to pinpoint the reasons behind their departures.
2. Actively attend the code of conduct committee review to hear firsthand what is being communicated and identify gaps in the dialogue.
3. Remain vigilant by recognizing the warning signs associated with turnover.

Addressing these issues through sound board policy, a comprehensive student code of conduct, and adequate funding that supports your superintendent in managing and implementing them will benefit the school community and learning environment.

Notes

Chapter 39

School Safety and Security

Meeting district needs regarding the safety and security of the students, staff, and schools should be approached with urgency and appropriate due diligence. Board duties encompass governance, budget allocation, establishing safety plans, monitoring progress, strengthening relationships with law enforcement, and formulating policies. The ultimate responsibility lies with the board when safety systems fail. A passive stance can lead to catastrophic failures in this area and should NOT be left solely to the superintendent and staff. The superintendent and the board must work proactively and promptly to address all shortcomings.

Good practices and student safety have become entangled in political debates for inexplicable reasons. Some stakeholders advocate for enhanced security measures, while others argue such safeguards create an environment that is not "nurturing or welcoming" for students. Concerns should be addressed through mental health solutions. No matter what side of the spectrum one falls on, the reality is it's all of the above. Political considerations should not interfere with a steadfast commitment to ensuring safety on school campuses.

Governance and Safety

As a board member, there are key questions for you to address:

1. What specific safety plan is in place?
2. Are safety needs and related plans being adequately addressed in the budget?
3. Is the board monitoring to ensure safety plans are being effectively implemented?
4. Are administrators conducting unannounced campus walk-throughs to verify safety protocols are being followed? Are the doors to hallways locked between classes? Are teachers limiting the students' wandering during class? Are doors propped open with rocks or other gadgets?
5. Is the security officer walking the campus looking for open gates, suspicious bags, and behavior?
6. Are regular, frequent drills being carried out?
7. Is local law enforcement familiar with district campuses and conducting routine active shooter drills with all essential stakeholders involved according to the safety plan?
8. As a board member, are you conducting your security audit to ensure that the board implemented policies have been implemented through protocols and reached the school campAs a board member, are you conducting a security audit to ensure that the policies implemented by the board are being followed through protocols and are reaching the school campuses? Has the board passed a policy giving board members access to campuses as illustrated in the following policy?

Policy: po0172
Section: 0000 Bylaws

VISITATION OF SCHOOLS BY INDIVIDUAL SCHOOL BOARD MEMBERS

0172 - **VISITATION OF SCHOOLS BY INDIVIDUAL SCHOOL BOARD MEMBERS**

An individual School Board member may, on any day and at any time at his/her pleasure, visit any school in the District. A member of the Legislature may visit any public school in the legislative district of the member. An individual visiting a school pursuant to this policy must sign in and sign out at the school's main office and wear his/her identification badge at all times while present on school premises. The Board, the school, or any other person or entity, including, but not limited to, the principal of the school, the Superintendent, or any other Board member, may not require an individual visiting the school pursuant to this policy to provide notice before visiting the school. The school may offer, but may not require, an escort to accompany an individual visiting the school pursuant to this policy during the visit. Another Board member or an employee, including, but not limited to, the Superintendent, the school principal, or his/her designee, may not limit the duration or scope of the visit or direct an individual visiting the school pursuant to this policy to leave the premises. No policy or practice may prohibit or limit the authority granted to an individual under this policy.

Following a visit to a school, a Board member may have suggestions and feedback regarding the visit. Recognizing that the Superintendent directs the work of staff, pursuant to F.S. 1001.51 and 1012.27(7), the Board member's feedback should be directed to the Superintendent, who will share it with staff, as appropriate. (See Bylaw 0149.3 *Board-Staff Communication*)

Revised 10/24/22

Adoption Date: **April 25, 2018**
Last Revised: **October 24, 2022**

Source: www.SDIRC.org

These visuals are easy to recognize and understand. To learn more about measures, members should use this excellent resource: the Safety and Governance Guide created by the California School Board Association (CSBA) for their members. Although it dates back to 2011, it continues to cover many topics that are relevant to current discussions. ***Scan the QR code for a guide on SAFE SCHOOLS: Strategies for Governing Boards.***

School Hardening

The board is responsible for ensuring schools have adequate defense mechanisms to prevent unauthorized intrusions and mitigate internal safety. The safety plan can identify soft and complex solutions such as perimeter fencing, secured and monitored entry points, metal detectors, and visible school resource officers on campuses. An emergency alert system can be installed to notify the campus of intruders or other critical situations.

Processes and Procedures

Safety plans should include regular drills to ensure students and staff know how to respond appropriately to emergencies. The board and superintendent should actively collaborate with law enforcement to conduct campus drills. Districts can establish a system for reporting. This will provide an understanding of any shortcomings during drills and a comprehensive process for ensuring issues are followed up and resolved.

Law Enforcement Relationships

Local law enforcement agencies must be involved in developing the safety plan and practicing drills. The superintendent should plan walkthroughs with law enforcement to familiarize them with the campuses and buildings. This collaboration can include local law enforcement, sheriff and city police chiefs, a safety team, the superintendent, and the board. ***Scan the QR code to read the President's Commission on Law Enforcement and Administration of Justice report on school shootings July 22, 2020.***

Setting Expectations

Regarding the critical issue of school safety, the board must take the lead in planning discussions and monitoring the procedures and protocols implemented by the superintendent. It is essential to conduct safety meetings with the superintendent, key safety staff, and local law enforcement. These meetings should be held as closed-door sessions due to their sensitive nature. It is advisable to refrain from publicizing these discussions during action agenda items when approving safety measures and plans. While transparency is vital in most areas, revealing vulnerabilities in safety protocols can undermine the effectiveness of safety measures, especially when unknown observers may be present.

To emphasize the importance of safety, board leadership will promote a culture that prioritizes keeping kids safe within the community and the school district. Everyone involved must be held accountable for maintaining safety standards, whether a disgruntled parent is trying to use the back gate for convenience, a negligent teacher fails to keep classroom doors locked, or an administrator hesitates to interrupt the learning environment with necessary safety drills.

Treating active shooter drills with the same seriousness and frequency as fire and tornado drills is imperative. Given the current climate, districts must learn from the tragic events of school shootings. The board's role is vital in mitigating loss of life and preparing the district for the reality that such incidents may occur in one of their schools.

While no school board wants to believe it will experience such a crisis, the risk increases when a comprehensive safety plan is not in place. Actively practicing and implementing drills can significantly enhance preparedness. Each shooting incident offers essential lessons that can help improve a district's response. Although it may be uncomfortable to contemplate, planning for these scenarios is essential to ensure the safety of students and staff.

Case Scenario: The Parkland, FL High School Shooting (2018)

On February 14, 2018, a previous student penetrated school security with a duffle bag of weapons and a massive amount of ammunition, resulting in the deaths of 17 individuals and injury to another 17. Numerous failures contributed to this horrific tragedy, highlighting the systematic issues that led to the loss of life.

In response to this shooting, the governor mandated that every school hire an armed security officer or guardian trained by law enforcement. While it's uncertain if or when such incidents will occur again, one thing is clear: **the faster a shooter is neutralized, the more lives can be saved**.

The board's role during the planning phase led to catastrophic failures. The situation surrounding their school resource officer revealed that he panicked and had been ill-prepared. Significant delays in the security camera feeds compounded this issue, severely hindering the ability to track the shooter for outside law enforcement entering the campus. Furthermore, the lack of effective communication with multiple city and county law enforcement agencies revealed considerable disorganization in response efforts. These problems were entirely avoidable with proper planning and foresight.

In 2022, after a four-year investigation, a report was released that resulted in the Governor of Florida removing four remaining school board members from that period for several reasons, including malfeasance, neglect of duty, and failure to perform their responsibilities. The report is a grim reminder to all board members on how complacency can lead to mass casualties. ***Scan the QR code to read the full report by the Marjory Stoneman Douglas Safety Commission.***

Case Scenario: Uvalde, TX Elementary School Shooting (2022)

On May 24, 2022, a perpetrator gained access to the school through an unlocked side gate, which ultimately led to the tragic shooting of 19 students and two teachers and injury of 17 others. Investigations into this incident revealed "systemic failures and egregious poor decision-making" by law enforcement, who did not follow their active shooter training protocols. This situation highlighted the urgent importance of following safety protocols on school campuses and the need for effective planning and rehearsing response protocols. Under extreme stress, quick decision-making becomes critical, and regular drills will prepare staff for such high-pressure scenarios. ***Scan the QR code to read the Texas House of Representatives Interim Report 2022.***

Case Scenario: Apalachee, GA High School Shooting (2024)

On September 4, 2024, a shooter entered the school armed with a knife and an assault rifle, killing two students and two staff members. Had metal detectors been installed, this incident could have potentially been prevented. However, the rapid response was facilitated by a wearable panic button that a teacher activated. The school had a comprehensive plan in place, collaborated with law enforcement and school resource officers, and conducted drills, which significantly reduced the loss of life. From the time the teacher's panic button was initiated to the first shot, the school resource officer was able to intervene within 8 minutes. Because of the active planning of this school board and district planning, lives were saved, unlike the previous case scenarios where the perpetrator had unprecedented time to commit a mass carnage of life. ***Scan the QR code to read the Georgia Bureau of Investigation (GBI) Report.***

7. Safety Dates & Activities

Important School Safety Dates & Activities that School Board Members Should Be Aware of:

Board members must be proactive in staying informed when it comes to campus safety.

1. Are the upcoming school safety review meetings on the board's calendar?
2. When was the last time the board reviewed the school safety plan with district staff and law enforcement?
3. What is the total budgeted amount allocated this school year for the school district's overall safety plan?
4. The local law enforcement familiar with your campuses? Have they conducted active shooter drills on your campuses? Does law enforcement have a detailed map for each campus and building in your district?
5. How many active shooter drills does your district conduct in a school year?
6. When are these drills conducted? Beginning of the school year? Each Quarter? Random times?
7. Are your substitute teachers and temporary staff required to take active drill training?

Board Member's Exercises — **Exercise 7**

Student Code of Conduct

The Student Code of Conduct (SCC) is an essential planning tool to help mitigate campus security and safety issues. The board, in setting policies, should address critical matters such as bullying, harassment, and fighting. This will establish clear expectations for students regarding safety protocols. Boards are presented with a SCC for annual approval (best practices), typically developed through committee meetings involving various stakeholders in the district. District staff guide the review process and propose all recommendations to the superintendent. If the superintendent approves these, they will be placed on the agenda for final approval by the board. However, before approving the code, the member is responsible for reviewing and seeking legal counsel to ensure it complies with applicable laws and does not conflict with existing board policies. If conflicts are identified, the board must address the conflicts before passing any new policies.

The SCC policy provides overarching controls for addressing safety and security issues within the school environment.

A lack of discipline, clear consequences, and adequate support systems can lead to an unsafe learning environment, diminishing students' and staff's sense of security. This lack of structure can also contribute to teacher burnout, as educators may struggle to teach effectively in an environment that lacks the necessary systems and support.

Students who experience heightened fears regarding their safety are likely to exhibit increased absenteeism. Use this to recognize the formulation and monitoring of these policies fall under your responsibilities and authorities and should not be delegated or taken lightly. This is not an area in which you can afford to be complacent.

One can never over-plan or over-emphasize the importance of safety. As the governing board, members are responsible for devising and funding safety measures while reviewing policies to support these plans. Establish a hotline for reporting safety concerns and suggestions, and ensure regular closed-door strategy sessions are held with the board, superintendent, key staff, and law enforcement for routine reviews.

The student code of conduct is an enforceable document that provides overarching guidelines for addressing safety and security issues. A lack of discipline and clearly defined consequences can lead to an unsafe learning environment, negatively impacting student well-being and teacher morale.

In addition, take the time to invest in learning about and monitoring the school district's safety plans and student code of conduct. A safe environment enables students to focus on learning. When rules, expectations, and consequences are articulated, teachers believe they are supported and valued in their professional role as educators rather than simply caretakers.

Chapter 40

Examining Political Cultural Issues in Schools

This section focuses on Critical Race Theory (CRT), an ideology that has been evoked by Diveristy, Equity, and Inclusion (DEI) and Anti-Racism initiatives within school districts, is a key example to illustrate how politically charged issues can undermine the culture and climate within public education. As school board members, it is vital to recognize that while students struggle with foundational skills such as reading, writing, and basic math, the discourse surrounding issues like CRT consumes valuable resources and attention away from teaching and learning.

The quality of education delivered to students rests on the board's shoulders. They must choose whether to become entangled in political debate or prioritize the education of students. Parents send their children to school for an education, and it is not the role of the board, district, or teacher to decide which political stance is correct. Instead, it is imperative that board members understand these issues and proactively mitigate their impact on the district through funding, policies, protocols, training, and attitudes. Decisions will directly affect the culture and climate of the community and school district. The Loudoun County School Board is a poignant example of what to do—and what not to do.

Case in Point

Since the COVID-19 pandemic, many parents across the United States have become increasingly concerned about their children's education and the curriculum being taught in schools. A significant source of dissatisfaction originally stems from implementing Critical Race Theory (CRT). Parents view CRT as concerning because it suggests the country is inherently racist and its institutions are irredeemably biased; that race will always play a role in students' everyday lives.

Parents have been vocal in demanding transparency from school board officials regarding CRT materials. Many scrutinize educational materials, insisting culture wars should not be a primary focus. School districts that dismiss these concerns risk losing students and experiencing significant enrollment declines, particularly in states with school choice options.

Understanding Critical Race Theory

CRT emerged in the post-civil rights era. It was developed by scholars like Derrick Bell, who sought to highlight systemic racism within American institutions, laws, and policies. Bell's perspective included skepticism about the effectiveness of landmark civil rights rulings like the 1954 case Brown v. Board of Education, which laid the groundwork for CRT and challenged the foundations of traditional civil rights discourse.

Critics of CRT argue that similar to Marxism, which divides people by class, CRT divides people by race. They contend that this division undermines the progress made toward racial equality and promotes a narrative of oppression rather than unity.

CRT advocates prioritize equity over equality, arguing for systemic changes to ensure equal outcomes among racial groups. This perspective has permeated various aspects of society, including K-12 education. Efforts have led to prioritizing equity initiatives that often overshadow the traditional concept of equality under the law. Critics warn that such approaches risk dividing students into arbitrary classifications, leading to government overreach.

Proponents argue that CRT questions the basis of equality and legal reasoning, moving beyond incremental progress to challenge the liberal order itself.

Opposing Beliefs

Parents

Many parents advocate for a truthful representation of history while recognizing the United States has an imperfect past. They emphasize the importance of teaching about historical injustices, such as slavery and Jim Crow laws, while also celebrating milestones like the Civil Rights Act of 1964, which aimed to eliminate discrimination based on race or ethnicity.

Opponents of CRT express concerns that certain associated practices, such as "privilege walks" or differential treatment based on race, violate the 14th Amendment, the Equal Protection Clause, and other civil rights laws. They argue these practices undermine progress since the Civil Rights Act and divert attention from the foundational principles of equality before the law.

Source: www.PennLive.com

Further Concerns from Opponents

CRT has several opponents ingrained in the education system. Though CRT has been in higher education for decades, it has recently filtered down into government training and K-12 education. This has allowed state and national organizations to promote CRT ideology and other ideologies that do not support learning and continue to cause division.

Trump (45) Administration

In September 2020, the Trump administration directed federal agencies to halt racial sensitivity training that covers topics such as white privilege and critical race theory, terming them as "divisive, anti-American propaganda."

In a letter to federal agencies, the director of the Office of Management and Budget (OMB), Russell Vought, stated the memo includes the following key points:

"All agencies are directed to begin to identify all contracts or other agency spending related to any training on 'critical race theory,' 'white privilege,' or any other training or propaganda effort that teaches or suggests either (1) that the United States is an inherently racist or evil country or (2) that any race or ethnicity is inherently racist or evil."

Trump (47) Administration

The latest update as of publication. On February 14, 2025, the acting US Assistant Secretary for Civil Rights issued a four-page "Dear Colleague" letter warning all educational institutions that receive federal funding to immediately halt all Diversity, Equity, and Inclusion (DEI) programs. Failure to comply could result in the loss of federal funding due to strict enforcement. ***Scan the QR code to read "Dear Colleague" letter***.

National Education Association

The National Education Association (NEA) is one of the biggest proponents of CRT. It has polarized itself with parents concerned about the ideological push into the classroom, making curriculum transparency even more critical.

Concerns arise from messaging put forth by the NEA. The organization claims it is working tirelessly to address these issues. They speak of dismantling systems of oppression that prevent children from accessing a tremendous public education because of race, gender, sexual orientation, culture, or nationality.

American Federation of Teachers

The American Federation of Teachers (AFT) is an influential teachers' union that has also been a leading proponent of CRT. Randi Weingarten, the current president, has come out in full support of teachers disciplined for teaching CRT outside of state and local guidelines and laws. Weingarten said, "Mark my words: Our union will defend any member who gets in trouble for teaching honest history.... Teaching the truth is not radical or wrong. Distorting history and threatening educators for telling the truth is what is truly radical and wrong." The advocates of CRT often claim it is simply about teaching history -- or even worse -- that those who oppose CRT want to suppress history.

Social and Emotional Learning

Opponents also express concerns about Social and Emotional Learning (SEL), claiming it serves as a vehicle for ideological teaching under the guise of promoting emotional intelligence. They argue SEL can usurp parental roles by addressing issues related to race and class status in ways families should manage. Opponents assert that while SEL may have positive intentions, it extends beyond basic childhood development. The ideology encroaches on values that should be taught within the family.

Professional Development

Teachers and administrators are not immune to this ideology. While the board should not support or promote a particular issue, it must also be mindful not to fund memberships or pay for professional development with associations or organizations that focus on political matters rather than improving skills.

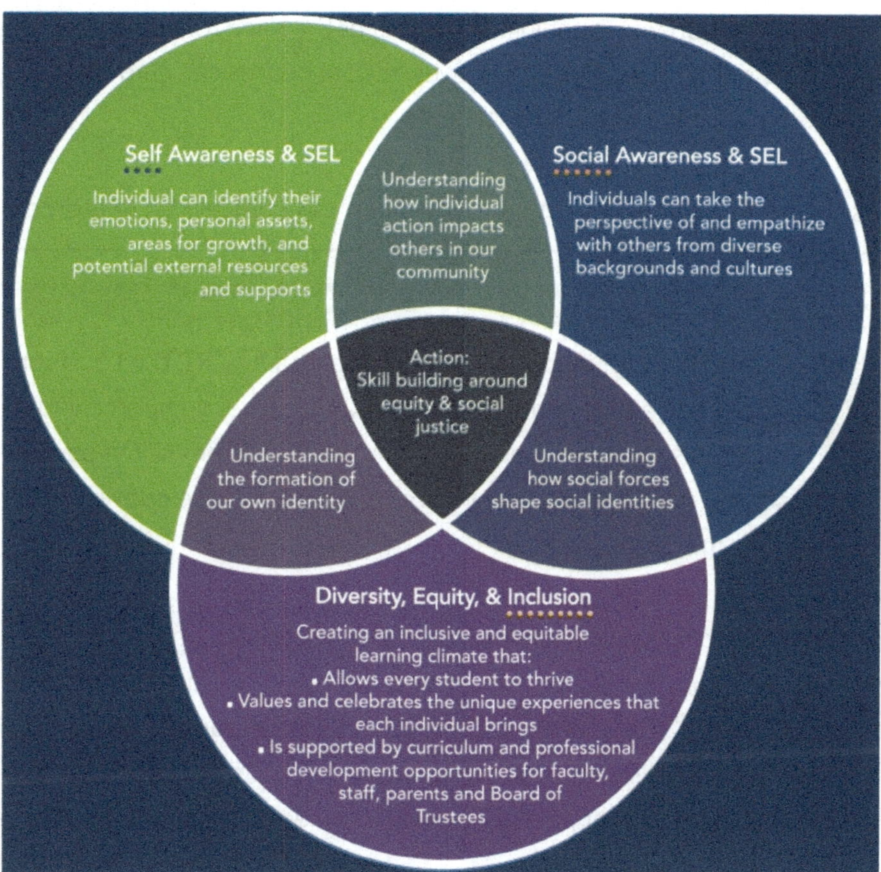

Source: Forest Ridge School of Sacred Heart

The Board's Role

Public statements from influential organizations, such as the NEA and AFT, create uncertainty among parents. As school board members, the primary responsibility is to ensure the learning environment remains free from political ideologies that compromise the educational experience.

The CRT example highlights a nationally divisive issue, but similar debates arise locally. Without boards creating a safe learning environment for all students, public trust in schools will continue to erode.

When adults disagree over educational content, parents must have the ultimate say in what their children are taught, regardless of differing beliefs. Board members must work diligently to rebuild trust to prevent divisive ideology from influencing the educational experience.

The district comprises a diverse population of Republican, Democrat, and Independent parents. Recent elections illustrate a nation divided, with voters fluctuating between parties. Parents are increasingly choosing to homeschool or enroll their children in private schools. The reasons are not due to facility issues or the food served in the cafeteria but because they oppose the political agendas. Earning parents' trust is essential to cultivating a climate that respects diverse beliefs and opinions by keeping these discussions out of the schools.

School board members are at the forefront of shaping the educational environment when addressing politically sensitive topics like CRT. It is important to focus on a student's academic needs rather than engage in political disputes that distract from the primary goal of education. Recognizing and addressing parents' concerns is a mandate for building trust within the community.

The conversations surrounding CRT highlight the need for transparency and open communication. By genuinely considering parents' perspectives, school boards can cultivate a respectful atmosphere that enhances the learning experience for all students.

As you contemplate these insights, consider how choices can reinforce or weaken trust in board leadership.

Case Scenario: The Polarization of Divisive Issues

In 2021, despite mounting concerns regarding CRT, the Loudoun County, VA School Board allocated nearly half a million dollars to programs addressing perceived systemic bias and oppression. These initiatives included coaching and training sessions some parents feared would further polarize the school environment. Many parents believed these conversations should remain discussions within families, not in school curricula.

In response to the pushback, Loudoun County school board members publicly expressed frustration on social media, urging colleagues to "call out statements and actions that undermine our stated plan to end systemic racism." This call to action escalated into a troubling practice: Teachers and community members began compiling a list of parents who opposed the district's focus on CRT. The list contained personal information about parents and created an atmosphere of fear, intimidation, and anger among the community.

As parents felt threatened and marginalized, their confidence in the board's commitment to providing a collaborative educational environment diminished, fracturing the sense of community and rippling distrust across the country.

Reflection Questions for School Board Members

Restoring Trust: How can the school board work to rebuild trust with parents who feel alienated by the actions of the school board member? What steps can be taken to ensure all voices are heard and valued in the decision-making process?

Encouraging Constructive Dialogue: What strategies can the board implement to promote respectful and constructive dialogue with parents? How can board members facilitate discussions that allow for differing opinions without resorting to divisive tactics?

Protecting All: What measures can the board take to protect the privacy and safety of students and parents who may feel targeted for their views? How can the board create a culture of respect and security within the school community?

Chapter 41
Equality vs. Equity

Framing Conversations

First, let's clarify and differentiate these two terms by exploring their meanings and their significant implications in K-12 education, particularly concerning policy, funding, and setting priorities. Remember the original intent discussed in the Critical Race Theories practicum as you read through this.

Equality as a Meritocratic Framework

Equality of opportunity is based on the belief that everyone should have equal chances to succeed, regardless of their background. This idea suggests talent varies among individuals, and recognizing and nurturing that talent is important for both personal and societal advancement. It argues no one should encounter obstacles to progress based solely on arbitrary characteristics unrelated to their abilities or merit. This principle aligns with meritocratic ideals, promoting success based on skills and contributions and a culture that values productivity and personal development.

Courts Reward High Education Merit-Based System

In June 2023, the US Supreme Court ruled against race-conscious admissions at colleges and universities, effectively dismantling affirmative action. Whether race or ethnicity should factor into admissions processes has been a contentious issue in higher education for decades.

On June 29, 2023, the Supreme Court deemed the intentional use of race in college admissions unconstitutional, particularly at Harvard University and the University of North Carolina (UNC) at Chapel Hill.

These challenges were brought before the court in October 2022 in two cases: *Students for Fair Admissions v. President and Fellows of Harvard College* and *Students for Fair Admissions v. University of North Carolina*. The lawsuits contend race-inclusive admission policies discriminated against Asian American applicants and, in the case of UNC, also White students.

Equity Original Intent

As defined by the National Equity Project, educational equity means every child receives the necessary resources to reach their full academic and social potential. Equity in education involves providing all students with the tools, opportunities, and support needed to fulfill their potential, regardless of socioeconomic background, race, ethnicity, gender identity, sexual orientation, or other factors that may contribute to educational disparities. Its goal was to level the playing field and close the achievement gap, ensuring every student has a fair chance to succeed.

However, the original intent has taken on various meanings within public education, and the term "equity" can be particularly contentious. While it is often promoted as a solution to address disparities in educational

outcomes, the concept has ignited intense debates among educators, policymakers, and parents. Although the intentions may be commendable, the implementation and interpretation of equity have resulted in a divided educational landscape. The following section explores the overreaches and ineffective solutions related to underperformance in the name of "equity" in public education. ***Scan the QR code to read the Opinion of the Supreme Court of the United States.***

Critique of Equity in its Implementation

Concerns about equity stem from differing interpretations of its meaning and application within educational systems. Equity was intended to focus on interventions and investments in disadvantaged communities to support marginalized students. However, school boards frequently resort to forced redistribution of resources and opportunities, which can negatively impact high-performing schools and students. This approach raises important questions about the effectiveness of equity initiatives. Achieving equitable outcomes without compromising the quality of education for others has become a significant challenge in discussing equity in education.

Reality of Implementation

A notable concern is the potential for discrimination. Some equity initiatives may prioritize specific groups to correct imbalances, leading to resentment among those who perceive themselves as overlooked. Additionally, the emphasis on equal outcomes can be seen as conflicting with individual merit and hard work principles. Critics argue promoting equity in this manner may undermine the recognition of students' efforts and achievements, potentially lowering overall educational standards and promoting a culture where merit is not adequately rewarded.

The debate around equity also intertwines with discussions of personal responsibility. While some emphasize the impact of external factors on students' progress, others advocate for a focus on individual accountability and the development of essential life skills. Furthermore, equity-driven funding models have sparked considerable controversy; some view these models as a socialistic approach aimed at redistributing resources from those who have to those who do not. This raises further questions about allocating resources—whether they should be evenly distributed or directed toward schools with more significant needs. These issues highlight the complexities and challenges of implementing equity fairly and effectively.

The Paradox of Equity

For board members, pursuing diversity conflicts with equity goals. When diversity is appreciated for its unique talents and perspectives, promoting equity—where outcomes are expected to reflect demographic proportions—can undermine the differences that diversity aims to celebrate. This contradiction raises questions about the effectiveness of equity as a guiding principle, as true diversity may naturally lead to varied outcomes.

You may have encountered a graphic created originally by Craig Froehle in 2012, which aims to help people understand that treating everyone equally does not always lead to equity - equally. This graphic illustration is intended to prove the concept of systemic racism.

Source: Interaction Institute for Social Change | Artist: Angus Maguire, madewithangus.com

On the left side of the image, there is an illustration representing **equality**. It depicts three boxes, each with individuals of varying heights and sizes. The concept of **equity** is illustrated on the right side of the image. In this scenario, the shortest individual requires additional boxes to see over a fence, while the tallest person does not need any boxes. A person of medium height requires just one box to see over the fence. This representation of equity highlights the idea of reallocating resources, suggesting some individuals have advantages based on their height or, in broader terms, their skin color.

The board members' approach needs careful examination, especially in light of current trends in education. A larger portion of Americans than not disagree with this model as a solution for improving academic outcomes. This disagreement comes from the model that defines equity as the reallocation of resources, which contrasts with the notion that true success in a school district should uplift all students without penalizing those perceived to have advantages. Ideologies that were once only taught in the universities have now emerged over the last decade nationwide into public school curriculum and teacher training. What has played out in the national media these last few years is some boards are taking away opportunities and not adding new opportunities that would ultimately lead to lifting up all. And, in essence school districts neglect other important issues and prove to lead to negative consequences. This is evident in the board policy, as illustrated in the two cases highlighted below.

Case Scenario: Lowell High School

In October 2020, Lowell High School in San Francisco, a prestigious magnet school, transitioned from a merit-based admissions system to a lottery system. This change was made in response to claims of "pervasive systemic racism" and aimed to promote more significant equity, diversity, and inclusion. As of 2021, the school's student demographic makeup was 52.4% Asian, 17.7% Hispanic, 16.5% White, and 2.7% Black.

This shift, intended to enhance diversity, ultimately led to a loss of opportunities for students. The school has recently reverted to a merit-based admissions system, meaning admissions will again be determined by grades and test scores instead of a lottery.

The decision by the San Francisco Unified School District to return to a merit-based system was sparked by some Asian parents, who believed the previous changes were unjust. They argued that merit should not be perceived as a form of racism.

Rather than focusing on preparing students from diverse backgrounds to perform at the same academic level as their peers, critics contended the school board was penalizing students who were admitted based on their natural abilities and achievements. The families and communities believe school boards should not take opportunities away from some students to fix broader educational disparities impact individuals of any race or socioeconomic status when the real solution lies in uplifting all students rather than reallocating resources from one group to another based on perceived inequalities—a common practice in the current emphasis on "equity."

Case Scenario: Thomas Jefferson High School for Science and Technology

Thomas Jefferson High School for Science and Technology, known for being one of the top public schools in the U.S., located in Alexandria, VA, has experienced a notable decline in academic achievement since it revised its admissions standards to pursue racial equity.

In 2020, school leaders began analyzing the underrepresentation of Black and Hispanic students at the magnet school and discussed how to move "toward greater equity, clearly distinguished from equality." Soon after, the school updated its competitive admissions process by replacing standardized tests with a holistic evaluation. This new approach considered factors such as attendance at underrepresented middle schools and eligibility for free lunch—criteria critics have labeled as racial proxies.

The new policy removed the previous reliance on standardized tests for filtering applicants. Instead, specific slots were allocated to each of the 28 middle schools that feed into Thomas Jefferson. Applicants are evaluated based on their grade point average (a minimum of 3.5), a "portrait sheet" outlining their skills, a problem-solving essay, and four experience factors. These "experience factors" include eligibility for free or reduced-price meals, status as an English Language Learner, eligibility for special education services, and attendance at a historically underrepresented public middle school. Essentially, these factors consider a student's socioeconomic status, English language proficiency, special needs, and whether they attended a school with a historically low number of students advancing to Thomas Jefferson.

Before the new admissions criteria were implemented, students of Asian-American descent represented three-quarters of Thomas Jefferson's overall enrollment. After the board adopted the new admission policy, the percentage of Asian students admitted to the school dropped from 73 to 54 percent.

Resources and students were reallocated in this situation, but the underlying issue was not addressed. The drop in national ranking suggests that while the student population has become more diverse, the quality of learning has not kept up.

Notes

Chapter 42
Curriculum Transparency Builds Trust

Transparency between board members and the parents is equally important. School districts frequently leave parents uninformed about the materials used in classrooms to educate students. Across K-12 schools nationwide, politically charged content is increasingly replacing academically rigorous, neutral instruction.

In response, state lawmakers in North Carolina, Arizona, Illinois, Texas, and Wyoming attempted to pass common-sense academic transparency bills requiring public schools to disclose classroom assignments. Unfortunately, none of these bills passed due to pushback from teachers' unions, special interest groups, and district administrators. However, boards can have home rules and pass policies to address the mistrust.

Opponents of these transparency measures argue they would create an administrative burden, forcing more teachers to leave the profession. They also claim they could breed distrust, encourage parental micromanagement, and stifle creativity in teaching. Indeed, K-12 educators often find themselves underpaid and overworked. However, greater transparency and cooperation between educators, parents, and communities help rebuild strained relationships.

Transparency Policies

Nicole Solas, a mother from Rhode Island, faced legal action from the National Education Association (NEA) for her persistent efforts to obtain information on the curriculum taught in her child's school. Concerned about topics addressed in the classroom, Solas filed over 200 public records requests after the school refused to answer her questions. Initially requesting a copy of the curriculum, her inquiries expanded to include emails between school officials, teachers, and union members.

The NEA's lawsuit sought to block the release of certain records, citing concerns over teacher privacy, while also requesting a judicial review of the public interest in these documents. Solas argued government employees, such as teachers, should not be immune from public scrutiny, stressing academic transparency is a parental right. School districts, however, have attempted to hinder similar efforts by increasing public record request fees. Despite this, Solas remained determined to uncover what her child is being taught, emphasizing the importance of transparency in education.

As school board members, we can help parents like Nicole by adopting an Academic Transparency policy so parents don't have to wonder or file public record requests to learn what their children are being taught daily. A model policy developed by the Goldwater Institute is available online. ***Scan the QR code to read Goldwater Institute's Academic Transparency Act Model Policy.***

Implementing this policy is straightforward and practical. District and school leadership can devise simple strategies for educators to post their learning materials online without adding extra burdens. Doing so can restore trust in our educational communities. Additionally, an online repository of course materials would allow educators to easily access successful resources from colleagues statewide, enhancing collaboration and professional development.

This approach would eliminate debates about divisive lessons, as the teaching materials would speak for themselves. Transparency would also let parents see whether their local schools are focused on academic excellence or activism, enabling them to make informed decisions about their children's education.

Enacting an academic transparency policy will hold schools accountable for what they teach, ensuring nothing is hidden. Parents would gain peace of mind knowing what their children are learning, while teachers would benefit from collaboration. This step offers school boards a powerful opportunity to lead and rebuild trust in the education system.

Student Enrollment Decline

Parents are so concerned about what their children are being taught that many are pulling their children out of the school district to homeschool or enroll them in a private school where they feel more comfortable with the curriculum. Personal ideologies do not have a place in the classroom or curriculum, and if parents are not given transparency, it could lead to a climate of distrust. Superintendents are eager to keep enrollment numbers up, and this is one of many actions you can take to address the issue of families leaving.

Chapter 43
Adapting to Change

School board members must shed the notion they are the sole providers of K-12 education. Just as corporate giants like Sears once seemed untouchable, so public school districts face a reckoning if they fail to adapt to the rise of school choice. Examining 10 iconic companies that fell victim to disruption provides a sobering parallel to the challenges facing today's school boards. Give your families a reason to stay and avoid the pitfalls that drive them away. Understanding the impact of a positive culture and climate is a powerful tool to ensure they don't leave; the same goes for your employees.

The stark reality is that 88% of Fortune 500 firms from 1955 no longer exist. This is a severe warning that even the most dominant organizations can quickly become irrelevant if they refuse to innovate. This same dynamic is unfolding in the education sector, where the growth of charter schools, private schools, and homeschooling is challenging the traditional public school model.

Many public school districts have been slow to recognize the threat posed by alternative education providers, much like how Blockbuster dismissed Netflix as a "small niche." Like Blockbuster, they risk missing the opportunity to adapt and innovate before it's too late. The Blockbuster CEO's dismissive attitude toward a new, emerging business model mirrors public school leaders' resistance toward school choice.

Representing the Entire Community

Board members must remember they have been elected to represent the interests of the entire community, not just those of district employees and traditional public school parents. While your primary role is to govern the school district, you also have a responsibility to make decisions that serve the needs of all students and families, including those who have chosen options outside the district.

This means shedding the mindset that school board members are elected solely to represent the district's interests. Your constituents include district staff and public school parents, taxpayers, senior citizens, young adults without children, homeschool parents, and families who have chosen private or charter schools. Failing to recognize this broader responsibility is a false premise.

Overcoming the Resistance to Change

Embracing school choice does not mean abandoning your commitment to public education. Instead, it represents an opportunity to strengthen your district by attracting back students and families seeking alternatives. Isolating themselves and promoting only their schools reflects a counterproductive, fear-based mindset.

In contrast, school districts and boards celebrating educational freedom for families symbolize a community that values every child's uniqueness. These inclusive approaches are a chance to attract new students and regain the trust of those who have left.

Governing with a sense of responsibility that "all means all" will build a culture of trust. When parents know their ability to choose the best educational path for their child is not a threat but a point of pride, they are more likely to remain engaged with the district.

Respecting Family Traditions and Beliefs

It's important to recognize the decision to leave a public school district is often rooted in deeply held family traditions and beliefs, not just the availability of school choice options. Many parents want their children to attend the same schools they did, with the same teachers, coaches, and extracurricular programs.

For example, in states like Texas and Kentucky, families are examples where the traditions and pride associated with their local public schools outweigh school choice measures. Overcoming this attachment can be challenging, even when alternative options are available.

Similarly, parents may leave a district if they feel their religious or political beliefs are not respected. These issues have driven a wedge between families and their local schools, leaving them with little choice but to seek alternatives.

As a board member, you must be willing to honor these family traditions and beliefs rather than imposing policies and practices that conflict with them, regardless of political affiliation. By doing so, you can build trust and demonstrate the district values each student and family's unique needs and preferences.

Embracing the School Choice Movement

School board members have a critical role in improving education for all students across the district. Embracing the school choice movement can benefit your entire community, but it requires a fundamental shift in mindset and approach.

The first step is to create a culture where parents are viewed as valued customers rather than adversaries. Your district should strive to provide a safe, nurturing environment and a quality education that meets the diverse needs of all students. When families see their child's well-being is the top priority, trust will be built and maintained.

For example, when hosting school choice fairs, open the doors to the entire educational ecosystem – including charters, private schools, and homeschool groups. This unlocks an opportunity to re-engage with students and families who have sought alternatives. These events demonstrate a willingness to collaborate and celebrate the freedom of educational choice.

EMBRACING SCHOOL CHOICE

Board members can take the following steps to embrace school choice and prevent further student attrition:

01 Maintain open communication with private, homeschool, and charter school families. Seek to understand their needs and concerns and demonstrate a willingness to work

02 Ensure your decision-making process considers the interests of all children in your constituency, not just those enrolled in district schools.

03 Hire a superintendent who honors and respects parents' rights to choose the learning environment that best fits their child's needs.

04 Set clear expectations with the superintendent that the district will cultivate a culture supportive of school choice.

05 Include non-traditional schools and students when setting legislative priorities and advocating for funding and resources.

06 Implement policies that require the district to provide families with comprehensive information about all available school choice options, including charters, private schools, and homeschooling. Consider hosting an annual School Choice Fair to showcase these alternatives.

The stakes are high, given the rise of school choice and a shift in the political landscape. Public school districts that fail to adapt to the post-COVID-19 landscape and the growing school choice movement risk becoming the next Blockbuster or Kodak – relics of a bygone era. As a board member, you can shape the future of public education in your community. Embrace a culture of innovation, constantly reinvent your district, and be willing to take bold steps to stay relevant and serve all students and families. Failure to do so could lead to a fate similar to the cautionary tales outlined.

Strategies to Win Back Families

Here are some key ways school boards can effectively communicate and collaborate with families who have chosen alternatives to traditional public schools:

Open and Ongoing Communication

- Establish regular communication channels with private, charter, and homeschool families to understand their needs and concerns.
- Host town halls, forums, and listening sessions for these families to provide input and feedback.
- Ensure district communication materials and outreach efforts include information on all available educational options, not just district schools.

Collaborative Partnerships

- Invite representatives from charter, private, and homeschool groups to participate in district-level planning and decision-making.
- Explore opportunities for shared professional development, resource-sharing, and co-programming between the district and alternative providers.
- Establish memoranda of understanding to facilitate collaboration and coordination on transportation, facility usage, and special education services.

Demonstrate Respect and Choice Inclusion

- Acknowledge and honor the diverse educational preferences and beliefs of all families in the community.
- Ensure board policies and practices do not disadvantage or discriminate against students in alternative settings.
- Celebrate student successes in private, charter, and homeschool environments and those in district schools.

Improve School Choice Information and Access

- Provide comprehensive, user-friendly information about all school choice options, including application processes and funding mechanisms.

- Host annual school choice fairs where families can learn about and connect with various educational providers.
- Ensure district staff are knowledgeable about school choice and can guide families through the selection process.

School boards can build trust and strengthen relationships with families who have opted out of the traditional public school system by embracing open communication, collaborative partnerships, respect for diverse educational preferences, and improved access to school choice information. This inclusive approach can attract and retain students while strengthening the entire community's academic outcomes.

Notes

Conclusion: **Stay the Course**

We hope you've found this book informative and inspiring. There is a lot of information to digest, and we understand the weight of this information can feel heavy, especially when faced with the realities of board service. Yet, amid all this, there's a vital message we want to leave you with: **Stay the Course.**

It's important to acknowledge burnout is a real and formidable challenge. Many of you may stand against the giants of bureaucracy, budget cuts, and community expectations. There may be days when you feel exhausted, overwhelmed, and ready to throw in the towel. But we urge you: **don't give up**. Every day you serve on the board, you have the opportunity to profoundly impact students' lives. Every decision you make contributes to their future. Every challenge you face is an opportunity to advocate for change.

The extensive knowledge shared throughout this book comes from over 40 years of board experience, wisdom, and lessons learned from the highs and lows of school board leadership and governance. We often don't know what we need until we need it, so we encourage you to refer back to this resource as frequently as necessary during your board journey.

The Importance of Your Role

We often hear the phrase, "It's for the kids," and it rings true now more than ever. Each child in your community deserves a chance to achieve the American dream, and your leadership plays a fundamental role in making that a reality. Consider this: the legacies of these children are being written right now, and you are an integral part of that story. Every time you sit at the board dais, you are not just a decision-maker but a champion for the next generation.

Navigating the complexities of a divided board can be daunting, especially when representing a minority opinion. Feeling isolated and frustrated is common when your insights seem lost amid dominant voices. However, please remember that perseverance can lead to meaningful change. You have the unique opportunity to influence initiatives and decisions far beyond your vote.

Strategies for Success

1. **Build Alliances:** Actively seek opportunities to forge strong relationships within the board and reach beyond it to form connections with trusted external networks, such as state coalitions and advocacy groups. This approach broadens your understanding of the issues at stake and creates a robust support network that can amplify your voice and help champion change on both state and local levels.

2. **Never Burn Bridges:** Cultivate a reputation of professionalism and approachability. Board dynamics can shift unexpectedly due to resignations, elections, or changes in focus. Maintaining positive relationships with all members despite your vote and views can position you favorably for the future. A contentious topic may arise that divides the board, allowing you to forge alliances that can strengthen your influence in decision-making.

3. **Leverage Your Perspective:** Your unique background and experience can offer invaluable insights that challenge the status quo. Use your viewpoint to propose innovative solutions and unveil opportunities others may have overlooked. This approach can showcase your leadership qualities and inspire constructive discussions that drive the organization forward.

4. **Communicate Effectively**: The ability to articulate your ideas clearly and confidently can improve board discussions. Tailor your message to resonate with your fellow members, ensuring your points align with the organization's presentation of your thoughts. This can capture attention and give you greater understanding and support.

5. **Attack Issues, Not Board Members:** Focus on the issues at hand rather than the personal shortcomings of fellow board members to cultivate an environment of respect and professionalism. Your authority doesn't require aggression; simply present your case cohesively and knowledgeably. Demonstrating a deep understanding of the subject matter will foster trust and mutual respect, even among those who may disagree with you.

6. **Focus on Data-Driven Decision-Making:** Come to meetings and discussions overprepared. Support your proposals with credible data and thorough research. Providing tangible evidence of your suggestions' potential impact enhances their likelihood of adoption. This emphasis on factual information can strengthen your arguments and persuade others to consider your perspective seriously.

7. **Stay Resilient:** Advocating for your beliefs and students as a minority member can be challenging. Maintaining resilience means navigating setbacks and frustrations. Use the setbacks presented by difficult situations as learning opportunities and remain steadfast in your commitment to your goals.

8. **Pick Your Battles:** Being a board member, particularly as a minority, requires strategic thinking when choosing which issues to advocate for fervently. By selectively choosing your battles, you can maximize your impact on board decisions while safeguarding your energy and motivation over time. This strategy allows you to stay focused and effective in your efforts.

Implementing these comprehensive strategies can significantly contribute to the objectives that resonate with you, ultimately supporting the board's success and growth. Your voice matters; you can create the lasting change you campaigned for with determination and strategic planning.

Embracing the Future

Looking ahead, the education landscape is evolving, and with that comes opportunities and challenges. Shifts in the national election—aiming to return control to local jurisdictions—empower you to lead your community toward an educational system that prioritizes your students in your community. Your leadership will ensure students meet academic standards and thrive beyond them, acquiring the skills necessary for success in their chosen paths.

We recognize the road ahead is not without its obstacles. The decline in academic performance within public schools and reduced funding due to students leaving districts present a formidable challenge. Yet, you have the tools and insights needed to turn the tide. Your leadership can drive excellence by applying your authority through accountability of the superintendent and their team, student-focused policies, and sound budgets. Don't shy away from school choice; it is here to stay. Successful districts will be the ones that embrace it as a pathway to empower families and enhance educational quality. When districts deliver, families will stay—it's that simple.

Commitment to Your Community

As you reflect on your commitments during your campaign, remember that your community is counting on you to fulfill those promises. Your students rely on you to secure the best teachers and educational resources, while the staff looks to you for fairness, transparency, and support. There has been a great awakening in our country since COVID-19 that finally realized the people they elected on the school board matter. The role of a school board member is crucial—not only for the present but also for the future of every child in your district.

All you were given was this term. Just to avoid scrutiny don't wait to do what you know needs to be done now. Avoid falling into that trap of making decisions based on your next election. Now is your time, and as the end of your term nears, you want to be able to look back with a sense of accomplishment, knowing you didn't waste time on the bureaucracy. Stand tall with integrity, lead with urgency, question with determination, and leave with no regrets.

A Call to Action

In closing, when in doubt or fatigued, we urge you to return to the very first chapter of this book to remember your "whys." Why did you run? What were your goals? What were your campaign promises?

Lastly, don't isolate yourself. When you join a community of like-minded school board members who share your passion for education, your focus will be sharpened. You will learn from others and realize the struggles or obstacles you are experiencing are not unique. You can gain valuable insights and support by connecting with those who have walked in your shoes. Being a school board member is not for the faint hearted. You do not have to do this alone. Know that you have "Best" friends rooting for your success – because our kids will be successful when you are successful. At www.BestInEd.org you can engage with fellow board members, participate in discussions, sign up for virtual or in-person professional learning sessions from Best In Ed Leadership Academy, be matched with a mentor, and connect to partner organizations in your state. ***Scan the QR code to learn more about Best In Ed's resources***

In the meantime, your legacy awaits. Stay steadfast in your commitment, and remember that the fruits of your labor and the seeds you sow today might not always be seen or appreciated. Don't let that deter you. Your work is taking root, changing lives, and creating lasting, purposeful change for this generation of young people. Stay the course, and show them they are worth the effort!

Appendix A: **School Board Members Roles and Authority by State**

SCHOOL BOARD MEMBERS ROLES AND AUTHORITY

STATE	FIRST	ARTICLE OR TITLE	BLAINE AMENDMENT LANGUAGE	STATUTES OR CODE	CONSTITUTION LINK	CODE/STATUTE LINK
Alabama	1819	Article XIV: Sections 256-270	Section 263	Title 16: Chapters 1-67		
Alaska	1959	Article VII: Sections 1-5	Section 1	Title 14: Chapters 3-60		
Arizona	1912	Article 11: Sections 1-11	Section 8	Title 15: Chapters 1-19		
Arkansas	1836	Article 14: Sections 1-4	None	Title 6: Subtitles 1-6		
California	1849	Article IX: Sections 1-16	Section 8	EDC: Titles 1-3		
Colorado	1876	Article IX: Sections 1-17	Section 7	Title 22: Articles 1-98		
Connecticut	1818	Article 8: Sections 1-4	None	Title 10: Chapters 163-184c		
Delaware	1897	Article 10: Sections 1-6	Section 3	Title 14: Chapters 1-94		
Florida	1838	Article IX: Sections 1-8	Section 6	Title XLVIII: Chapters 1000-1013		
Georgia	1777	Article VIII: Sections I-VII	Section VI	Title 20: Chapters 1-18		
Hawaii	1959	Article X: Sections 1-6	Section 1	Title 18: Chapters 296-319		

STATE	FIRST	ARTICLE OR TITLE	BLAINE AMENDMENT LANGUAGE	STATUTES OR CODE	CONSTITUTION LINK	CODE/STATUTE LINK
Idaho	1890	Article IX: Sections 1-11	Section 5	Title 33: Chapters 1-61		
Illinois	1818	Article X: Sections 1-3	Section 3	Chapter 105: Articles 1-36		
Indiana	1816	Article 8: Sections 1-8	Section 3	Title 20: Articles 1-51		
Iowa	1857	Article IX: 1st Sections 1-15; 2nd Sections 1-7	None	Title VII: Chapters 256-305B		
Kansas	1855	Article 6: Sections 1-7;	Section 6(c)	Chapter 72: Articles 1-99		
Kentucky	1792	Sections 183-189	Section 189	Title XIII: Chapters 156-170		
Louisiana	1812	Article VIII: Sections 1-16	None	Title 17: 17.1 - 17.5122		
Maine	1820	Article VIII. Part First: Sections 1-2	None	Title 20: Parts 1-6		
Maryland	1776	Article VIII: Sections 1-3	None	Sections 1-26		
Massachusetts	1780	Chapter V: Article I-III & Section II	N/A	Part 1: Title XII: Chapters 69-78A		
Michigan	1835	Article VIII: Sections 1-9	Section 2	Act 451-1976: Articles 1-4		
Minnesota	1857	Article XIII: Sections 1-3	Section 2	Chapters 120-137		
Mississippi	1817	Article 8: Sections 201-213B	Section 208	Title 37: Chapters 1-181		

STATE	FIRST	ARTICLE OR TITLE	BLAINE AMENDMENT LANGUAGE	STATUTES OR CODE	CONSTITUTION LINK	CODE/STATUTE LINK
Missouri	1820	Article IX: Sections 1-10	Section 8	Chapters 160-186		
Montana	1889	Article X: Sections 1-11	Section 6	Title 20: Chapters 1-32		
Nebraska	1875	Article VII: Sections 1-17	Section 11	Chapter 79: 101-2704		
Nevada	1864	Article 11: Sections 1-10	Section 10	Title 34: Chapters 385-400		
New Hampsire	1776	Part Second: Article 6-b	Article 83	Title XV: Chapters 186-200N		
New Jersey	1947	Article VIII: Section IV	None	Title 18A: Sections 1-66		
New Mexico	1911	Article XII: Sections 1-13	Section 3	Chapter 22: Articles 1-35		
New York	1777	Article XI: Sections 1-3	Section 3	EDN: Titles 1-9		
North Carolina	1776	Article IX: Sections 1-10	None	Chapter 115C: Sections 1-598		
North Dakota	1889	Article VIII: Sections 1-6	Section 5	Title 15.1: Chapters 1-38		
Ohio	1803	Article VI: Sections 1-6	Section 2 (IJ - none	Title 33: Chapters 01-85		
Oklahoma	1907	Article XIII: Sections 1-8	Section 1a	Title 70: 1-8005		
Oregon	1857	Article VIII: Sections 1-8	Sections 2 & 4	Volume 9: Chapters 326-365		

STATE	FIRST	ARTICLE OR TITLE	BLAINE AMENDMENT LANGUAGE	STATUTES OR CODE	CONSTITUTION LINK	CODE/STATUTE LINK
Pennsylvania	1776	Article IIIB: Sections 14-15	Section 15	Title 24: Parts I-VI		
Rhode Island	1790	Article XII: Sections 1-4	None	Title 16: Chapters 1-109		
South Carolina	1776	Article XI: Sections 1-4	Section 4	Title 59: Chapters 1-156		
South Dakota	1889	Article VIII: Sections 1-20	Section 16	Title 13: Chaptes 1-65		
Tennessee	1796	Article XI: Section 12	None	Title 49: Chapters 1-50		
Texas	1836	Article VII: Sections 1-20	Section 5	Titles 1-6		
Utah	1895	Article X: Sections 1-9	Section 9	Title 53B-G		
Vermont	1777	Chapater II: Section 68	None	Title 16: Chapters 1-133		
Virginia	1776	Article VIII: Sections 1-11	Section 10	Title 22.1: Chapters 1-25		
Washington	1889	Article IX: Sections 1-5	Section 4	Title 28A: Chapters 150-900		
West Virginia	1863	Article XII: Sections 1-12	None	Chapter 18: Articles 1-32		
Wisconsin	1848	Article X: Sections 1-8	Section 3	Chapters 115-121		
Wyoming	1889	Article 7: Sections 1-23	Section 8	Title 21: Chapters 1-24		

Glossary of Acronyms and Terms

K-12 Education Acronyms

504: Section 504 of the Rehabilitation Act
AA: Associate in Arts
AACC: American Association of Community Colleges
AAP: Affirmative Action Plan
AAPI: Asian American and Pacific Islander
AAS: Associate in Applied Science
AASA: American Association of School Administrators
AASPS: American Association of State Policy Services, affiliated with the National School Boards Association (NSBA)
AAV: Adjusted Assessed Valuation
ABE: Adult Basic Education
ACC: Articulation Coordinating Committee
ACE: Adult and Community Education or American Council of Education
ACEE: Area Centers for Educational Enhancement
ACENET: Adult and Community Education Network
ACF: Administration for Children and Families
ACRN: America's Career Resource Network
ACT: American College Testing
ACTE: Association for Career and Technical Education
ADA: Americans with Disabilities Act
ADHD: Attention Deficit/Hyperactivity Disorder
ADM: Average Daily Membership
AEA: Adult Education Act
AFDC: Aid to Families with Dependent Children
AG: Attorney General
AGE: Adult General Education
AHS: Adult High School
AJB: America's Job Bank
ALMIS: America's Labor Market Information System
ALP: Advanced Learning Programs
AP: Advanced Placement
AS: Associate in Science
ASE: Adult Secondary Education
ASET: Assistant Secretary of Employment and Training
ASL: America's Service Locator
ATD: Applied Technology Diploma
ATP: Adult Training Programs

BAT: Bureau of Apprenticeship and Training
BIPOC: Black, Indigenous, People/Person of Color
BLS: Bureau of Labor Statistics
BRG: Business Relations Group
BSL: Base Support Level
BYOD: Bring Your Device
CAA: College and Career Readiness
CAAHE: Council for Adult and Experiential Learning
CAEP: Council for the Accreditation of Educator Preparation
CAP: College Access Program
CAR: Comprehensive Assessment Report
CBE: Competency-Based Education
CC: Common Core
CCA: College and Career Awareness
CCE: Community Colleges of Education
CCL: Community College Learning
CCR: College and Career Readiness
CDA: Child Development Associate
CE: Continuing Education
CEM: Center for Educational Management
CED: Council for Education Development
CEP: Community Eligibility Provision
CF: Comprehensive Framework
CFS: Child and Family Services
CHAMP: Comprehensive Health and Mental Health Assessment and Management Program
CHIP: Children's Health Insurance Program
CIE: Center for Innovative Education
CITE: Center for Instructional Technology and Education
CLC: Community Learning Center
CLD: Culturally and Linguistically Diverse
CLP: Career Ladder Program
CMT: Comprehensive Monitoring Tool
CNE: Certified Nurse Educator
COT: Community Outreach Team
CRC: Career Resource Center
CTE: Career and Technical Education
CTP: Child Tax Credit Program
DAP: Developmentally Appropriate Practice
DBT: Dialectical Behavior Therapy

DAA: District Additional Assistance
DEI: Diversity, Equity, and Inclusion
DESE: Department of Elementary and Secondary Education
DOLETA: Department Of Labor Employment & Training Administration Federal
DOSO: Division of One-Stop Operations or One-Stop Division, part of the US Labor Employment & Training Administration
DSS: Department of Social Services
ECE: Early Childhood Education
EDIM: Education Data Integration Model
EEP: Extended Education Program
EFL: English as a Foreign Language
ELA: English Language Arts
ELD: English Language Development
ELL: English Language Learner
EL: English Learner
ELP: English Language Proficiency
EMIS: Education Management Information System
EOC: End-of-Course
EOG: End-of-Grade Assessment
EOP: Educational Opportunity Program
EP: Educational Plan
ESE: Exceptional Student Education
ESL: English as a Second Language Oral Assessment
ESOL: English for Speakers of Other Languages
ETA: Employment and Training Administration
ETAD: Employment Task Force for Adults with Disabilities
ETR: Educational Technology Resources
EZ: Enterprise Zone
FAPE: Free and Appropriate Public Education in IDEA
FERPA: Family Educational Rights and Privacy Act
FFL: Federal Family Education Loan
FSA: Free Application for Federal Student Aid
FRL: Free and Reduced Price Lunch
FTE: Full-Time Equivalent
FY: Fiscal Year
GED: General Education Diploma
GNP: Gross National Product
GPA: Grade Point Average
GSA: Government Services Administration
HHS: US Department of Health & Human Services

HQT: Highly Qualified Teacher
IAA: Individualized Assessment and Accountability
IB: International Baccalaureate
IDEA: Individuals with Disabilities Education Act
IDAEP: Individual Disabled Adult Education Plan
IEP: Individual Education Plan
IHE: Institute of Higher Education
IIS: Instructional Improvement System
IEL: Intensive English Language
ILP: Individual Learning Plan
IM: Instructional Materials
ILC: Instructional Leadership Council
ILT: Instructional Leadership Team
LD: Learning Disability
LEA: Local Education Agency
LEP: Limited English Proficient
LRE: Least Restrictive Environment
LMS: Learning Management System
M&O: Maintenance and Operations
MOA: Memorandum of Agreement
MOE: Maintenance of Effort
MOU: Memorandum of Understanding
MTSS: Multi-tiered System of Supports
NAEP: National Assessment of Educational Progress
NAICS: National American Industry Classification System
NAS: National Apprenticeship System
NASWA: National Association of State Workforce Agencies
NAWB: National Association of Workforce Boards
NCES: National Center for Education Statistics
NCLB: No Child Left Behind Act
NCWD: National Collaborative on Workforce and Disability
NESS: National Educational Support Services
NGA: National Governors Association
NLA: National Literacy Act
OATELS: Office of Apprenticeship Training Employer and Labor Services
OCO: Other Capital Outlay
OCP: Occupational Completion Point
ODEP: Office of Disability Employment Policy under the US Department of Labor
OES: Occupational Employment Statistics
OJC: Office of Job Corps under the US Department of Labor Employment & Training Administration

OJT: On-the-Job Training
ONP: Office of National Programs under the US Department of Labor Employment & Training Administration
OPDER: Office of Policy Development Evaluation and Research under the US Department of Labor Employment & Training Administration
OPPAGA: Office of Program Policy Analysis & Government Accountability
OPS: Other Personnel Services
OSHA: Occupational Safety and Health Administration under the US Department of Labor
OST: Occupational Skills Training
OYS: Office of Youth Services under the US Department of Labor Employment & Training Administration
PBIS: Positive Behavioral Interventions and Supports
PBB: Performance Based Budgeting
PBIF: Performance-Based Incentive Funding
PECO: Public Education Capital Outlay
PEPC: Post Secondary Education Planning Commission
PIC: Private Industry Council
PISA: Program for International Student Assessment
PL: Personal Learning
PLT: Project Learning Tree
PMT: Performance Management Team
PMP: Project Management Plan
POS: Program of Study
PP: Professional Development Plan
PRO: Performance and Results Office under the US Department of Labor Employment & Training Administration
PSAV: Post Secondary Adult Vocational
PSV: Post Secondary Vocational
PSVC: Post Secondary Vocational Certificate
PY: Program Year
RAIMS: Registered Apprenticeship Information Management System (formally AIMS)
REDI: Rural Economic Development Initiative
RFB: Request For Bid
RFP: Request For Proposal
RFQ: Request For Quotation
RTI: Response to Intervention
RWDB: Regional Workforce Development Board
SAC: Southern Association of Colleges
SACs: State Apprenticeship Councils
SAIL: System for Applied Individualized Learning (changed to VPI)
SBC: State Board of Community Colleges
SBE: State Board of Education

SBNCE: State Board of Nonpublic Career Education Employment & Training Administration
SDA: Service Delivery Area
SGA: Solicitations for Grant Applications Federal
SIC: Standard Industrial Classification
SOC: Standard Occupational Classification
SSI: Supplemental Security Income
STW: School-To-Work
SUS: State University System
TA: Technical Assistance
TABE: Test of Adult Basic Education
TAG: Technical Assistance Guide
TANF: Temporary Assistance for Needy Families
TEGL: Training and Employment Guidance Letter
TEIN: Training and Employment Information Notice
TEN: Training and Employment Notice
TO: Table of Organization
UC/UI: Unemployment Compensation/Insurance
USES: US Employment Service under the US Department of Labor Employment & Training Administration
VESIL: Vocational Education for Speakers of Other Languages
VET: Veterans' Employment and Training Service under the US Department of Labor Employment & Training Administration
VPI: Vocational Preparatory Instruction
VSO: Vocational Student Organization
WIOA: Workforce Innovation and Opportunity Act
WSP: Workforce Solutions Partnership
WST: Work Skills Training
WTP: Welfare Transition Program
XAP: eXperience America Program
YAP: Youth Apprenticeship Program
YCC: Youth Conservation Corps
YIN: Youth Interventions Network
YRP: Youth Resource Program
ZTC: Zero Textbook Cost

K-12 General Education Terms

504 Plan: A special needs learning plan derived from Section 504 of the Rehabilitation Act of 1973, which states, "Any person who (a) has a physical or mental impairment which substantially limits one or more of such person's major life activities, (b) has a record of such an impairment, or (c) is regarded as having such an impairment."

Academic Bankruptcy: The status of a school district demonstrating low educational achievement.

Academic Performance: The measurement of student achievement across various academic subjects, typically assessed through classroom performance, graduation rates, and standardized test results.

Achievement Gap: The difference in academic performance or graduation rates between groups of students, often influenced by various societal factors.

Adult General Education (AGE): Educational programs designed for adults to improve basic skills or obtain a high school diploma.

Adult High School (AHS): A program that offers high school diplomas or equivalency for adult learners.

Adult Secondary Education (ASE): Programs that offer education to adults seeking to complete their high school education.

Adult Training Programs (ATP): Programs designed to provide training and education for adult learners.

Advanced Learning Programs (ALP): Programs designed to challenge and enhance the learning experiences of advanced students.

Advanced Placement (AP): A program that allows high school students to take college-level courses and exams for potential college credit.

Age Appropriate: Refers to the suitability of content based on a child's age.

Aid to Families with Dependent Children (AFDC): A federal assistance program that provides financial aid to families with children in need.

Allied Health Program: A program that provides education and training for health professionals.

America's Job Bank (AJB): A resource for job seekers to find employment opportunities.

America's Labor Market Information System (ALMIS): A system that provides labor market data and resources for job seekers and employers.

America's Service Locator (ASL): A resource for job seekers to find workforce services and programs.

American College Testing (ACT): A standardized test used for college admissions in the United States.

American Federation of Labor – Congress of Industrial Organizations (AFL-CIO): A federation of unions that advocates for labor rights and workers' interests.

Applied Learning Skills (ALS): Communication, problem-solving, critical thinking, research, personal/ social responsibility, and interpersonal skills across all disciplines and courses.

Applied Technology Diploma (ATD): A credential awarded for completing a program in a technical field.

Assistant Secretary of Employment and Training (ASET): A government position overseeing employment and training programs.

Associate in Science (AS): A two-year degree focused on science and mathematics coursework.

Association for Career and Technical Education (ACTEONLINE): An organization dedicated to promoting career and technical education.

At-Risk: A student is considered "at-risk" if the school is concerned about their potential to fail or drop out.

Audiologist: A specialist who studies hearing, administers hearing assessments, and assists individuals with hearing loss.

Augmentative and Alternative Communication Device (AAC): A tool that uses communication methods other than speech to express thoughts, needs, and ideas.

Authorizer: Entities that set rules for starting and maintaining charter schools. Most authorizers are local education agencies, but they can also be universities, state education agencies, independent boards, municipalities, or nonprofit organizations.

Base Support Level (BSL): A measure of the primary funding necessary to support a school district's operations.

Baseline: A student's starting point is determined by data collected through screening tools to measure progress over time.

Behavior Intervention Plan (BIP): A written plan that outlines specific strategies and interventions that will be implemented to promote positive behaviors and reduce problem behaviors

Benchmark: Milestones that allow parents, students, and educators to track a student's progress throughout the academic year.

Best Practices: An everyday phrase that describes solid, reputable, state-of-the-art work in a field. If employees follow best practices, they are knowledgeable about current knowledge, technology, and procedures.

Black, Indigenous, People/Person of Color (BIPOC): A term that acknowledges and represents the diverse racial and ethnic identities of individuals.

Blaine Amendment: Refers to a proposed constitutional amendment in 1875 to prevent public funds from supporting private education, particularly in parochial schools.

Blended Learning: A formal education program that combines online or web-based components with traditional teaching methods.

Block Scheduling: An organizational system for middle or high school schedules with longer class periods than the traditional schedule.

Blue Ribbon School: A designation awarded by the US Department of Education to recognize schools demonstrating exceptional academic excellence or significant progress in closing achievement gaps.

Brick-and-Mortar Education: Refers to education conducted at a physical school rather than in a virtual environment.

Bring Your Own Device (BYOD): A policy that allows students to bring personal electronic devices to school for educational purposes.

Budget Expenditures: Typical expenses incurred by school districts, including salaries, employee benefits, supplies, utilities, maintenance, and miscellaneous expenditures.

Bureau of Apprenticeship and Training (BAT): A division of the U.S. Department of Labor that oversees apprenticeship programs.

Bureau of Labor Statistics (BLS): A government agency that provides data on employment, wages, and economic conditions.

Business Relations Group (BRG): A group that aims to facilitate collaboration between businesses and educational institutions.

Career and Technical Education (CTE): Educational programs that prepare students for specific careers through hands-on learning.

Centers for Medicare and Medicaid Services (CMS): A federal agency overseeing healthcare programs.

Certificate of Initial Mastery (CIM): Academic achievement in mathematics and English language arts, the ability to apply academic learning, and possessing essential work habits.

Charter Schools: Publicly funded schools that operate independently, often with a specific educational focus or approach.

Child Find Program: A program mandated by IDEA that continuously seeks out and evaluates children who may have disabilities.

Children's Health Insurance Program (CHIP): A program that provides health coverage to eligible children in low-income families.

Classical Education: An educational philosophy rooted in the liberal arts, ancient histories, and classic literature.

College and Career Ready: Describes students or educational programs that equip students with the necessary knowledge and skills for success in college or careers.

Common Core State Standards (CCSS): A national set of educational standards for K-12 students in subjects like math and English language arts not fully vetted before being adopted by states that took the Race to the Top Federal grant dollars under the Obama administration

Common Tasks: It connects to a standard, GLE, or GSE endorsed by the district or the state.

Consolidated Resource Plan (CRP): The Consolidated Resource Plan (CRP) provides the opportunity to move towards a fuller integration in using resources and your other state and local funds.

Consolidated School District: A school district formed by combining two or more existing districts.

Core Curriculum: Colleges use standardized curricula to impart specific skills or knowledge to all students.

Cost of Living Allowance (COLA): An adjustment made to salaries to account for changes in the cost of living.

Critical Race Theory (CRT): An ideology based on the framework for examining race and racism's impact on culture and institutions in the US, arguing that systemic racism is embedded in legal and social structures.

Curriculum alignment: The process of ensuring that the curriculum, content standards, instructional and assessment methods, educational materials, learning outcomes, and other elements are all coherent, unified, and consistent.

Curriculum-Based Measurement (CBM): Curriculum-based measurements are short, regular assessments to monitor student performance.

Curriculum: A formal plan for an educational course that defines how students will learn what they should learn.

Differentiated Instruction (DI): A method of teaching that focuses on creating varied experiences that meet students' different learning levels and needs in a class.

District Corrective Action: The NCLB classification for a district that has been "In Need of Improvement" for three or more years.

Diversity, Equity, and Inclusion (DEI): Initiatives tied to CRT practices aimed at promoting diverse, equitable, and inclusive environments in schools and workplaces.

Dual Enrollment: A program allowing high school students to earn college credit while working toward their high school diploma.

Dual-language Program: Students receive a significant amount of weekly instruction in a partner language (a language other than English).

Early and Periodic Screening, Diagnostic, and Treatment (EPSDT): A program that provides comprehensive health services for children enrolled in Medicaid.

Early College Program: See Dual Enrollment.

Early Intervention Program (EIP): Services designed to address developmental delays in young children.

EdTech: "EdTech" is short for education technology.

Education Savings Account: Parents who enroll in an education savings account program can receive public education funds for various approved education costs.

Education Savings Accounts (ESA): Programs that allow parents to use public funds for educational expenses, such as private school tuition or tutoring.

Elementary and Secondary Education Act (ESEA): A federal law aimed at improving education opportunities for disadvantaged students.

Emotional Disturbance (ED): An emotional condition used to describe a diagnosable mental, behavioral, or emotional disorder that lasts for a significant duration and affects educational performance.

Emotional/Behavior Disorder (EBD): A classification for students whose emotional or behavioral functioning negatively impacts their educational performance.

End of Grade Assessment (EOG): Tests administered to evaluate student performance at the end of a grade level.

End-of-Course (EOC): Assessments are given to students at the end of a course to measure their understanding of the material.

English for Speakers of Other Languages (ESOL): Programs designed to teach English to non-native speakers.

English Language Arts (ELA): The subject area focuses on reading, writing, speaking, and listening skills.

English Language Learner (ELL): A term used to describe students who are learning English as an additional language.

Equity: Equity ignores a merit-based system and fairness in education by shifting resources to some students within an identified category based on race to give them access to the resources and opportunities they need to succeed.

Every Student Succeeds Act (ESSA): A federal law that replaced No Child Left Behind, emphasizing equal opportunity and flexibility for states in education.

Family Educational Rights and Privacy Act (FERPA): A federal law regulating the management of student records and disclosure of information from those records.

Fiscal Year (FY): One year used for financial reporting and budgeting.

Free and Reduced Lunch (FRL): A program that provides free or discounted meals to eligible students from low-income families.

Full-Time Equivalent (FTE): A measure used to represent the workload of an employed person in a way that makes workloads comparable across various contexts.

Functional Behavior Assessment (FBA): A problem-solving process for addressing inappropriate behavior that impedes a child's learning or the learning of others.

Gamification: An instructional approach that brings elements of playing a game into a classroom.

Gifted Program: A gifted program is designed to bring unique support to academically exceptional students whose needs are unmet in a traditional learning environment.

Grade Level Expectations (GLEs): A blueprint for developing and implementing a state-level assessment that identifies the content knowledge and skills expected of all students.

Health and Human Services (HHS): A federal department responsible for protecting the health of all Americans and providing essential human services.

Higher Order Thinking Skills (HOTS): The cognitive domain in Bloom's taxonomy categorizes learning into six major divisions.

Highly Qualified Teachers: The federal definition of a highly qualified teacher meets all the following criteria: the teacher must be fully certified and/or licensed by the state, hold at least a bachelor's degree from a four-year institution, and demonstrate competence in each core academic subject area.

Inclusion: Term used to describe services that place students with disabilities in general education classrooms with appropriate support services.

Independent Educational Evaluation (IEE): By law, a school district must conduct assessments of students who may be eligible for special education.

Individualized Education Program (IEP): A legal roadmap for what individualized supports and services a child with disabilities will receive.

Individualized Family Service Plan (IFSP): A process of providing early intervention services for children ages 0-3 with special needs.

Individualized Transition Plan (ITP): This plan starts in the 9th grade or before age 16 and addresses areas of post-school activities, post-secondary education, employment, community experiences, and daily living skills.

Individuals with Disabilities Education Act (IDEA): A law ensuring students with disabilities receive a free and appropriate public education.

Institute of Higher Education (IHE): Institutions that provide post-secondary education and training.

Instructional Improvement System (IIS): Designed to help educators improve instructional practices and student outcomes.

Intensive English Language (IEL): Programs designed to provide focused English language instruction to non-native speakers.

International Baccalaureate (IB): An internationally recognized educational program that offers a rigorous curriculum for students aged 3-19.

Intervention: An instructional strategy or method of instruction used to increase student skills.

Learning Disability: A disorder in one or more basic psychological processes involved in understanding or using language.

Learning Management System (LMS): Software that helps educators create, deliver, and manage educational courses and training programs.

Least Restrictive Environment (LRE): A requirement that students with disabilities be educated with their non-disabled peers to the maximum extent possible.

Limited English Proficient (LEP): A term used to describe individuals who are not fluent in English.

Local Education Agency (LEA): A term that can refer to any school program conducted by a public school or agency.

Mainstreaming: The term describes integrating children with special needs into regular classrooms for part of the school day.

Maintenance and Operations (M&O): Refers to the expenditures necessary to maintain and operate educational facilities.

Major Life Activities: Include caring for oneself, performing manual tasks, walking, seeing, hearing, speaking, breathing, learning, and working.

Manifestation Determination/Hearing: Within 10 school days of any decision to change the placement of a child with a disability because of a violation of school code.

Medical Report/Information: This form may document relevant medical findings, health problems, medication, and other medical information to determine eligibility.

Memorandum of Agreement (MOA): A document outlining the terms and details of an agreement between parties.

Memorandum of Understanding (MOU): A formal agreement between two or more parties outlining their intentions and responsibilities.

Modifications: Changes were made to curriculum expectations to meet the student's needs.

Multi-tiered System of Support (MTSS): A framework for providing varying levels of support to students based on their needs.

Multidisciplinary Evaluation and Eligibility Group Summary (MEEGS): The multidisciplinary evaluation must include relevant and functional information from the home and school.

Multiple Disabilities: An IEP term defines a combination of disabilities that cause severe educational needs that require multiple special education programs.

National Assessment of Educational Progress (NAEP): A long-term assessment of student performance in various subjects across the United States.

National School Board Association (NSBA): An organization that represents school boards and advocates for public education.

National School Lunch Program (NSLP): A federally assisted meal program that provides children nutritionally balanced, low-cost, or free lunches.

No Child Left Behind Act (NCLB): Federal legislation aimed to improve disadvantaged students' educational outcomes.

Notification of Meeting (NOM): Notification of Meeting is used by the LEA to take steps to ensure that parent(s) are allowed to participate in the special education process.

Obsessive-Compulsive Disorder (OCD): An anxiety disorder that presents itself as recurrent obsessions or compulsions.

Office for Civil Rights (OCR): Ensures equal access to education and promotes educational excellence throughout the nation.

Office of Special Education Programs (OSEP): This division of the U.S. Department of Education is entirely focused on special education.

Online Learning Exchange (OLE): A platform for sharing resources and information about online education.

Open Educational Resources (OER): Teaching, learning, and research resources that are freely available for use.

Oppositional Defiant Disorder (ODD): A child who defies authority by disobeying, talking back, arguing, or being hostile.

Orthopedic Impairment: Term used to define impairments caused by congenital anomaly, impairments by diseases, and impairments by other causes.

Other Health Impaired (OHI): A term described as limited strength, vitality, and alertness resulting in limited educational ability.

Parent Consent: Special education term used by IDEA that states you have been fully informed in your native language.

Parents Rights in Special Education: Notice of Procedural Safeguards.

Performance Evaluation Instrument (PEI): Tools used to assess and evaluate employee performance.

Personal Protective Equipment Grant (PPE): Funding provided to help schools purchase necessary protective equipment.

Physical Therapy (PT): Physical therapy is instructional support and treatment of physical disabilities.

Positive Behavior Intervention and Support (PBIS): A framework for improving student behavior and promoting a positive school culture.

Preliminary SAT/National Merit Scholarship Qualifying Test (PSAT/NMSQT): A standardized test that provides practice for the SAT and qualifies students for scholarships.

Race to the Top (RTTT): A federal program providing funding to encourage state education reform by implementing CCSS and integrated longitudinal databases with the Federal Department of Education under the Obama administration.

Reevaluation: In special education, a reevaluation is an assessment that occurs at least every three years.

Referral: A referral concerning special education is the official request to begin a formal process.

Related Services: Services that a school is required to provide under IDEA.

Resource Room: A room separate from the regular classroom where students with disabilities can receive specialized assistance.

Resource Specialist Program (RSP): This term describes a program that provides instruction, materials, and support services to students with identified disabilities.

Resource Specialists Provide instructional planning, support, and direct services to students whose needs have been identified in an IEP.

Response to Intervention (RTI): An educational approach providing early, systematic assistance to struggling students.

Revenue Control Limit (RCL): A limit on the revenue a school district can generate.

Review of Existing Data (RED): When a student is requested to be evaluated initially, the LEA staff must conduct a Review of Existing Data.

Scaffolding: In education, scaffolding is an instructional technique that helps students progressively build on knowledge.

Scholarship Granting Organization (SGO): Non-profit organizations that manage contributions from donors or grants for educational scholarships.

Scholastic Aptitude Test (SAT): A standardized test widely used for college admissions in the United States.

School Psychologist: Assist in identifying students' intellectual, social, and emotional needs.

School-based System (SBS): Refers to programs or initiatives implemented at the school level.

Science, Technology, Engineering, and Mathematics (STEM): An educational approach emphasizing these four disciplines.

Science, Technology, Engineering, Arts, and Mathematics (STEAM): An educational approach integrating arts into the STEM fields.

Secretary of Education: The Federal Secretary of Education leads the Department of Education and advises the President.

Self-Advocacy: A skill set that allows students to take charge of their education.

Self-Directed Learning: An educational style in which students can choose their activities and experiences.

Social-Emotional Learning (SEL): A trend in K-12 education that emphasizes the development of emotional and interpersonal skills. This focus on SEL can sometimes be polarizing, leading to debates about what is appropriate for students' age and what should be the responsibility of parents versus the school district.

Socratic Method: The Socratic method is a teaching method in which a teacher asks questions to help students reason more clearly.

Special Education (SpEd): Instruction specifically designed to meet the unique needs of a student with a disability.

Special Purpose Local Option Sales Tax (SPLOST): A tax used to fund specific school projects or improvements.

Specially Designed Instruction (SDI) is an instruction that has been adapted in content or delivery method to address specific learning needs.

Speech and Language Impairments: Communication disorders such as stuttering, delayed speaking, impaired articulation, language impairment, or voice impairment.

Speech and Language Specialists: Assesses students for possible delayed speech and language skills and provides direct services.

Standardized Testing: Used to ask students in the same grade level across a state or country to answer the same questions under the same time limit and conditions.

State Educational Agency (SEA): A state educational agency in charge of supervising public schools in a state.

STEM Education: STEM education focuses on innovation and active learning through science, technology, engineering, and mathematics.

Student Assistance Team/Student Support Team: This team of professionals and parents meet to discuss any problems students have in their general education classroom.

Substance Use Disorder (SUD): A condition characterized by an individual's inability to control their use of substances, leading to significant impairment.

Synchronous Learning: In synchronous learning, a student goes through learning material with the teacher in real-time.

Tax Credit Scholarships (TCS): Scholarships funded by donations that provide tax credits to donors and allow families to attend private schools.

Teacher Certification: The state requires most or all teachers in public schools to be certified or licensed to teach.

Teaching and Learning Division (T&L): A division within an education agency focused on enhancing teaching and learning practices.

Title I: A federal program that provides extra funding to schools with high percentages of low-income children.

Title II: A federal law aimed at supporting the development of teachers and school leaders.

Title IX: A civil rights law that protects students from discrimination based on sex, especially in school athletics and sports.

Transition Meeting: In special education, a transition meeting is a meeting of the Individualized Education Program (IEP) or ARD team.

Transition Plan: A plan specific to an Individualized Education Plan (IEP).

Transportation Revenue Control Limit (TRCL): A limit on the revenue generated for school transportation.

Transportation Support Level (TSL): Funding provided to support transportation services in educational settings.

Triennial Review: A triennial review is an Individualized Education Program (IEP) meeting every three years.

United States Education Department (USED): The federal agency responsible for national education policy and funding.

Universal Screening Tool: An assessment used to identify or predict students who may be at risk for not meeting benchmarks.

University Model Education: A model that blends aspects of homeschooling, public schooling, and private schooling.

Unschooling: A type of homeschooling that focuses on nurturing a child's innate curiosity and interests.

Voucher: Families eligible for vouchers can use all or some of the public funding available for their child's education to attend a private school.

Waldorf: Waldorf education is one philosophy and method of education.

Weighted Grades: A weighted grade is the average of a group of grades, each making up a different percentage of the final grade.

Welfare Information Network (WIN): A network providing information and resources related to welfare programs.

Welfare Transition Program (WTP): Programs aimed at helping individuals transition from welfare to work.

Whole Child Education: Whole child education is a trend in education that takes on the role of caregiver beyond academics to provide emotional and health care, creating a community approach to raising the child.

Women's Bureau (WB): US Department of Labor: An agency that promotes the interests of working women and advocates for their rights.

Work And Gain Economic Self-sufficiency (WAGES): A program aimed at helping individuals achieve economic independence.

Work Opportunity Tax Credit (WOTC): A tax credit for employers hiring individuals from certain target groups.

WorkForce Development (WFD): Initiatives and programs to improve workforce skills and job readiness.

Workforce Development Board (WDB): A group that oversees workforce development programs and initiatives.

Workforce Development Education Fund (WDEF) supports education and training programs to enhance workforce skills.

Workforce Development Implementation Team (WDIT): A team executing workforce development initiatives.

Workforce Development Information Systems (WDIS): Systems that manage and analyze data related to workforce development.

Workforce Education (WE): Education programs focused on preparing individuals for careers and employment.

Workforce Education and Outcome Information Services (WHOIS): Services that provide information on workforce education outcomes.

Workforce Investment Act (WIA): Legislation designed to improve the workforce development system in the United States.

Workforce Investment Board (WIB): A board that oversees local workforce development initiatives and funding.

Wraparound Services: In education, wraparound services refer to when a school seeks to support students that "wrap around" into all areas of life.

Year-round School: Like it sounds, year-round schooling without summer break.

Zone (Attendance Zone): In many areas where a family lives, it determines what public school they are automatically assigned or zoned to.

Finance and Budget Terms

AAA Bond Rating: There are three major rating agencies for municipal bonds: Moody's Investors Service, Standard & Poor's, and Fitch Ratings. Standard & Poor's and Moody's rate over 80% of the three rating agencies' municipal and corporate bonds. In assigning a rating for general obligation bonds, the rating agencies assess the following factors: economy, debt structure, financial condition, demographic characteristics, and management practices of the governing body/administration. "AAA/Aaa" – Municipalities rated triple-A demonstrate the strongest creditworthiness relative to other US municipal or tax-exempt issuers or issues—the higher the credit rating, the lower the yield on the bonds issued to that municipality.

Academic Performance Index (API): The API scale measures student achievement on specific standardized tests. Schools' API scores and their improvement, as reflected by API scores, form the basis for funding in several Governor's Initiative programs.

Account: A descriptive heading that lists recorded financial transactions similar to a given frame of reference, such as function, object, or source.

Account Code: A number that classifies sources of revenues or purposes of expenditures in either a school district budget or the reports districts submit to the California Department of Education. The account code classifies expenditures according to the types of items purchased or services obtained, as well as revenues by the general source and kind of revenue.

ADA: Average Daily Attendance

Adequacy: An approach to school funding based on the idea that the funding schools receive should be based on some estimate of the cost of achieving the state's educational goals. It tries to answer two questions: How much money would be enough to achieve those goals, and where would it best be spent?

Adequate Yearly Progress (AYP): A collection of performance measures that a state, its school districts, and subpopulations of students within its schools should meet if the state receives Title I, Part A federal funding. In California, the measures include: (1) specified percentages of students scoring "proficient" or "advanced" on California Standards Tests in English language arts and math; (2) participation of at least 95% of students on those tests; (3) specified Academic Performance Index scores or gains; and (4) for high schools, a specified graduation rate or improvement in the rate. (See No Child Left Behind Act and Title I.)

ADM: Average Daily Membership

Administrative Budget Component: One of three general fund budget categories that school districts must report. This category includes expenditures in such areas as curriculum development; property and casualty insurance; costs associated with the Board of Education, District meetings, and the offices of the Superintendent, business, and assistants for instruction and personnel, including all salaries and benefits for certified school administrators who spend 50 percent or more of their time performing supervisory duties, e.g., building principals and assistant principals; office supplies; data processing; and legal fees other than those relating to student matters.

Administration (Function 201): This function funds activities associated with regulating, directing, and controlling the school system, such as the Superintendent, Deputy Superintendent, other professional staff, and secretaries and clerks. Some offices included in this category are the Board Office, Business Management Services, Internal Audit, Information Technology, and Human Resources.

Additional and Replacement Equipment: Funds athletic equipment, cafeteria equipment, computers, office furniture and equipment, and security alarm systems.

Adult Education: School districts, community colleges, and other public and private organizations offer classes for residents 18 years or older who are not enrolled in a high school. State law requires that specific courses, including citizenship and English, be provided free, while others may charge a fee. Adult Education revenues and expenditures must be tracked separately from a school district's general fund.

Allocation: Dollars directed to schools or students based on various factors, including student need and enrollment.

American Recovery and Reinvestment Act (ARRA): also known as the Federal Stimulus Bill, was signed into law in February 2009. The legislation is designed to stimulate the US economy and provide additional funding for education nationwide from 2009 to 2011. The funds are also intended as an incentive for states to improve in four reform areas: 1) increasing teacher and principal effectiveness and equitable distribution of adequate staff; 2) establishing data systems and using data for improvement; 3) adopting rigorous college- and career-ready standards and high-quality assessments; and 4) turning around the lowest-performing schools. The governor of each state had to commit (or give "assurances") that the state would pursue reform in these areas before the state was eligible for the funds.

Appropriations: Funds set aside or budgeted by the state or local school district boards for a specific period and purpose.

Appropriated Fund Balance: The portion of a district's total fund balance from the previous fiscal year applied as revenue to the following year's general fund budget. This reduces the amount of money that taxes must generate.

Academic Performance Index (API): A number summarizing the performance of a group of students, a school, or a district on the state's standardized tests. A school's number (or API score) is used to rank it among schools of the same type (elementary, middle, high, or small) and among the 100 schools of the same kind that are most similar in terms of students served, teacher qualifications, and other factors. (See Standardized Testing and Reporting Program.)

Apportionments: According to specific formulas, federal or state governments distribute funds to local education agencies or other governmental units.

Assembly Bill (AB) 1200: Legislation passed in 1991 that defined a fiscal accountability system for school districts and county offices of education to prevent bankruptcy. The law requires districts to make multi-year financial projections, identify funding sources for substantial cost increases, such as employee raises, and make public the cost implications of such increases before approving employee contracts. County offices review district budgets, and the state reviews countywide school districts.

Assessed Value: The value of your property as determined by your local property assessor. This value can change based on your municipality's equalization rate and the market or if your municipality undergoes a reassessment. It determines the amount of taxes you pay and the amount of STAR exemption you receive.

Assessment Roll: A list of properties and their assessed value in your municipality. This public document can be accessed at your local assessor's office.

Associated Student Body (ASB) Funds: One name for money earned/spent (usually in cash) from school-based student activities. For example, this may include PTA/PTO fundraisers, after-school sports/clubs, school dances or BBQs, concessions at a football game, etc.

Audit: An examination of documents, records, and accounts for (1) determining the propriety of transactions, (2) ascertaining whether transactions are appropriately recorded, and (3) determining whether statements drawn from accounts reflect an accurate picture of financial operations and financial status for a given period of time.

Basic Aid: The minimum general-purpose aid guaranteed by the state's constitution for each school district in some states. For example, the amount is $120 per pupil (ADA), with a minimum of $2,400 per district for small districts.

Basic Aid School District: The historical name for a district in which local property taxes equal or exceed the district's revenue limit. These districts may keep the money from local property taxes and still receive constitutionally guaranteed state basic aid funding.

BCBA: The Board Certified Behavior Analyst (BCBA) is a graduate-level certification in behavior analysis. BCBA professionals provide behavior-analytic services and supervise the work of Board-Certified Assistant Behavior Analysts, Registered Behavior Technicians, and others who implement behavior-analytic interventions in schools.

Base Amount: The state allocates the minimum guaranteed dollar amount per student to each district using a student-weighted funding formula.

Base proportions: The NYS Office of Real Property Services (ORPS) determines the distribution of the tax burden between residential and commercial properties in the town. Changes in the base proportion do not affect the overall district tax levy; instead, they affect the percentages paid by homeowners and commercial Property owners.

Base Revenue Limit: The basic state funding for K-12 education. It is expressed as an amount per ADA or as a dollar amount. The district's most important funding source, Base Revenue Limit funding, comprises a combination of State tax revenues and local property tax allocations.

Bond Measure: See General Obligation (G.o.) Bonds.

Bonus/Performance Pay: Extra money for school district employees who perform extra duties or are considered exemplary. In some states, performance pay incentivizes teachers to improve their students' performance.

Board Budget: Spending plan adopted by the Board of Education.

Board Sources: Funds received from non-government sources, including tuition (e.g., non-resident students), fees (e.g., reimbursements for community building use), interest earnings on cash investments, and other miscellaneous revenues (e.g., sales of assets).

Bond: Money borrowed to pay for school district expenditures. Typically, the money is used for capital expenditures, such as the purchase of buses or the construction or renovation of a building. However, in some cases, school districts also issue bonds for other large expenditures, such as the repayment of back taxes in a certiorari settlement. The goal of borrowing is to spread the cost out over the years and lessen the cost to taxpayers in any single year. By definition, a bond is a written promise to pay a specified sum of money, called the face value or principal amount, at a specified date in the future (the maturity date), together with periodic interest at a specified rate.

Balanced Budget: A balanced budget is a budget where expenditures equal revenue.

Before and After-School Fund: A special revenue fund for financial transactions related to providing school-age child care services before and after school hours.

Block Grant: An allotment of money that is the sum of multiple special-purpose funds combined into one. A block grant tends to have fewer restrictions on how the money is spent than the original, disparate funding streams, and it often combines funds with similar purposes.

Bridge to Excellence Master Plan (Master Plan): This long-range action plan guides the system in preparing students to be prosperous citizens in the 21st century. It reflects the school system's mission and addresses its priority goals.

Budget Act: A constitutionally established, one-year statute for the state's budget appropriations. It is the only bill allowed to have more than one appropriation. The state Constitution requires that it be passed by a two-thirds vote of each house and sent to the governor by June 15 each year. The governor may reduce or delete, but not increase, individual items.

Budget Adjustment (or "Budget Transfer"): A change among budgeted items.

Budget: A financial plan for the operation of a school district, outlining the estimates of proposed expenditures for a fiscal year to meet the goals of the district and the proposed means of financing those expenditures.

Budget Calendar: The schedule of key dates that the school district, Board of Education, and administrators follow in preparation, adoption, and administration of the budget.

Budget Cap: State law prohibits school districts from increasing spending annually by more than four percent. Some areas, such as debt repayment, are excluded from that cap.

Budget Timeline: The schedule of key dates that the school district, Board of Education, and administrators follow in preparation, adoption, and administration of the district's budget.

Budget Year: The fiscal year immediately following the current year.

Building Fund A: District funds must be used only for buildings. The money comes from sources such as bonds and the sale or rental of property.

Categorical Aid/Categorical Programs: Allocations from the state or federal government generally fall into three categories: specific programs, specific students, and specific characteristics of school districts. All districts receive categorical aid in varying amounts in addition to the funding they receive for their general education program. In most cases, districts have limitations on using these funds.

Certificated/Credentialed Employees: Employees who are required by the state to hold some type of teaching credentials, including most administrators and full-time, part-time, substitute, and temporary teachers.

Child Find Program: A special education program mandated by IDEA that continuously searches for and evaluates children who may have a disability. Child Find Programs can vary widely from school district to school district.

Class Size Reduction (CSR): Incentive programs that fund schools with class sizes of no more than 20 students per teacher. CSR was initiated in the 1996–97 school year for kindergarten through third grade. A separate program supports smaller classes for core academic subjects in 9th grade.

Classified Employees: School employees who are not required to hold teaching credentials, such as bus drivers, secretaries, custodians, instructional aides, and some management personnel.

Collective Bargaining: The process of negotiating workers' wages, hours, benefits, working conditions, etc., between an employer and some or all of its employees, represented by a recognized labor union. Cohasset Public Schools has five bargaining units: teachers, paraprofessionals, secretaries, custodial and cafeteria workers.

Con App (Consolidated Application): The application districts can use to apply for about 20 state and federal categorical programs. Most, if not all, districts use the "con app" to secure funding from at least some of the programs on the application. These programs tend to be on roughly the same timeline and are relatively straightforward to apply for, such as the federal Title I program and the state School Improvement Program (SIP).

Consolidation: Combining two or more elementary or high school districts with adjoining borders to form a single district. (See Unification and Unionization.)

Chart of Accounts: The structure and logic for accounting codes, which organize dollars by funding source, cost center, function, and other relevant information segments.

Referring to the Chart of Accounts as both the logic for how each segment fits together and the structure and hierarchies within a segment (for example, Locations -> High Schools = 100 -> JFK High School = 101)

Carryover (or Carryforward): Unexpended balances are carried forward from one fiscal year to the next by programmatic or district guidelines. Funds may be carried forward at a particular location or may be carried forward and redistributed as part of a new year's allocation, depending on program guidelines.

Categorical Aid: Financial support from state and federal governments targeted for particular categories of students, special programs, or special purposes.

Categorical Funds/Aid: Also known as direct funding. States distribute funds based on student characteristics or program needs. Funds may be allocated using grants or reimbursements. For example, a state may provide a funding supplement for a tutoring program.[4]

Categorical Programs: Funds from the state or federal government are granted to qualifying schools or districts for specific children with special needs, certain programs, such as Class Size Reduction, or special purposes, such as transportation. Special Education and Class Size Reduction are two of the largest state programs in dollars. Schools or districts must spend the money for a specific purpose. This money is in addition to the funding schools receive for their general education programs.

Certificated Salaries: Are given to employees required by the state to hold some teaching credentials, including most administrators and full-time, part-time, substitute, and temporary teachers. The requirements for a fully credentialed teacher include having a bachelor's degree, completing additional required coursework, and passing the California Basic Educational Skills Test (CBEST). However, teachers who have not yet acquired a credential but have an emergency permit are allowed to teach in the classroom and are counted in this category.

Charter School: Under State law, a school operates semi-autonomously from the district. A "fiscally independent" charter school receives funding from the State and utilizes the funds to serve the needs of its students best; an "affiliated" charter school continues to receive funding from the district but develops a curriculum that may differ from that of the district.

Classified Salaries: Salaries for school employees who are not required to hold teaching credentials, such as transportation, clerical, custodial, and some management personnel.

Coding: A system of numbering, or otherwise designating, accounts, entries, invoices, vouchers, etc., in such a manner that the symbol used quickly reveals specific required information.

Capital Projects: Investments in buildings and infrastructure. These are typically funded through a bond or other one-time funds and budgeted for separately from the general fund.

Capital Budget Component: One of three categories that school districts must show in their proposed general fund budgets, which include the following categories: debt service and lease expenditures; any bus purchases; legal judgments and settled claims; custodial, maintenance, security, and grounds salaries and benefits, and all facility-related costs, including service contracts, supplies, utilities, maintenance, repairs, minor construction or renovations; and any transfers to the Capital Fund for significant construction projects.

Capital Outlay: An expenditure generally exceeds $20,000, resulting in the ownership, control, or possession of assets intended for continued use over long periods. Examples: the construction or acquisition of buildings and equipment, initial equipment of buildings or additions, or the initial acquisition of library books and research periodicals for a new school building.

Cost Center: The department or other units (often schools) within the district to which costs may be charged for accounting purposes.

Consumer Price Index (CPI): An index of prices used to measure the change in the cost of basic goods and services compared to a fixed base period. It is also called the "cost-of-living" index.

Cost-of-living Adjustment (COLA): An increase in funding for schools from the state or federal government to compensate for inflation. In California, the law states that schools should receive a certain COLA based on the Implicit Price Deflator for State and Local Government Purchases of Goods and Services.

County Office of Education (COE): The agency that provides, in general, educational programs for certain students; business, administrative, and curriculum services to school districts; and financial oversight of districts. These services are affected by the size and type of districts within the county, the geographical location and size of the county, and the special needs of students not met by the districts. Each of California's 58 counties has an office of education.

Capital Reserve: A district's reserve account may be established to pay bonds, transportation, and facility project expenses.

Consumer Price Index (CPI): This index measures the change in the cost of basic goods and services compared to a fixed base period. It is also called the "cost-of-living" index. The CPI does not consider many of the items that cause school district budgets to rise, such as the increasing cost of health insurance, liability insurance, and contributions to the State's employee retirement systems.

Contingency Budget: Under state law, school boards can submit a budget to voters a maximum of two times in one year. If the initial proposed budget is defeated, the board may submit the same budget to the voters again, submit a revised budget to the voters, or go directly to a contingency budget immediately after the first budget defeat. Under a contingency budget, the board may not increase the tax levy above the amount previously authorized by the voters in the prior year. No exemptions, exclusions, or growth factor options are permitted within this budget. Under a contingency budget, the percentage of the budget devoted to administrative costs cannot increase from what it was in the prior year's budget or the last defeated budget, whichever is less. Once a contingency budget is established, community residents are no longer allowed to petition boards of education to put additional items up for a separate vote. Further, any costs associated with the community's use of a district's facilities must be paid for by the community organization or member who is granted such use, and no new equipment may be purchased or new capital construction permitted.

Debt Service: Loan repayments, typically budgeted for separately from the general fund.

Deficit Spending: When actual expenditures are more significant than actual revenues (also referred to as an operating deficit).

Discretionary: Dollars that a school principal or department head has complete autonomy over and can use as they deem best.

Debt Exclusion: Results in a temporary increase in a municipality's levy limit (and possibly the levy ceiling) when a municipality's voters elect to exclude the payment of a particular debt service from the constraints of Proposition 2 1/2. The debt service is then added to the levy limit for the life of the debt only. To place a debt exclusion question on the ballot requires a 2/3 vote of the entire Board of Selectmen. A simple majority vote by the voters is necessary for passage.

Developer Fees: A charge per square foot on residential and commercial construction within a school district based on the premise that new construction will lead to additional students. School districts decide whether to levy the fees and at what rate up to the maximum allowed by law. Proceeds are used for building or renovating schools and for portable classrooms.

Deferred Maintenance: Major repairs of buildings and equipment that school districts postponed. Some matching state funds are available to districts establishing a deferred maintenance program to proceed with these repairs.

Deficit Factor: The percentage by which an expected allocation of funds to a school district or county office of education is reduced. The state may apply deficit factors to revenue limits and categorical programs when the appropriation is insufficient based on the funding formulas specified by law.

Direct Services: Services—including business, attendance, health, guidance, library, and supervision of instruction (K–8 only)— performed without cost by county offices of education for small districts, which are defined as fewer than 901 (elementary), 301 (high school), and 1,501 (unified) students based on ADA.

Economic Impact Aid (EIA): State categorical funds for districts with concentrations of children who are transient, from low-income families, or need to learn English.

Education Code: The body of law that regulates education in California. Additional education regulations are contained in the California Administrative Code, Titles 5 and 8, the Government Code, and general statutes.

Elementary and Secondary Education Act (ESEA): The principal federal law affecting K-12 education. The No Child Left Behind Act (NCLB) is the most recent reauthorization of the ESEA. Originally enacted in 1965 as part of the War on Poverty, ESEA was created to support the education of the country's poorest children, which remains its overarching purpose. Congress must reauthorize it every six years. Each reauthorization of ESEA has made some changes, but NCLB was the most dramatic revision of the act since its creation. Its provisions represent a significant change in the federal government's influence in public schools and districts throughout the United States, particularly regarding assessment and teacher quality.

Encroachment: The expenditure of a local education agency's general-purpose funds for mandated special-purpose programs in which the cost of providing the programs exceeds the state or federal funding provided.

Enrollment: A count of the students enrolled in each school and district on a given day in October. The number of pupils enrolled in the school is usually larger than the average daily attendance (ADA) due to factors such as students moving, dropping out, or staying home because of illness. (See Average Daily Attendance.)

Equalization Aid: Funds allocated, on occasion, by the Legislature to address perceived inequalities and raise the funding level of school districts with lower revenue limits toward the statewide average based on size and type of district.

Employee Benefits: Amounts paid by the district on behalf of employees. These amounts are not included in employees' gross salary. They are fringe benefits and, while not paid directly to employees, are part of the cost of employees. Employee benefits include the district cost for health insurance premiums, dental insurance, life and disability insurance, Medicare, State retirement contributions, social security, and tuition reimbursement.

Employee Benefit Accrued Liability Reserve (EBALR): This reserve accounts for the value of accrued benefits due to employees upon termination of service, such as vacation, sick leave, personal leave, etc.

Encumbrance: Purchase orders, contracts, salaries, or other commitments chargeable to an appropriation and for which a part of the appropriation is designated. They cease to be encumbrances when paid, when an actual liability is established, or at the end of the budget year. An encumbrance may be re-established in the subsequent year's budget.

Encumbrance Reserve: This reserve account allows the district to pay for budget items from one fiscal year to the next. For example, suppose the district orders new technology equipment in June 2024, but the purchased items do not arrive until July (when the new fiscal year begins). The purchase order can be paid from the reserved funds without affecting the new year's school budget.

Enrollment: The total number of students. This may refer to the district's total student population, the school's total student population, or a sub-group of the student population, such as special education.

Equalization Rate: Represents the state's judgment of how closely assessed values in your town match the "true market value" of the properties. It is a ratio of a municipality's total assessed value to its market value. Regarding school taxes, the equalization rate helps determine how the school tax levy is shared among a district's municipalities. A municipality with an equalization rate of 100 percent means that the municipality is assessing property at full market value. Thus, property owners are paying the most accurate share of that municipality's tax burden, including school taxes.

Equalization Aid: Funds provided by the State to improve the revenue equity between districts receiving relatively low revenue limit amounts per ADA and districts receiving relatively higher amounts. Equalization aid is typically provided based on the type and size of school districts; small elementary district revenue limits are compared with other small elementary districts; large unified districts such as LAUSD are compared with other large unified districts, etc.

ESEA: The Elementary and Secondary Education Act is a significant piece of legislation reauthorized every five years at the federal level that guides federal policy regarding K-12 education. Each authorization may have a separate, more popular name (e.g., No Child Left Behind, ESSA).

ESSA: Every Student Succeeds Act. This is the latest (2015) reauthorization of ESEA. It is especially relevant to our work because it includes provisions related to equity and finance, such as reporting per-pupil spending.

Expenditure: Payment of cash or transfer of property or services to acquire an asset or service.

Expenditures Per Pupil: The amount of money spent on education by a school district or the state divided by the number of students educated.

FAPE (Free and Appropriate Public Education): The education to which every student is entitled under IDEA (Individuals with Disabilities Education Act). Every student is entitled to an education appropriate to their unique needs and provided free of charge.

Free Cash: Town Meetings can appropriate free cash, which results from unexpended appropriations, revenue overestimates, and property tax collections from prior years. However, the amount is not available for appropriation until it has been certified by the Department of Revenue (DOR). This is done when the Town submits its balance sheet to the DOR. Free cash is sometimes referred to as the Undesignated Fund Balance.

Fiscal Year: A fiscal year is the accounting period on which a budget is based. For example) The New York State fiscal year runs from April 1 to March 31. The fiscal year for all New York counties, towns, and most cities is the calendar year. School districts in New York State operate on a July 1 through June 30 fiscal year.

Free or reduced-price lunch (FRPL): An indicator of poverty. Students qualify for FRPL when their family income falls below a standard poverty level. FRPL is a metric used to calculate a district's Title I funding.

Fund Balance: A fund balance is created when the school district has money left over at the end of its fiscal year from underspending the budget and/or taking in additional revenue. Part of the fund balance (appropriated fund balance) may be applied as revenues to the district's budget for the following year. A portion may also be set aside (unappropriated fund balance) to pay for emergencies or other unforeseen needs (as determined by the Board of Education) and, if not used, becomes a part of the following year's fund balance.

Fund: Defined as "a sum of money or other resources set aside to carry on specific activities or attain particular objectives."

FTE (Full-Time Equivalent): Often misunderstood to mean Full-Time Employees, in school finance, FTE stands for Full-Time Equivalent. Regarding the people employed in a district, it is the ratio of a person who works out of the 40 possible hours in a workweek. Someone working 60 hours a week would be 1.5 FTE, and someone working 10 hours a week would be .25 FTE. In higher education, FTE relates to a student's class load, where full time may be 14 hours of classwork per week, and a student enrolled ½ time would be considered .5 FTE.

Funding Source: Where revenue dollars originate. Some familiar funding sources are federal grants related to legislation such as the Individuals with Disabilities Education Act, state tax revenue like state lottery proceeds, and local tax receipts, primarily from property taxes.

Funding Formula: A customized combination of enrollment and staffing ratios and/or student-based funding weights to calculate funding allocations to districts or schools. Funding formulas generally aim to make funding fair and equitable based on the student's needs.

Fundamental Operating Budget (FOB): The total amount required to pay for current year programs, staffing, and services at next year's prices — i.e., what the following year's budget would be if the current year's budget were simply "rolled over."

Guaranteed Tax Base (see also Wealth Equalization): Sometimes referred to as Tax-Levy Equalization or School Finance Equalization, funding levels are determined by a formula that equalizes the taxes paid on the base amount of property within the district.[3]

General Fund Budget: The budget is placed before the voters of a school district for their consideration and approval, including the revenues to support the budget. Most districts also develop and operate budgets for the school lunch/breakfast program, the capital fund, and the special aid fund (related to programs for students with special needs).

General Fund: The unrestricted annual operating budget includes state and local revenue. *Note: These dollars are unrestricted because the district chooses how to spend them without specific external restrictions.*

General Local Aid (also called Unrestricted General Government Aid or UGGA): Cities and towns use general local aid to fund general government services, with broad leeway to distribute this money for programs across their local budgets. General local aid came in two forms for many years: Lottery Aid (revenue from state lottery profits) and Additional Assistance.

Gifted and Talented Education (GATE): A State-funded program within the General Fund that provides supplementary funding for identified qualifying students.

Goal: The result or achievement toward which effort is directed; aim; end. See S.M.A.R.T Goal. Governor's Budget - The Governor's Proposed State Budget, or "Governor's Budget," is published each January and represents his initial public disclosure of his financial assumptions and spending priorities for the coming fiscal year.

Grant: A contribution, either in money or material goods, made by one governmental agency to another. Grants may be for specific purposes or, rarely, for general purposes.

Governmental Fund: A classification of funds which include the General Fund, Special Revenue Funds, Debt Service Fund, Permanent Funds, and Capital Project Funds.

Hybrid Model: Hybrid models often combine aspects of student-based budgeting models, resource allocation models, and various cost factors.

IEP (Individualized Education Program): A legal document that defines special education services to be provided by the district to a student with disabilities.

IDEA (Individuals with Disabilities Education Act): Legislation that guarantees educational rights to all students with disabilities and makes it illegal for school districts to refuse to educate them based on their disabilities.

Inclusive Classroom: For individuals with a disability and/or in special education, inclusion secures opportunities for students with disabilities to learn inside general education classrooms. General education classrooms in which students with disabilities learn are known as inclusive classrooms.

Individuals with Education Disabilities Act (IDEA): This federal law requires that all children with disabilities receive a free and appropriate education from infancy through age 21.

Instructional Components: The state allocates funding based on the cost of resources, such as staffing, classroom supplies, or other educational materials. Funding is sometimes provided for a bundle of resources. Resources are often allocated based on the size of the student population, with some references to student characteristics like English learner status.

Interfund Transfers: Permanent transfers within the same fund from one account to another.

Least Restrictive Environment (LRE): The environment in which students with disabilities must be educated, as IDEA mandates. Students with disabilities must be educated in a classroom near the general education setting.

Level Service Budget: A no-growth budget that continues appropriations for programs and services at their current year levels. The appropriation to maintain programs and services may still increase due to inflation or other factors.

LEA: Local Education Agency. The local unit of school administration, such as a school district or a charter organization.

Levy: The total of taxes or special assessments a governmental unit imposes—also, the act of imposing taxes or special assessment.

Local Receipts: Town revenue is based on local taxes and fees such as motor vehicle excise, utility, local permits, and license fees.

Limited: See "Onetime."

Local Match: The required share of total formula funds that local jurisdictions must allocate to schools for each school district to receive its state-funded share of dollars. Some states do not require their districts to contribute to making a local match to receive state funding for operating expenses (e.g., North Carolina).

Local Revenue: Local revenue is generated by a combination of property tax, sales tax, and income tax and is a significant funding source for many school districts across the country.

Maintenance of Effort: These laws require local funding bodies to allocate at least the same amount of funding to school districts as was budgeted the previous year for operating expenditures, excluding capital outlay and debt service, unless there is a decline in student enrollment. Maintenance of effort laws ensures that financial contributions by one funding body are used to enhance existing financial support from another. For example, these laws ensure that new or increased state funding provides additional support to schools and does not result in simply replacing existing local funding, also known as supplanting.

Mill: A rate used in calculating property taxes expressed in units of one-tenth of one cent or 0.001 of one dollar instead of reporting tax levies in terms of mileage.

Norms: Most district schools receive base allocations of teachers, school administrators, school clerical positions, and various resources based on Board-approved "norms," which determine the resources to be allocated to individual schools. Most norms are based on the number of students on "norm day," generally the Friday of the fourth week of school. Still, other factors may be used in norm allocations (e.g., the allocation of custodians is based on a complex formula that includes the size of the school). The district norms are published as "norm tables," describing the factors determining the individual norms.

Ongoing Revenue or Expenditure: Line items expected to continue into the subsequent year.

Operational Budget: The positions and other resources that enable an operating unit (a district) to perform the functions for which it is responsible.

Other Outgoing Expenditures: for debt service, transfers between funds within a district, and transfers to other agencies.

Outcomes-based funding: Otherwise known as performance-based funding, it's used primarily in post-secondary policy. In this type of funding, a portion of a funding formula is allocated based on performance, often including student outcomes such as assessment scores. Additionally, it may more heavily weigh students from low-income backgrounds, students with disabilities, English learners, and other groups.

Insurance Reserve: This reserve is used to pay liability, casualty, and other types of losses, except those incurred for which the following types of insurance may be purchased: life, accident, health, annuities, fidelity and surety, credit, title residual value, and mortgage guarantee.

Per-Pupil Expenditures: The dollars a school district *spends* in one fiscal year divided by the number of students the district is responsible for educating. This differs from per-pupil revenue because districts can contribute and withdraw money from "rainy day" funds (see Fund Balance), so revenues will not always reflect expenditures. The Every Student Succeeds Act requires that districts report per-pupil actual expenditures at the school level broken down by federal, state, and local fund sources.

Per-Pupil Revenue: The dollars a school district *receives* from all funding sources in one fiscal year divided by the number of students the district is responsible for educating.

Position Control: The act of planning for the salary and benefits of employees at a district to be sure that the district can afford the employees they expect to pay.

Program Budget Component: The district's proposed budget must include one of the three categories. These include the salaries and benefits of teachers and supervisors who spend most of their time teaching, instructional costs such as supplies, equipment, and textbooks, and all transportation operating costs, excluding bus purchases.

Proposed Budget: Also called the Administrative Budget Proposal, the spending plan was developed by school administrators before Board adoption. (i.e.) New York State requires school districts to show their proposed budgets in three categories: administrative, program, and capital.

Preliminary Budget: The district's first budget, published annually, is intended to assist in financial planning by providing Board Members and the public with information regarding available revenues and expenditure requirements for the coming fiscal year. The Preliminary Budget is based on information from the Governor's Proposed Budget and other sources.

Primary Funding Model: Money is provided for general purposes to cover basic education costs, such as teacher salaries and instructional materials. Models include student-based, resource allocation, and hybrid (See respective terms for definitions).[4]

Property Tax: A tariff is assessed to the value of real estate levied by the governing authority and paid by the property owner. Property taxes are subject to assessed value calculations, millage rates, and personal or privately owned property tax policies.[4]

Revenue: Sources of income financing the operation of the school district.

Reimbursement System: Districts submit receipts of eligible expenditures to the state, reimbursing districts for all or a portion of those expenditures.

Resource-Based Allocation: This type of allocation occurs when all districts receive a minimum base amount of resources. These resources could be staffing, services, or programs and are often based on a ratio of staff to students.

Reassessment: A reassessment is a systematic analysis of all locally assessed properties (commercial and residential) to achieve a uniform percentage of value. The goal of a reassessment is to ensure that each assessment reflects current market prices and that each property owner pays only their fair share of the tax burden. With a reassessment comes a shift in the tax burden to those whose property values have risen faster than average. This process does not result in a windfall of new revenue for the town, county, or school district, nor does the reassessment change the total taxes the school district must collect; it merely redistributes who pays them. In theory, rising assessments will decrease the tax rate (everything else being equal), as there is now a larger tax base from which the school may generate the same amount of tax dollars. If a property owner's assessment doubles, their tax bill will not double – in fact, it may remain about the same, increase slightly, or even decrease depending on the final tax rate.

Retirement Contribution Reserve Fund: This reserve funds employer retirement contributions.

Restricted Fund: State or federal allocations with restrictions on who or what money can be spent. For example, some dollars may be restricted for spending on low-income students or certain resources, such as literacy materials.

Segment: (as it relates to the chart of accounts) A piece of the account string that contributes meaning/a definition of that account. Common examples are Funds (denote the source of dollars), Objects (denote what dollars are being spent on, such as salaries, benefits, and supplies), Locations (denote the locations where dollars are spent), Cost Centers (denotes who holds and controls the dollars), Projects (denotes if money is targeted at a specific project), and Functions (denotes why resources are spent, such as instruction, support staff, etc.)

Site- or School-Based Management (SBM): A system by which some level of autonomy is given to site leaders (e.g., principal, teachers, community) in the budgeting process. This autonomy is not reliant on the former two movements.

S.M.A.R.T. Goal: *Specific, Measurable, Attainable, Relevant, Time*. This type of goal is clear and realistic. It allows schools to assess progress toward student achievement better when the goal in mind is clear. Special Education Program – Programs to identify and meet the educational needs of children with emotional, learning, or physical disabilities. Federal law requires that all children with disabilities be provided a free and appropriate education according to an Individualized Education Program (IEP) from infancy until 21 years of age.

Special Education (SPED): Students who qualify for targeted funding and services under the Individuals with Disabilities in Education Act (IDEA).

Special Funds: Separate financial entities within the budget that provide for specified activities, as defined in the (State) Education Code. Examples are the Adult Education Fund, Building Fund, and Cafeteria Fund.

State Education Agency (SEA): The agency primarily supervises a state's public elementary and secondary schools.

Student-Based Budgeting (SBB): A system in which the funding available to a school is based on the overall enrollment of the school. In its simplest form, it is an assigned dollar amount allocated per pupil and multiplied by enrollment to determine a total budget allocation.[4] Often, student-based budgeting includes funding students at differing levels based on their characteristics (e.g., low income, English learner, special education status, or rurality).

Student-Based Foundation: Districts receive a base amount of funding per student, with additional money or weights added to provide additional resources to students with higher needs. (See also Base Amount above.)

Stakeholder: A person or group that has an investment or interest in the success of our schools and district.

Stimulus: See American Recovery and Reinvestment Act.

Supplant: To replace (one thing) with something else. Federal funding supplanting occurs when a state or local government reduces funds for an activity because federal funds are available to fund the same activity—typically frowned upon in most grants.

Supplementing: This is when federal funds are used to enhance existing or local funds, which differs from federal supplanting.

Supplement: Something added to complete a thing, supply a deficiency, or reinforce or extend a whole.

Student-Based Budgeting (SBB): A system in which the funding available to a school is based on the overall enrollment of the school. In its simplest form, it is an assigned dollar per pupil multiplied by enrollment to determine a total budget allocation.

Support Services: The personnel, activities, and programs that enhance instruction and provide for the general operation of the school district. This includes attendance, guidance, and health programs; library personnel and services; special education services provided by speech and language pathologists, physical therapists, and occupation therapists; professional development; transportation; administration; buildings and ground operations; and security.

Teacher or Instructional Unit: Funding is distributed by setting the number, or target number, of teachers or instructional support staff that state funds will support based on a ratio. Teacher or instructional unit funding is often calculated based on student enrollment.[4]

Tax Base: Assessed value of local real estate that a school district may tax to fund yearly operations.

Tax Effort: The level of taxation needed to generate the same amount of tax revenue as another governmental entity. Because some governmental entities have wealthier tax bases, they can tax a smaller percentage and still generate the same level of resources as an area with a smaller tax base.

Tax Levy: Total sum to be raised by the school district after subtracting out all other revenues, including state aid and appropriated fund balance and the use of reserve funds. The tax levy determines the tax rate for property owners in the district.

Tax Levy Limit: The amount the district's tax levy may increase without requiring a supermajority to approve a proposed budget (60 percent of votes plus one). Each district must use a state formula that begins with an increase of 2 percent or the level of inflation (whichever is less) and add back certain exemptions. The result is often a number higher than 2 percent.

Tax Rate: The tax paid for each $ unit of assessed property value. In districts that cover just one municipality, the tax rate is figured simply by dividing the total assessed property value by 1,000 and then dividing that again into the tax levy (the amount of money to be raised locally). The formula for figuring the tax rate is more complicated in districts encompassing more than one municipality. It involves assigning a share of the total tax levy to each municipality by applying equalization rates, which consider the different assessment practices in each municipality.

Title I Funding: Federal dollars allocated to school districts based on the number of low-income (defined as qualifying for Free or Reduced Priced Lunch) students in the district. These are often highly restricted funds. NOTE: Title I funding refers to Title I under ESEA.

Three-Part Budget: School districts must divide their budgets into three components – administrative, capital, and program – and each year, they must show how much each portion has increased in relation to the budget. A further definition of the three components is as follows:

> **Administrative Budget Component:** These expenditures include office and administrative costs, salaries, and benefits for certified school administrators who spend 50 percent or more of their time performing supervisory duties, data processing, public information, legal fees, property insurance, and school board expenses.
>
> **Capital Budget Component:** This covers all school bus purchases, debt service on buildings, leasing expenditures, tax certiorari, and court-ordered costs, as well as all facility costs, including salaries and benefits of the custodial staff, service contracts, maintenance supplies and equipment, and utilities.
>
> **Program Budget Component:** This portion includes salaries and benefits of teachers and supervisors who spend the majority of their time teaching, instructional costs such as supplies, equipment, and textbooks, cocurricular activities and interscholastic athletes, staff development, and transportation operating costs.

Unappropriated Fund Balance: A school district can keep a portion of its total fund balance, up to 4 percent of the following year's budget. These monies are kept in a separate fund, which may be used to pay for emergency repairs and other unforeseen occurrences, as determined by the Board of Education. Unused monies within this fund become part of the following year's total fund balance.

Unemployment reserve: The district's financial reserve account is used to pay unemployment insurance benefits as determined by the State and Federal government.

Unrestricted: Refers to funding that may be used for any educational purpose at the discretion of the Board of Education.

Wealth Equalization: A policy tool utilized in some states to reduce funding gaps between districts by redistributing resources more equally. This approach is sometimes called district power equalization because it allows each district to tax and spend as if they had the same or more equalized local property tax base. Equalization policies can help eliminate the inequities that foundation funding can produce by providing additional levels of funding to school districts with higher tax efforts rather than distributing solely based on student characteristics.[9]

Weighted Student Funding (WSF): A student-based funding system by which individual students, based on their characteristics (e.g., low income, English learner, or special education status, or rurality), are given additional funding in the form of a "weight," suggesting they need a percent of funding over the base level of funding. For example, a student from a low-income background may be funded with a weight of .4, meaning the funding for that student will be 1.4 times the base level of funding.

Workers Compensation Reserve Fund: This reserve funds workers' compensation expenses, including medical, legal, and self-insurance administrative costs.

Terms Commonly Associated with Critical Race Theories

(CRT) Critical Race Theory: A theory that examines and critiques the appearance of race and racism across dominant cultural modes of expression. Critical race theorists hold that the law and legal institutions in the United States are inherently racist insofar as they function to create and maintain social, economic, and political inequalities between whites and nonwhites, especially African Americans.

It's important to understand that these ideas formed in the 1990s are based on a Marxist background that sought to divide individuals by class. In today's culture, they have replaced class with race. What we're left with is any disparate outcomes among races being termed systemic racism and/or white oppression. This theory has evolved into an ideology that has permeated many areas of American society, including schools, businesses, government agencies, and human resources protocols.

CRT has been rebranded as Diversity, Equity, and Inclusion (DEI), Anti-Racism, Anti-Bias, Belonging, Leveling, Opportunity and Access, and Workplace and Wellbeing initiatives. While many school districts may claim that they do not teach Critical Race Theory (CRT), it is important to note that CRT is not a formal curriculum. Instead, it is an ideology integrated through various practices, lessons, trainings, and discussions. To identify the presence of CRT in your district, you can look for commonly associated terminologies and curricula. Below is a glossary of terms commonly associated with Critical Race Theory utilized in class.

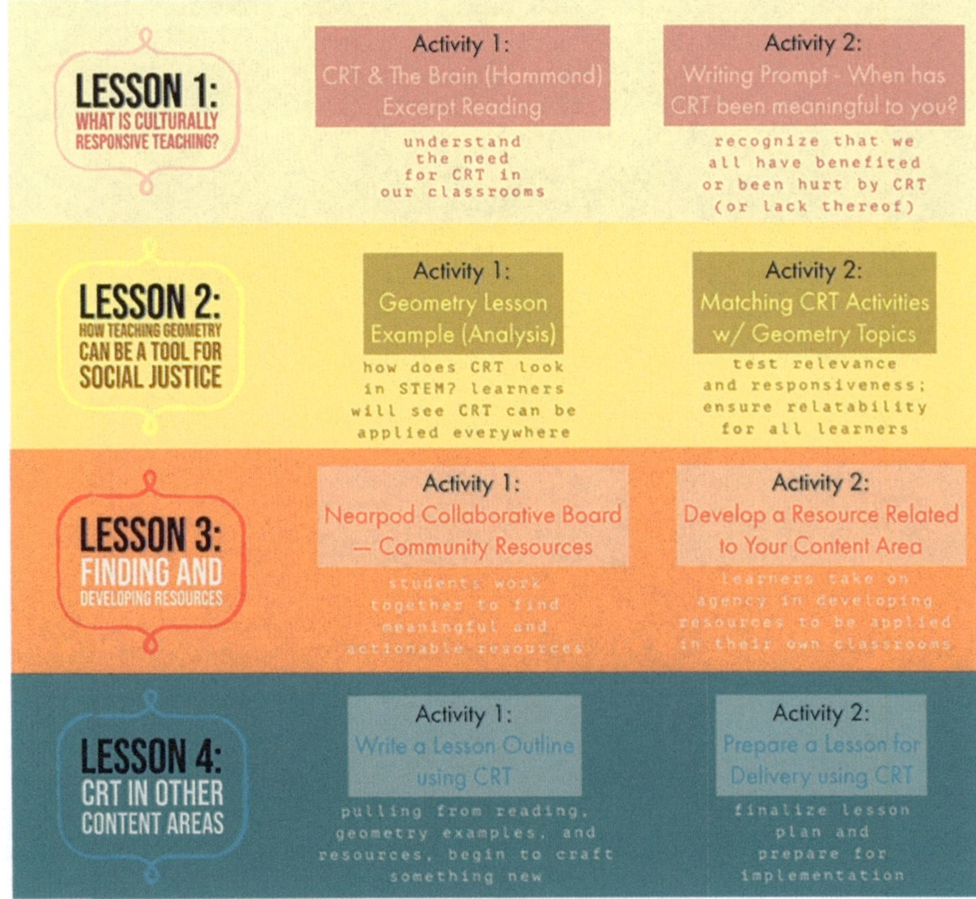

Source: www.knilt.arcc.albany.edu/Designing_a_Culturally_Responsive_Geometry_Curriculum

Terminology and Curriculum

1619 Project. A series of essays now morphed into K-12 school curricula, produced by *The New York Times* and based on the assertion that the seminal date of United States history isn't 1776 but 1619 – when enslaved Africans arrived in Virginia. It argues that slavery dictates all aspects of current American society, including culture, economics, diplomacy, etc., and results in systemic racism that cannot be overcome without totalitarian efforts. (The project has been debunked by prominent historians of different political persuasions.)

Abolitionist Teaching: Teaches that white abolitionism is the optimum level of whiteness for a white person. *For more information, see Whiteness: The 8 Levels to Identify.*

Action Civics: A model of teaching civics that downplays America's founding principles and governmental structure and pushes students to become political activists. Approved projects may include lobbying for or against legislation and/or participating in political demonstrations. As a practical matter, all projects are directed toward leftist activism. *Synonyms: New Civics or Project-Based Civics.*

Anti-Racism: i) The practice of dismantling a system marked by white supremacy and anti-Black racism through deliberate action. ii) A theory that explains and exposes multiple forms of racism: overt and covert, interpersonal and institutional, historical and present day, and persistent and nascent.

Colorblind Racism: i) The worldview that suggests that since race should not matter, it does not matter. ii) An ideology that insists that everyone be treated equally without regard to race, accompanied by a denial of the causes and consequences of racism.

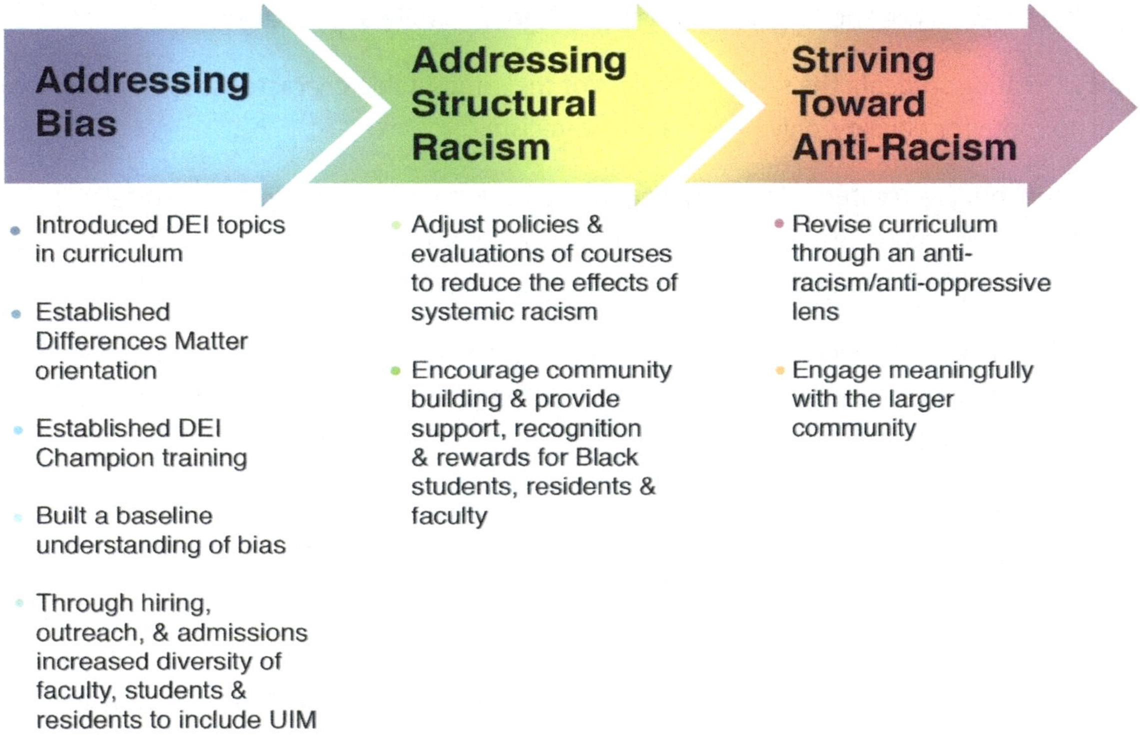

Addressing Bias

- Introduced DEI topics in curriculum
- Established Differences Matter orientation
- Established DEI Champion training
- Built a baseline understanding of bias
- Through hiring, outreach, & admissions increased diversity of faculty, students & residents to include UIM

Addressing Structural Racism

- Adjust policies & evaluations of courses to reduce the effects of systemic racism
- Encourage community building & provide support, recognition & rewards for Black students, residents & faculty

Striving Toward Anti-Racism

- Revise curriculum through an anti-racism/anti-oppressive lens
- Engage meaningfully with the larger community

Source: www.knilt.arcc.albany.edu/Designing_a_Culturally_Responsive_Geometry_Curriculum

Co-Optation: i) Taking an idea, disassembling it, and then reassembling it with original pieces and retro-fitting ones; giving the modified idea a different name from the original and then claiming originality. ii) Appropriation: falsely claiming rights to or innovation of something as one's own

Colorism: i) A practice whereby privileges and disadvantages are systematically doled out based on skin color, with a disproportionate amount of advantage provided to lighter-skinned people. *Synonym: light-skin privilege*

Courageous Conversations: A training curriculum used to "address racial disparities through safe, authentic, and effective cross-racial dialogue." The curriculum operates from a starting point that racial disparities are equal to systemic racism.

Culturally Responsive Teaching: A pedagogy that emphasizes including students' cultural references in all curricula. For example, works by William Shakespeare and Jane Austen may be replaced with those of Maya Angelou and Sandra Cisneros and related to Action Civics and Critical Race Theory.

Diversity, Equity, and Inclusion (DEI): A series of buzzwords that promote the same tenets as Critical Race Theory. The focus is to teach equating disparities with oppression.

Diversity Training: Programs designed to facilitate intergroup interaction. The goal is to presuppose that there is implicit discrimination and prejudice amongst a group. Implies that interactions should be different based on their identity groups.

Dehumanization: i) The notion that some people are less than human ii) The routine association of Blacks with demons and animals, such as apes.

Epistemology of Ignorance: i) A militant, aggressive willingness to not know ii) A process of knowing designed to produce not knowing about white privilege and white supremacy

Equality: Treating students the same regardless of their immutable characteristics. In today's groupthink, there is no room for equality, only racism and anti-racism.

Equity: Students are treated differently depending on their membership in historically "privileged" or "oppressed" racial groups. Students from oppressed groups are to be given special treatment because of their race, with the ultimate goal of ensuring equal outcomes for all groups regardless of merit or effort.

False Equivalence: i) A logical fallacy whereby two opposing sides of an argument are deemed equivalent when they are not. ii) A reliance on feeble similarities to moot the more important observation and effect of the glaring differences.

Ibram X. Kendi: The modern-day leader of the antiracism (racist) movement. He teaches that the only remedy to past discrimination is present discrimination, and the only remedy to present discrimination is future discrimination. See Kendi's Book, *How to Be an AntiRacist*

ICivics: A politically biased curriculum that promotes civics education and encourages students to become active citizens. Emphasis is placed on promoting activism among students, and critical theories and equity are commonly used as the basis for student engagement.

Institutional Oppression: The systematic mistreatment of people within a social identity group, supported and enforced by the society and its institutions, solely based on the person's membership in the social identity group. Oppression is often conflated with "inequity". When this happens, groups blame institutions because outcomes are not identical and insist that they manipulate their practices until outcomes are identical.

Implicit/Explicit Bias: Refers to attitudes or stereotypes that unconsciously affect our understandings, actions, and decisions, making them difficult to control. Teachings focus on identifying the root of bias.

Unconscious Bias: A professional training emphasizing social stereotypes about certain groups of people from outside their conscious awareness. Everyone holds unconscious beliefs about social and identity groups.

White Fragility: An emotional response or reaction including dismissiveness, anger, resentment, defensiveness, and more by white people when introduced to teaching concepts like white privilege or bringing up social injustices against the Black community. There are a variety of common phrases "they" use: i) "I have a Black friend/ family member, so I'm not racist." ii) "Racism ended with slavery." iii)"I am colorblind, so I'm not racist."[1] See Robin DiAngelo's book, *White Fragility.*

Peggy McIntosh, activist and scholar, coined the term "white privilege" in 1988 in her paper "White Privilege- *Unpacking the Invisible Knapsack.*" She described it as the dominant culture's unspoken advantage over people of color. In other words, power, benefits, and other advantages are distributed unequally among different social groups. Specifically, concerning white privilege, the advantage rests with white people.

WHITE PRIVILEGE

A term used to describe the cultural and social advantages that white people face in today's Western societies compared to non-white counterparts.

INVISIBLE KNAPSACK

The term is most closely associated with Peggy McIntosh's article "White Privilege: Unpacking the Invisible Knapsack" in which she stated:

"I observe white privilege as an unearned box of opportunities that can be cashed out on any day, but about it, I meant to remain oblivious" (Amico, 2019).

EXAMPLES

1. I'm Not Discriminated Against when Interviewing for Jobs
2. I can Spend Most of my Time with People of my Own Race
3. I Don't Face Housing Discrimination
4. I am Unlikely to be Harassed by Police due to my Race

HELPFULPROFESSOR.COM

The 8 White Identities

By Barnor Hesse

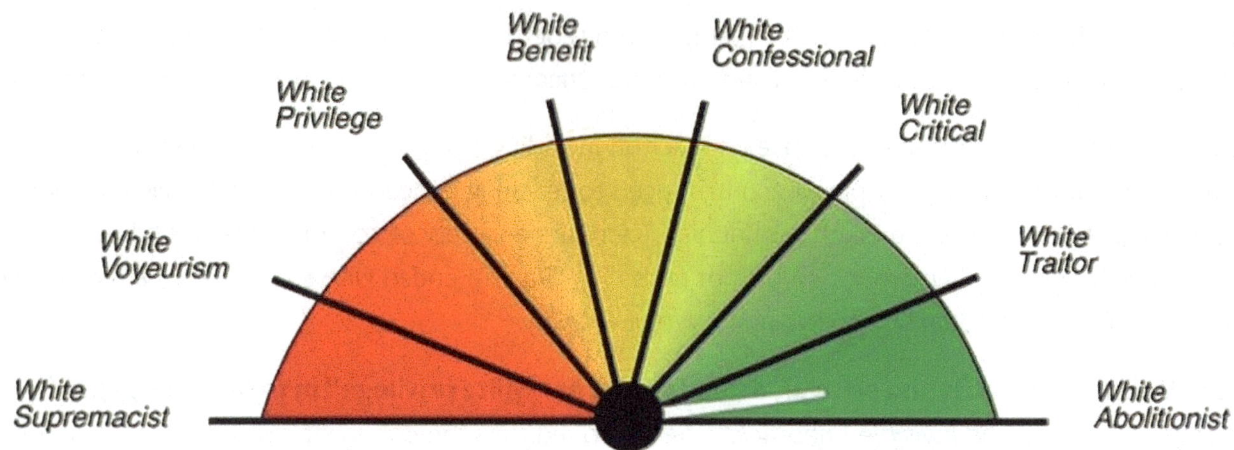

Source: www.camosun.libguides.com/action/whitePrivilege

8 White Identities

1. **White Supremacist.** Marked white society that preserves, names, and values white superiority.
2. **White Voyeurism.** Wouldn't challenge a white supremacist; desires non-whiteness because it's interesting and pleasurable; seeks to control the consumption and appropriation of non-whiteness; fascination with culture (ex., consuming Black culture without the burden of Blackness).
3. **White Privilege.** It may critique supremacy, but it is a deep investment in questions of fairness/equality under the normalization of whiteness and white rule, the sworn goal of 'diversity.'
4. **White Benefit.** Sympathetic to a set of issues but only privately; won't speak/act in solidarity publicly because benefitting through whiteness in public (some POC [People of Color] are in this category as well).
5. **White Confessional.** Some exposure to whiteness takes place, but as a way of being accountable to POC after, seek validation from POC.
6. **White Critical.** Take on broad criticisms of whiteness and invest in exposing/marking the white regime, refusing to be complicit with the regime, and whiteness speaking back to whiteness.
7. **White Traitor.** Actively refuses complicity; names what's going on; the intention is to subvert white authority and tell the truth at whatever cost; need them to dismantle institutions.
8. **White Abolitionist.** Changing institutions, dismantling whiteness, and not allowing whiteness to reassert itself.

References

Onboarding

National School Board Association to President Biden. (n.d.). Document Cloud. *https://www.documentcloud.org/documents/21094557-national-school-boards-association-letter-to-biden*

Owings, W. A., & Kaplan, L. S. (2006). *American Public School Finance.* Thomson Learning/Wadsworth.

Transparency

Open My Government. (n.d.). Open My Government: A Citizen's Guide to Public Records Request. Retrieved 2024, from *https://www.openmygovernment.org*

Ballotpedia. (n.d.). *Open Records.* Retrieved 2024, from *https://ballotpedia.org/Open_records*

Suffolk City School Board, et al., against Record No. 201334 Circuit Court No. CL20-1263

Sherri D. Story. (2022, January 20). Supreme Court of Virginia. *https://vacourts.gov/static/courts/scv/orders_unpublished/201334.pdf*

Student Press Law Center. (2023, September). *Looking Back On Key Student Free Speech And Expression Cases.* Constitution Day Free Speech Expression SCOTUS Cases. Retrieved 12, 2024, from *https://splc.org/2023/09/constitution-day-free-speech-expression-scotus-cases/*

Searles, C. (2024, April 15). *Olathe Public Schools First Amendment Lawsuit.* www.Johnson County Post. Retrieved 2024, from *www.johnsoncountypost.com*

Tennessee Coalition for Open Government. (2021, July 19). *6th Circuit Says School Boards Public Comment Rules Violate First Amendment.* www.TCOG.org. *https://tcog.info/6th-circuit-says-school-boards-public-comment-rules-violate-first-amendment/*

Authorities and Roles

Parental Rights. *Parental Rights Per State.* www.ParentalRights.org. *https://parentalrights.org/states/.*

Fiscal Responsibility

Hartman, W. T. (2003). *School District Budgets* (second ed.). Assn of School Business Officials. ISBN-10 1578860687

U.S. Department of of Education. *Grants and Programs.* *https://www.ed.gov/grants-and-programs/formula-grants/response-formula-grants/covid-19-emergency-relief-grants/elementary-and-secondary-school-emergency-relief-fundhttps://www.ed.gov/grants-and-programs/formula-grants/response-formula-grants/covid-19-emerg*

Weaver. (2021, 4 28). *From Fishing Trips to Phishing Scams: Today's Top School District Fraud Traps And How To Avoid Them.* Weaver. *https://weaver.com/resources/fishing-trips-phishing-scams-todays-top-school-district-fraud-traps-and-how-avoid-them/*

Financial Accounting for Local and State School Systems: 2009 Edition - Chapter 6: Account Classification Descriptions — Fund Classifications. From *https://nces.ed.gov/pubs2009/fin_acct/chapter6_1.asp*

Financial Transparency, Mahoning County, OH. *https://auditor.mahoningcountyoh.gov/980/Financial-Transparency*

Bellwether Education. (n.d.). *https://bellwethereducation.org*

PreK-12 Federal Funding Resources, e-Learning Infographics, from *https://elearninginfographics.com/prek-12-federal-funding-resources/*

Funding. www.readycoach.net. Retrieved 12, 2024, from *https://readycoach.net/funding/*

Elementary and Secondary School Emergency Relief Fund, U.S. Department of Education. from *https://oese.ed.gov/offices/education-stabilization-fund/elementary-secondary-school-emergency-relief-fund/?ref=mathspace-blog*

K!2 Prospects.. School District Purchasing Cycle-Timing is Everything. https://www.k12prospects.com/school-districts-purchasing-cycle-timing-everything/

Hatfield, M. (2021, 12 16). *Brian Busby & Anthony Hutchinson Indicted Houston ISD FBI Raid*. ABC13.com. *https://abc13.com/brian-busby-indicted-houston-isd-anthony-hutchison-fbi-raid/11348104*

Holsman, M. E. (2020, 7 16). Brian Burkeen was guilty of grand theft and sentenced to 12 years in prison. *TCPalm. https://www.tcpalm.com/story/news/crime/indian-river-county/2020/07/16/brian-burkeen-convicted-grand-theft-sentenced-12-years-prison/5441953002/*

The Guardian. (2024, 8 12). *Chicago Food Director Steals 11,000 Cases of Chicken Wings Valued Over $1.5 Million. https://www.theguardian.com/us-news/article/2024/aug/12/chicago-woman-stolen-chicken-wings-sentencing*

Internal and External Influence

The American Presidency Project. (1937, 8 16). *Letter The Resolution Federation Employees Against Strikes Federal Services. https://www.presidency.ucsb.edu/documents/letter-the-resolution-federation-federal-employees-against-strikes-federal-service#ixzz1RH7XH5ug*

Janus v. American Federation of State, County, and Municipal Employees, Council 31, et al. (2018) *https://www.supremecourt.gov/opinions/17pdf/16-1466_2b3j.pdf*

Friedrichs v. California Teachers Assn., 578 U.S. (2016), from *https://supreme.justia.com/cases/federal/us/578/14-915/*

Knox v. Service Employees Int'l Union Local 1000, 567 U.S. 298 (2012), from *https://supreme.justia.com/cases/federal/us/567/298/*

Memorandum of Understanding. Kimberly. *https://www.kimberly.edu/sites/default/files/school_board/MEMORANDUM%20OF%20UNDERSTANDING%20Kimberly%20ll.pdf*

Melbourne SRO. Brevard County School District. *https://agenda.brevardschools.org/content/files/melbourne-sro-mou-2023-24-revised-approved-by-pg-6223.pdf*

Culture and Climate

Manhattan Institute. (2019, March). Safe And Orderly Schools**:** UPDATED GUIDANCE ON SCHOOL DISCIPLINE. Eden, M., from *https://media4.manhattan-institute.org/sites/default/files/R-ME-0319.pdf*

FINAL REPORT OF THE FEDERAL COMMISSION ON School Safety. (2018, 12-18). www.Ed.gov. *https://www.ed.gov/sites/ed/files/documents/school-safety/school-safety-report.pdf*

Dee, T. S. (2023, August 10). Higher Chronic Absenteeism Threatens Academic Recovery from the COVID-19 Pandemic. *https://doi.org/10.31219/osf.io/bfg3p*

Urban Institute. Everyday violence: Gunfire near DC schools. *https://apps.urban.org/features/everyday-violence/#:~:text=For%20some%20DC%20students%2C%20nearby,a%20profound%20effect%20on%20children.*

American University Radio WAMU 88.5. (2024, 3 20). School absenteeism rates in D.C. are alarmingly high. What's the city doing about it? *https://wamu.org/story/24/03/20/how-is-dc-addressing-chronic-absenteeism/*

DC.gov. DC School Report Card -Ballou High School. *https://schoolreportcard.dc.gov/lea/1/school/452/report*

Alaska Public Media. (2023, 8 11). Alaska Sees Worst School Attendance As Rates Tank Nationwide. *https://alaskapublic.org/2023/08/11/alaska-sees-worst-school-attendance-as-rates-tank-nationwide/*

National Education Association. (NEA). Advocating For Change, Radical Social Justice. EdJustice. *https://www.nea.org/advocating-for-change/racial-social-justice*

White House. (2020, 9 28). EXECUTIVE OFFICE OF THE PRESIDENT OFFICE OF MANAGEMENT AND BUDGET. Ending Employee Trainings that Use Divisive Propaganda to Undermine the Principle of Fair and Equal Treatment for All*https://www.whitehouse.gov/wp-content/uploads/2020/09/M-20-37.pdf.*

US News. (2024, 8 8). What the Supreme Court's Affirmative Action Ban Means for College Admissions Colleges and universities can't intentionally consider race in the admissions process. *https://www.usnews.com/education/best-colleges/applying/articles/how-does-affirmative-action-affect-college-admissions*

Suchy, R. W. (1992). A concept of the secondary principal and the school: A reflective essay. *https://core.ac.uk/download/571433620.pdf*

SF Examiner. (2023, 6 23). *San Francisco School Board votes to restore merit-based admissions to Lowell High. https://www.sfexaminer.com/news/san-francisco-school-board-votes-to-restore-merit-based-admissions-to-lowell-high/article_ded63b9e-f29e-11ec-828b-5f8fbe85ad0e.html*

Duggan, L. (2024, 10 29). *Top high school's standards slip following DEI policy*. UnHerd. *https://unherd.com/newsroom/top-high-school-sees-major-decline-following-dei-admissions-policy/*

Parents Defending Education. (2024, 9 24). *Thomas Jefferson High School's number of students named national merit semifinalists decreases by over half year to year. https://defendinged.org/incidents/thomas-jefferson-high-schools-number-of-students-named-national-merit-semifinalists-decreases-by-over-half-year-to-year/*

Acronyms and Glossary Terms

COHASSET PUBLIC SCHOOLS. GLOSSARY: District & Budget Terms. *https://resources.finalsite.net/images/v1715257143/cohassetk12org/edxzcelcbza2pbzhyqfu/School_Budget_Terms_Glossary_FY18.pdf*

East Greenbush CSD, Budget Glossary. *https://egcsd.org/budget/budget-glossary/*

FLDOE. Apprenticeship Toolbox. Acronyms. *https://www.fldoe.org/academics/career-adult-edu/apprenticeship-programs/apprenticeship-toolbox/acronyms.stml*

George's County Public. Glossary of Budget Terms. *https://www.pgcps.org/offices/budget-and-management-services/glossary-of-budget-terms*

A Glossary of Education Terms for School Board Members. (n.d.). Iowa Association of School Boards. Retrieved January 6, 2025, from *https://www.ia-sb.org/docs/default-source/toolbox/board-development/educationtermsglossary.pdf*

Mayfield Central School District.Budget terminology, *https://www.mayfieldk12.com/budget-and-taxes/school-budget-terminology/*

Spencerport Central School District.Key Budget Terms. *https://www.spencerportschools.org/departments_and_programs/business_office/2024-25_budget_section/key_budget_termshttps://www.spencerportschools.org/departments_and_programs/business_office/2024-25_budget_section/key_budget_terms*

What Is White Privilege. (2023, May 9). www.VeryWellMind.com. *https://www.verywellmind.com/what-is-white-privilege-5070460*

Project READY: Reimaging Equity for Diversity Youth. (2024). https://ready.web.unc.edu/. *https://ready.web.unc.edu/section-1-foundations/module-10-2/*

Index